Date Due

NOV 4 1982		
FEB 2 1984	JAN 2 3 1996	
JAN 19/90 RECEIVED	JAN 0 9 1996	
MAR 27 1990	OCT 1 0 2000	
MAY 1 1 1990	3 1 MAY 2001	
NOV 7 1991		

The Annual handbook for
group facilitators.

SERIES
IN
HUMAN
RELATIONS
TRAINING

THE
1972
ANNUAL
HANDBOOK
FOR
GROUP
FACILITATORS

Edited by

J. WILLIAM PFEIFFER, Ph.D.
Human Relations Consultant
La Jolla, California

JOHN E. JONES, Ph.D.
Human Relations Consultant
La Jolla, California

UNIVERSITY ASSOCIATES
Publishers and Consultants
7596 Eads Avenue
La Jolla, California 92037

PREFACE

This first edition of the *Annual Handbook for Group Facilitators* has grown out of the work which we did in preparing the three volumes of the *Handbook of Structured Experiences for Human Relations Training*. The *Handbook* has been well received, and we have been very gratified to hear of its impact on the human relations training field. The need that we have been feeling increasingly over the past three years has been to supply theoretical and practical suggestions for the use of structured experiences as well as the directions necessary for their immediate use. There is a growing number of practitioners who are using intensive small groups in a variety of fields, and there is a need not only for training tools but also theory and practical application input to those workers.

This is an annual handbook that will be largely written by practitioners for practitioners. In this series, we hope to record the development of structured experiences, instruments, theoretical positions, and ideas for applications as they emerge in the future. To that end we invite inquiries from users of the *Annual* concerning our policies regarding incorporating their work in future editions. Users are encouraged to submit structured experiences, instruments that they have developed, and papers which they have written that might be considered for inclusion in later volumes. In addition, users may submit critiques of new materials and other such information that might be of interest to practitioners in the area of human relations training. In this manner, the annual series can serve a clearinghouse function for ideas developed by group facilitators. The notebook is designed to hold the extra pages of materials that facilitators accumulate.

We have learned a great deal from our work in collecting and disseminating information about structured experiences. Our communications with users have indicated that the intensive small group experience is becoming an increasingly common part of training and education designs in a variety of settings and that a very large number of people are becoming involved as facilitators of small group interaction. We have learned that there is no easy way to help people grow, that training designs in and of themselves are not sufficient to insure growth and learning, and that in large part the skill and expertise of the facilitator are more powerful than the designs which he devises.

We have had some concern about the use by untrained group leaders of the materials which we published, but we have come to believe that the personality and life style of the individual facilitator, regardless of his training background, are the critical variables in determining whether or not he is harmful. In other words, if the facilitator is a healthy person, psychologically mature and congruent, he is very unlikely to be harmful in his use of the materials available in human relations training. On the other hand, if he is a person whose adjustment is precarious and whose motives for the use of human relations training designs are based on his own needs rather than on the learning needs of his participants, there is a high likelihood that he will be harmful. There is no inherent harm in the materials themselves nor in the exercises which are available for use by the facilitator; they are neither helpful nor harmful except in terms of how they are used and by whom.

This annual is copyrighted, but there are few implied restrictions concerning the reproduction of its contents. Users should feel free to duplicate and/or modify the forms, charts, structured exercises, descriptions and instruments for use in education/training designs. However, reproduction of sections of the book in other publications should be done with the permission of the editors. Innovation in human relations training is a norm that has been very well established, and adaptation of the learning experiences that have been described in this book is expected. We seldom use an exercise the same way twice, and we anticipate that users will adapt this material for their own particular training purposes.

We want to acknowledge the contributions of our wives, who have spent a great deal of time in making it possible for us to free ourselves for the hours required to edit such a volume. They also have been invaluable in assisting us in the editing task.

We have made considerable effort to determine the authorship of these materials, but we continue to have concern over the accuracy of our research into finding the people who develop particular exercises. An interesting phenomenon occurs in the human relations training field that aggravates the authorship problem. A facilitator uses a structured experience or an instrument for several years, it becomes a part of his training repertoire, and he forgets where he originally attained it. He sees another facilitator using a version of it, and he feels that he is not being acknowledged for something which he "owns." As one consultant put it, "I have been using my own version for such a long time, that I simply assumed it was the only one in the world."

We had hard deadlines for the development of this book, and the persons whose names appear in it responded positively to short notices. We took liberties in editing their work; we recognize that their contributions represent a considerable part of their professional development, and they were very gracious in permitting us wide latitude in handling their ideas. We are deeply appreciative of the patience with which contributors have interacted with us over the past few years.

J. William Pfeiffer
John E. Jones

Iowa City, Iowa
January, 1972

TABLE OF CONTENTS

GENERAL
INTRODUCTION
TO THE
1972 ANNUAL

Group facilitators typically have bulky files of materials containing hundreds of loose papers that they have picked up at conventions, workshops, and laboratories. This *Annual* was designed to become a vehicle for sharing such materials. Theory, information, and practical application ideas are brought together in an organized, yet flexible, way. One of the most important criteria in judging the worth of a given theory is its utility in guiding behavior, and we have attempted to place a pragmatic emphasis on all of the materials in this handbook.

The first section of this *Annual* continues the publication of structured experiences which was initiated in our three-volume series. Included are twelve items which can be used in personal growth designs and in organization development efforts. The format of these activities is the same as the one employed earlier.

A number of instruments have been developed for use with groups of participants, and the second section contains four which show promise of being useful, not only in research, but also in teaching, sensing, and providing feedback. This set of instruments extends the list of twelve that were included in the volumes of the *Handbook*.

Lecture materials are contained in the third section, in response to the expressed need on the part of group facilitators for readily accessible cognitive inputs that could be coordinated with the structured experiences. The intent is to provide basic ideas that can be used in a variety of training efforts.

The fourth section, "Theory and Practice," contains a collection of papers most of which were prepared especially for this *Annual*. Contributors were asked to address themselves to the practitioner rather than to the scholar. Those papers, along with the brief pieces in the "Lecturettes" section, are cogent background reading for persons interested in working with small groups.

The intent of the fifth section, "Resources," is to provide access to tools — books, films, products, and professional associations. The personalized critiques of resources available to the facilitator should provide guidance to him as he selects from a confusing array of group-oriented materials and organizations.

Contributors to this edition of the *Annual* are listed alphabetically in the final section of the book. Their mailing addresses and telephone numbers are provided in order that users may communicate directly with them.

The materials in the *Annual* are clearly uneven: in some cases they represent adaptations of "old" ideas and in some cases they are theories which are still very much "in progress." The sole intent is to provide stimulating ideas for the group facilitator.

INTRODUCTION
TO THE STRUCTURED
EXPERIENCES SECTION

This section continues the effort that was initiated in the three-volumes of *A Handbook of Structured Experiences for Human Relations Training*. In those volumes the materials are numbered consecutively from 1 through 74. In this section of the *Annual* the numbering of the exercises continues with 75. As in the preceeding *Handbook*, these exercises have been rank-ordered in terms of their complexity and the needed skill and background of the user of such exercises. The first structured exercise in this series, "Frustrations and Tensions," requires considerably less background on a part of the facilitator than do "Growth and Name Fantasy" or "Nonverbal-Closure" that end the section. This ordering represents our assessment of the impact of these exercises, and it is somewhat arbitrary.

We think that it is useful to make a distinction between games and structured experiences. In casting about for a name for our original *Handbook of Structured Experiences for Human Relations Training* we discarded a number of terms, among which were games, training materials, techniques, and exercises. We decided to use the term "structured experiences" because we wanted to point out that the materials were designs for experience-based learning. We also wanted the term to provide a connotation of guiding the participants in learning about human interaction. However, the term "structured" does not imply that participants are being manulipated; it simply means that the intended learning is facilitated by a design. The term "games" generally connotes play, and the term "structured experience" hopefully connotes working and learning. It sometimes happens that in structured experiences participants have fun, but the major difference between games and structured experiences is that the learning goals of the latter are specifiable before hand.

A game is engaged in not for the purpose of generating data for processing, but for the experience itself. A game also connotes competition rather than collaboration. The materials that we have compiled in the *Handbook* and those that are included in this section should not be considered games in the sense that they are to be played. Rather, they are designed for the serious business of helping participants to learn about themselves, about how they relate to each other, about how groups operate, and about the human side of organizations.

It is important that the facilitators keep in mind that the most significant aspect of the learning experience is not the exercise itself but the processing which should immediately follow. The user should be ready to accept the responsibility of insuring that all of the data that are generated by the structured experience are adequately talked through, sifted out, and integrated. This processing skill is perhaps the most important characteristic of the facilitator who uses such devices. It is important that he help participants to develop generalizations and learnings from the experience. He should be prepared to inject theory and practical applications of the learning. Some structural interventions, such as the following, are suggested to provide for adequate processing.

1. Participants interviewing each other about what was learned.

2. Sub-grouping.

3. Having one group observe another group in a group-on-group design.

4. Using an empty-chair design to have people talk about what they learned.

5. Having reports from observers who used process observation sheets such as the one which is included in exercise 79, "What to look for in Groups."

6. Establishing panels, *i.e.*, a group of observers who will interact after the structured experience in discussing their independent observation of the event.

Particular attention should be paid to the need to adequately process the outcome of experiences that are based on fantasy or nonverbal communication. Many people do not respond well to these activities, and it is important that the facilitator permit people to opt out of such activities. Fantasy and nonverbal techniques can be very powerful interventions in the learning experience of participants, but it is important that considerable time be allowed for participants to talk through their learning. In effect, the processing is more important than the experience itself. Some participants may need considerable assistance in integrating the learning derived from fantasy and nonverbal exercises into their own view of themselves. The use of such methods should be based on a well-thought-out theory of learning held by the facilitator, and he should be careful to introduce such activities in a timely way, *i.e.*, the use should be based on a diagnosis of the learning needs of the group at a particular time rather than a pre-planned "schedule of events."

It is not intended that these exercises must always be carried out in exactly the manner in which they are described. Rather, it is important that the facilitator adapt each exercise to his own group situation. That is, he takes into account the type of group he is working with, its developmental phase, the readiness of members to engage in particular types of activities, the learning needs of members, and the particular goals of the group with which he is working. All of these data can be used in creative adaptation of the learning experiences. When such designs are used in an organization development effort, the processing can be made in terms of the application of the learning to the organization, *e.g.*, its internal communication and its power relations. The adaptations for T-groups should be in terms of the goals of that particular group.

The exercises selected for inclusion in this section reflect the development within the field of human relations training of increasing activity and interest in organization development. A number of the exercises, particularly 80, 81, 82, and 83 lend themselves directly to organizational diagnosis, clarification of interpersonal relations within and between teams.

75. FRUSTRATIONS AND TENSIONS

Goals

    I. To help participants to become aware of their responses to tense, frustrating situations.

    II. To study alternative responses to such situations.

Group Size

    Six to twelve participants. A number of groups may be directed simultaneously in the same room.

Time Required

    Approximately forty-five minutes.

Materials Utilized

    I. Frustrations and Tensions Worksheet I.

    II. Frustrations and Tensions Worksheet II.

    III. Pencils.

Physical Setting

    Groups should be seated around tables, or lapboards should be provided.

Process

    I. The facilitator explains the goals of the experience.

    II. Worksheet I is handed to each of the participants, and they are instructed to fill in the missing dialogue in the two cartoons and to briefly note the assumptions that they are making about each situation.

    III. Each group then discusses the responses made by its members to each of the situations, exploring the probable effects of each response.

    IV. Worksheet II is distributed. Again each participant works independently on the two situations depicted in the cartoons.

    V. Groups discuss members' responses to the second set of situations and try to derive generalizations about effective responses in tense, frustrating interpersonal situations.

    VI. The facilitator opens the discussion to all participants, drawing out the generalizations from each of the groups.

    An alternative would be to have group members create their own cartoons on posters. These may be instances in which they have been actually frustrated and/or tense. Group members may suggest responses, and the group member who was actually involved may compare the response which he actually made to what is suggested.

Another variation might be to use the cartoons as a vehicle for feedback to individual group members. Members may be asked to predict what one particular member might say in each of the four situations.

Assumptions that you made about the situation:

Assumptions that you made about the situation:

Assumptions that you made about the situation:

Assumptions that you made about the situation:

76. QUAKER MEETING

Goals

I. To generate a large number of ideas, suggestions, approaches to a problem or topic when the group is too large to employ brainstorming techniques.

II. To gather data quickly for a large group to process.

Group Size

Any group larger than fifty participants; for example, a professional meeting, church congregation, etc.

Time Required

Fifteen minutes for the actual "Quaker meeting" and whatever time seems appropriate to the processing chosen for the particular group.

Materials Utilized

I. Paper and pencils for those taking notes.

II. Chalkboard, newsprint and felt-tipped markers, or mimeographing materials.

Physical Setting

Large meeting room.

Process

I. The facilitator explains that it is necessary to hear total group reactions to a given problem or topic.

II. He instructs the group concerning the structure that will be employed in gaining the reactions.

A. As a group participant formulates a thought, suggestion, or reaction, he is to speak out to the entire group. Verbalizing is to be limited to a few words (10 to 15) so that as many can speak in the fifteen minutes as possible.

B. Participants must not interrupt each other, but they must be ready to inject their thoughts quickly.

C. The participant is to feel free to express even "far out" suggestions, since they may trigger other, more practical ones for other participants.

D. Each reaction from a participant will be recorded; however, there will be *no* processing of individual ideas at this point.

III. The facilitator asks several participants to take notes on the data generated. He may ask them to take turns writing down what they hear expressed by the other participants.

IV. He then presents the problem or topic and asks participants to begin verbalizing as quickly as ideas form.

V. The facilitator may change the dynamics slightly by asking participants to stand as they verbalize. This will focus on individuals as well as ideas and may be appropriate to given situations; however, the process will be slower if he approaches it in this manner.

VI. The facilitator may process the data gathered in any way that is appropriate to the group. He may wish to list ideas on a chalkboard or newsprint for the entire group to process, or he may mimeograph lists and distribute them to smaller groups or committees to process.

77. TEAM IDENTITY

Goals

    I. To develop cohesion within work groups established as part of a larger training group.

    II. To explore the dynamics of group task accomplishment.

Group Size

    Unlimited. Subgroups are best established to have five to seven members each. Any number of such teams can be directed simultaneously in the same room.

Time Required

    Approximately one and one-half hours.

Materials Utilized

    I. Newsprint and felt-tipped pens (various colors), and masking tape.

    II. Team Identity Poster Formats.

    III. Team Identity Processing Guides.

    IV. Pencils or pens.

Physical Setting

    There should be room enough for groups to work independently. Wall space should be adequate for hanging a poster for each group in different locations around the room.

Process

    I. The facilitator introduces the structured experience by explaining the goals of the activity and by giving a brief overview of the design. Participants should be given the expectation that this activity will be both fun and productive.

    II. Groups are formed by any convenient method (numbering off, choosing each other, forming homogeneous groups, etc.).

    III. The facilitator explains that these groups will function as task teams from time to time throughout the training. He indicates that there can be a large difference between a *group* and a *team* and that this activity is intended to promote a sense of identification with one's task team.

    IV. The facilitator distributes a copy of the Team Identity Poster Format to each participant. He instructs the teams to create a name for themselves, a symbol (logo), and a motto. They have thirty minutes to complete the planning and production of this task. As soon as they have completed their planning, they should send a representative to the facilitator to get newsprint and colored pens.

    V. At the end of the task phase the facilitator distributes a copy of the Team Identity Processing Guide to each participant and reads aloud the instructions printed on the form. The facilitator gives the participants five minutes to make notes privately.

VI. Teams are instructed to discuss each of the items on the Team Identity Processing Guide and to select a different member to prepare to summarize each of the five items. (Twenty minutes.)

VII. The facilitator calls for summary statements to each item from all teams. The large group is instructed to listen for common themes in these reports. (Fifteen minutes.)

VIII. The facilitator instructs the teams to put their posters on the walls, considerably apart from each other. Each team designates one member to stay with the poster to answer questions that members of other teams might have about the poster.

IX. Team members are instructed to break up their groups and to go individually to the posters of all the other teams. They may ask questions and give reactions. The team members assigned to stay at these "stations" (one at each poster) are instructed to answer the other participants' questions and to note their reactions. (Twenty minutes.)

X. As soon as everyone has seen all the posters, the teams are instructed to reassemble. They then hear and discuss a summary of reactions noted by their representatives who stayed with the posters. (Five minutes.)

XI. The facilitator invites each team to make a statement about itself to the larger group.

XII. Each team has a brief discussion of learnings about cohesion and about group task functioning.

XIII. The facilitator conducts a large-group discussion of learnings from the structured experience.

This structured experience was contributed by John E. Jones.

TEAM NAME

(acronym or other memorable
designation)

TEAM LOGO

(diagram, picture, words, colors)

TEAM MOTTO

(a saying or slogan related to the team's
purpose, values, composition, or preferred
way of working)

TEAM MEMBERS

(may include titles)

TEAM IDENTITY PROCESSING GUIDE

Now that you have completed the development of your team's identity, take a few minutes to look back at the interaction that occurred. Each of you should write notes on this form before you discuss how your group worked on the task of making your poster. Then look for patterns in the perceptions of the members of your team. The facilitator will call for a report from your team on each of the following items. You will be instructed to designate a different member to give the summary for each item. Again, work *independently* first, then discuss each of these questions as a group.

1. *Organization*

    a. How did your group organize itself to accomplish the task?

    b. How did you feel during this getting-started phase?

2. *Involvement*

    a. How involved were all of the members during the problem solving?

    b. How did you feel about your own involvement?

3. *Creativity*

    a. What creative processes were used or occurred spontaneously?

    b. What was happening with you during the creative activity?

4. *Conflict*

    a. If there were disagreements, how were these handled by the team?

    b. How did you feel when there was group tension?

5. *Closure*

    a. How did the group decide that its task was done?

    b. How did you feel at the end of the team's production phase?

78. UNEQUAL RESOURCES

Goals

  I. To provide an opportunity for observing group use of resources which have been distributed unequally.

  II. To observe bargaining processes.

Group Size

  This task may be done with clusters of "groups" of from one to four members each. If more than one cluster of four groups is used, the facilitator may add the dimension of competition between as well as within clusters. The facilitator may ask that several participants volunteer to be process observers.

Time Required

  Approximately one hour, depending upon the number and complexity of the tasks assigned and the ages of the group members.

Materials Utilized

  I. Scissors, ruler, paper clips, glue, black felt-tipped markers and construction paper in six colors (as used in the sample task illustrated here).

  II. Unequal Resources Task Sheet for each group.

  III. Large envelopes to hold each group's resources. In the example below, the envelopes will contain the following resources as designated by group:

  Group   I — scissors, ruler, paper clips, pencils and two 4″ squares of red paper and two of white.

  Group II — scissors, glue and 8½″ x 11″ sheets of paper (two blue, two white, two gold).

  Group III — felt-tipped markers and 8½″ x 11″ sheets of paper (two green, two white, two gold).

  Group IV — 8½″ x 11″ sheets of paper (one each: green, gold, blue, red and purple).

Physical Setting

  Table and chairs for each group. These should be placed far enough away from each other so that each group's bargaining position is not betrayed by casual observation.

Process

  I. The facilitator asks groups to be seated at their individual tables and distributes an envelope of materials and a Tasks Sheet to each group.

  II. The facilitator asks the group not to open their materials until he tells them to begin the task. He then explains that each group has different materials but that each group must complete the same tasks. He explains that they may bargain for the use of materials and tools in any way that is mutually agreeable. He emphasizes that the first group to complete all tasks is the winner. (If clusters are competing, there will be both a group winner and a cluster winner.)

III. The facilitator gives the signal to begin and attempts to observe as much group and bargaining behavior as he can, so that he can supply some of the feedback during the final phase.

IV. The facilitator stops the process when winners have been declared and groups have been allowed to complete ongoing tasks.

V. During the discussion, the participants may make process observations concerning utilization of resources, sharing, bargaining, and competition, using the facilitator (and process observers) as an outside consultant to supply feedback on individual and group behavior.

VI. The facilitator may alter the complexity of tasks and distribution of resources to fit many different kinds of groups and age levels. This experience is appropriate for children as well as adults. When it is being used as a teaching tool, analogies may be drawn between this experience and how minority groups or underdeveloped nations relate to these with more power.

UNEQUAL RESOURCES TASKS SHEET

Each group is to complete the following tasks:

1. Make a 3″ by 3″ square of white paper.
2. Make a 4″ by 2″ rectangle of gold paper.
3. Make a four-link paper chain, each link in a different color.
4. Make a T-shaped piece 3″ by 5″ in green and white paper.
5. Make a 4″ by 4″ flag, in any three colors.

The first group to complete all tasks is the winner. Groups may bargain with other groups for the use of materials and tools to complete the tasks on any mutually agreeable basis.

79. WHAT TO LOOK FOR IN GROUPS:
AN OBSERVATION GUIDE

Goal

    To assist group members in understanding and being more perceptive about group process.

Group Size

    Two groups of at least ten members each.

Time Required

    Three hours.

Materials Utilized

    I. Handout for each member, "What to Look for In Groups."

    II. Scratch paper and pencil for each member.

Physical Setting

    Large room with movable chairs.

Process

    I. The facilitator distributes the handout and leads a thirty-minute theory session on group process based upon the material in the handout.

    II. The facilitator asks the group members to number off, one through ten (and begin with one again if their are more than ten members in a single group). He assigns the "ones" the section in the handout entitled "Participation," "twos" the section entitled "Influence," etc.

    III. The facilitator then names one group "A" and the other "B." He explains that each group will complete some appropriate task which will provide the groups with "group process" to observe, each member observing in terms of his assigned section of the handout.

    IV. Group A completes an assigned task while Group B observes. This phase of the experience should take no more than thirty minutes.

    V. The facilitator asks Group A to give feedback to Group B based upon the handout. (approximately fifteen minutes).

    VI. Group B is given ten minutes in which to respond to the feedback from Group A.

    VII. The facilitator asks everyone to take a fifteen minute break.

VIII. The experience resumes with Group B observing Group A completing an assigned task, Group B giving feedback to Group A, and Group A responding to the feedback with the same time indications as above.

IX. Each group processes the feedback from the entire experience separately. The facilitator may move between groups to observe and assist in the processing of feedback.

This structured experience and the accompanying observation guide were contributed by Philip G. Hanson, V. A. Hospital, Houston, Texas.

WHAT TO LOOK FOR IN GROUPS

In all human interactions there are two major ingredients — content and process. The first deals with the subject matter or the task upon which the group is working. In most interactions, the focus of attention of all persons is on the content. The second ingredient, process, is concerned with what is happening between and to group members while the group is working. Group process, or dynamics, deals with such items as morale, feeling tone, atmosphere, influence, participation, styles of influence, leadership struggles, conflict, competition, cooperation, etc. In most interactions, very little attention is paid to process, even when it is the major cause of ineffective group action. Sensitivity to group process will better enable one to diagnose group problems early and deal with them more effectively. Since these processes are present in all groups, awareness of them will enhance a person's worth to a group and enable him to be a more effective group participant.

Below are some observation guidelines to help one process analyze group behavior.

Participation

One indication of involvement is verbal participation. Look for differences in the amount of participation among members.

1. Who are the high participators?
2. Who are the low participators?
3. Do you see any shift in participation, e.g., highs become quiet; lows suddenly become talkative. Do you see any possible reason for this in the group's interaction?
4. How are the silent people treated? How is their silence interpreted? Consent? Disagreement? Disinterest? Fear? etc.
5. Who talks to whom? Do you see any reason for this in the group's interactions?
6. Who keeps the ball rolling? Why? Do you see any reason for this in the group's interactions?

Influence

Influence and participation are not the same. Some people may speak very little, yet they capture the attention of the whole group. Others may talk a lot but are generally not listened to by other members.

7. Which members are high in influence? That is, when they talk others seem to listen.
8. Which members are low in influence? Others do not listen to or follow them. Is there any shifting in influence? Who shifts?
9. Do you see any rivalry in the group? Is there a struggle for leadership? What effect does it have on other group members?

Styles of Influence

Influence can take many forms. It can be positive or negative; it can enlist the support or cooperation of others or alienate them. *How* a person attempts to influence another may be the crucial factor in determining how open or closed the other will be toward being influenced. Items 10 through 13 are suggestive of four styles that frequently emerge in groups.

10. Autocratic: Does anyone attempt to impose his will or values on other group members or try to push them to support his decisions? Who evaluates or passes judgment on

other group members? Do any members block action when it is not moving the direction they desire? Who pushes to "get the group organized"?

11. Peacemaker: Who eagerly supports other group members' decisions? Does anyone consistently try to avoid conflict or unpleasant feelings from being expressed by pouring oil on the troubled waters? Is any member typically deferential toward other group members — gives them power? Do any members appear to avoid giving negative feedback, i.e., who will level only when they have positive feedback to give?

12. Laissez faire: Are any group members getting attention by their apparent lack of involvement in the group? Does any group member go along with group decisions without seeming to commit himself one way or the other? Who seems to be withdrawn and uninvolved; who does not initiate activity, participates mechanically and only in response to another member's question?

13. Democratic: Does anyone try to include everyone in a group decision or discussion? Who expresses his feelings and opinions openly and directly without evaluating or judging others? Who appears to be open to feedback and criticisms from others? When feelings run high and tension mounts, which members attempt to deal with the conflict in a problem-solving way?

Decision-Making Procedures

Many kinds of decisions are made in groups without considering the effects of these decisions on other members. Some people try to impose their own decisions on the group, while others want all members to participate or share in the decisions that are made.

14. Does anyone make a decision and carry it out without checking with other group members? (Self-authorized) For example, he decides on the topic to be discussed and immediately begins to talk about it. What effect does this have on other group members?

15. Does the group drift from topic to topic? Who topic-jumps? Do you see any reason for this in the group's interactions?

16. Who supports other members' suggestions or decisions? Does this support result in the two members deciding the topic or activity for the group (handclasp)? How does this effect other group members?

17. Is there any evidence of a majority pushing a decision through over other members objections? Do they call for a vote (majority support)?

18. Is there any attempt to get all members participating in a decision (consensus)? What effect does this seem to have on the group?

19. Does anyone make any contributions which do not receive any kind of response or recognition (plop)? What effect does this have on the member?

Task Functions

These functions illustrate behaviors that are concerned with getting the job done, or accomplishing the task that the group has before them.

20. Does anyone ask for or make suggestions as to the best way to proceed or to tackle a problem?

21. Does anyone attempt to summarize what has been covered or what has been going on in the group?

22. Is there any giving or asking for facts, ideas, opinions, feelings, feedback, or searching for alternatives?

23. Who keeps the group on target? Who prevents topic-jumping or going off on tangents?

Maintenance Functions

These functions are important to the morale of the group. They maintain good and harmonious working relationships among the members and create a group atmosphere which enables each member to contribute maximally. They insure smooth and effective teamwork within the group.

24. Who helps others get into the discussion (gate openers)?

25. Who cuts off others or interrupts them (gate closers)?

26. How well are members getting their ideas across? Are some members preoccupied and not listening? Are there any attempts by group members to help others clarify their ideas?

27. How are ideas rejected? How do members react when their ideas are not accepted? Do members attempt to support others when they reject their ideas?

Group Atmosphere

Something about the way a group works creates an atmosphere which in turn is revealed in a general impression. In addition, people may differ in the kind of atmosphere they like in a group. Insight can be gained into the atmosphere characteristic of a group by finding words which describe the general impressions held by group members.

28. Who seems to prefer a friendly congenial atmosphere? Is there any attempt to suppress conflict or unpleasant feelings?

29. Who seems to prefer an atmosphere of conflict and disagreement? Do any members provoke or annoy others?

30. Do people seem involved and interested? Is the atmosphere one of work, play satisfaction, taking flight, sluggishness, etc.?

Membership

A major concern for group members is the degree of acceptance or inclusion in the group. Different patterns of interaction may develop in the group which give clues to the degree and kind of membership.

31. Is there any sub-grouping? Some times two or three members may consistently agree and support each other or consistently disagree and oppose one another.

32. Do some people seem to be "outside" the group? Do some members seem to be "in"? How are those "outside" treated?

33. Do some members move in and out of the group, e.g., lean forward or backward in their chairs or move their chairs in and out? Under what conditions do they come in or move out?

Feelings

During any group discussion, feelings are frequently generated by the interactions between members. These feelings, however, are seldom talked about. Observers may have to make guesses based on tone of voice, facial expressions, gestures, and many other forms of nonverbal cues.

34. What signs of feelings do you observe in group members: anger, irritation, frustration, warmth, affection, excitement, boredom, defensiveness, competitiveness, etc.?

35. Do you see any attempts by group members to block the expression of feelings, particularly negative feelings? How is this done? Does anyone do this consistently?

Norms

Standards or ground rules may develop in a group that control the behavior of its members. Norms usually express the beliefs or desires of the majority of the group members as to what behaviors *should* or *should not* take place in the group. These norms may be clear to all members (explicit), known or sensed by only a few (implicit), or operating completely below the level of awareness of any group members. Some norms facilitate group progress and some hinder it.

36. Are certain areas avoided in the group (*e.g.*, sex, religion, talk about present feelings in group, discussing the leader's behavior, etc.)? Who seems to reinforce this avoidance? How do they do it?

37. Are group members overly nice or polite to each other? Are only positive feelings expressed? Do members agree with each other too readily? What happens when members disagree?

38. Do you see norms operating about participation or the kinds of questions that are allowed (*e.g.*, "If I talk, you must talk"; "If I tell my problems you have to tell your problems")? Do members feel free to probe each other about their feelings? Do questions tend to be restricted to intellectual topics or events outside of the group?

80. ENERGY INTERNATIONAL: A PROBLEM-SOLVING MULTIPLE ROLE-PLAY

Goals

    I. To study how task-relevant information is shared within a work group.

    II. To observe problem-solving strategies within a group.

    III. To explore the effects of collaboration and competition in group problem solving.

Group Size

    Unlimited groups of five participants each. These groups may be directed simultaneously in the same room.

Time Required

    Approximately two hours.

Materials

    I. A set of five Energy International Data Sheets for each group of participants. Each sheet is coded by the number of dots ranging from one to five following the second sentence in the first paragraph. Each sheet contains data unique to that sheet.

    II. Energy International Candidate Summary Sheet for each participant.

    III. Energy International Briefing Sheet for each participant.

    IV. Energy International Problem Solution for each participant.

Physical Setting

    One room large enough so that the individual groups of five can work without being disrupted by other groups and without being influenced by solutions to the problem overheard from other groups. An alternative physical setting would be a room large enough to hold all participants comfortably during instructions and post problem-solving processing and several smaller rooms where individual groups could work undisturbed during the problem-solving.

Process

    I. The facilitator explains to the participants that they will be doing an exercise in problem-solving.

    II. He then divides participants into groups of exactly five each by any convenient and appropriate method. (The use of observers is optional.)

    III. The facilitator instructs the groups to choose the correct candidate for an executive position based upon the data they will receive. He suggests that there is one correct solution and cautions them that they must reach their solution independent of the other groups. He indicates that when groups have completed the problem-solving and have given their solution to the facilitator, participants may observe other groups still in process; however, they may not join another group or influence another group's process in any way.

IV. The facilitator then distributes Candidate Summary Sheets, Briefing Sheets and individual Data Sheets to each participant, taking care that all five differently coded sheets (number of periods at the end of the first paragraph) have been distributed in each group.

V. The groups begin the problem-solving process when the facilitator gives the signal. He may incorporate an element of competition by posting groups' solutions in order of completion and may even wish to post the number of minutes used by each group in solving the problem.

VI. When all groups have found a solution to the problem, the facilitator distributes the Problem Solution to each participant and processes the experience with the groups, focusing on problem-solving strategies employed, the effects of collaboration and competition, and the sharing process.

Note: It is expected that the facilitator will adapt these materials to fit the needs of particular groups. Any appropriate problem with a unique solution could be generated from the background of the participants; then, the facilitator could "work backwards" to create the individual briefing sheets with varied information that, when shared, can result in the correct solution. The experience can be designed to be simple or complex by decreasing the redundancy of the information so that groups using more complex versions must share more unique data to find the solution. Another possible variable could be group size.

ENERGY INTERNATIONAL DATA SHEET

Your group is a committee made up of the General Managers of Energy International, a young, medium-sized, growing organization. The prime mission of E.I. is to locate and develop mineral claims (copper, uranium, cobalt, etc.).

The company's business has grown very rapidly, especially in South America, where your organization has been made welcome by the governments. In a recent meeting, the board of directors decided to develop a new property near Fortaleza, in northeastern Brazil. This operation will include both mining and milling production.

The date is April 1, 1972. You have come from your respective plants in different locations. This is the initial session of your annual meeting. Your first order of business today is to select a new General Manager for the Brazilian plant from among the candidates on the attached list.

Fortaleza, Brazil, has a hot climate, one railroad, a scheduled airline, a favorable balance of trade, a feudal attitude toward women, considerable unemployment, a low educational level, a low literacy rate, and a strongly nationalistic regime.

The government has insisted that the company must employ Brazilian elements in all posts except that of General Manager. The government has also installed an official inspector who will make monthly reports to the government. This report must be signed by the company's representative, who must be a Fellow of the Institute of Mineralogy.

There are a number of schools offering degrees in mineralogy; the most recently founded is the New Mexico Institute of Earth Sciences. This Institute was established under a special grant and opened in 1945.

In order to earn a bachelor's degree in mineralogy, this school requires geology, seismology, and paleontology, in addition to the usual courses.

ENERGY INTERNATIONAL DATA SHEET

Your group is a committee made up of the General Managers of Energy International, a young, medium-sized, growing organization. The prime mission of E.I. is to locate and develop mineral claims (copper, uranium, cobalt, etc.)..

The company's business has grown very rapidly, especially in South America, where your organization has been made welcome by the governments. In a recent meeting, the board of directors decided to develop a new property near Fortaleza, in northeastern Brazil. This operation will include both mining and milling production.

The date is April 1, 1972. You have come from your respective plants in different locations. This is the initial session of your annual meeting. Your first order of business today is to select a new General Manager for the Brazilian plant from among the candidates on the attached list.

Fortaleza, Brazil, has a hot climate, one railroad, a scheduled airline, a favorable balance of trade, a feudal attitude toward women, considerable unemployment, a low education level, a low literacy rate, and a strongly nationalistic regime.

The government has ruled that the company must employ Brazilians in all posts except that of manager. It has also installed an official inspector, who will make a monthly report which must be countersigned by the General Manager. By law, the General Manager must have had at least three years' experience as a manager in charge of a mining operation.

There are a number of schools offering a degree in mineralogy, a degree essential to qualify for General Membership in the Institute of Mineralogy. The smaller universities require three, the larger four, of the following special subjects as a part of their graduation requirements: geology, geophysics, oceanography, paleontology, seismology. The smallest is a women's university.

ENERGY INTERNATIONAL DATA SHEET

Your group is a committee made up of the General Managers of Energy International, a young, medium-sized, growing organization. The prime mission of E.I. is to locate and develop mineral claims (copper, uranium, cobalt, etc.) . . .

The company's business has grown very rapidly, especially in South America, where your organization has been made welcome by the governments. In a recent meeting, the board of directors decided to develop a new property near Fortaleza, in northeastern Brazil. This operation will include both mining and milling production.

The date is April 1, 1972. You have come from your respective plants in different locations. This is the initial session of your annual meeting. Your first order of business today is to select a new General Manager for the Brazilian plant from among the candidates on the attached list.

Fortaleza, Brazil, has a hot climate, one railroad, a scheduled airline, a favorable balance of trade, a feudal attitude toward women, considerable unemployment, a low educational level, a low literacy rate, and a strongly nationalistic regime.

The government has ruled that the company must employ Brazilians in all posts except that of manager. It has also installed an official inspector, who will make a monthly report which must be countersigned by the company's representative. None of the government inspectors can read or write any language but his own.

There are a number of schools offering degrees in mineralogy, but a passing grade in paleontology is essential to qualify for General Membership in the Institute of Mineralogy. The largest university is the New York School of Mines, which requires the following special subjects for graduation: geology, paleontology, geophysics, and seismology.

ENERGY INTERNATIONAL DATA SHEET

Your group is a committee made up of the General Managers of Energy International, a young, medium-sized, growing organization. The prime mission of E.I. is to locate and develop mineral claims (copper, uranium, cobalt, etc.). . . .

The company's business has grown very rapidly, especially in South America, where your organization has been made welcome by the governments. In a recent meeting, the board of directors decided to develop a new property near Fortaleza, in northeastern Brazil. This operation will include both mining and milling production.

The date is April 1, 1972. You have come from your respective plants in different locations. This is the initial session of your annual meeting. Your first order of business today is to select a new General Manager for the Brazilian plant from among the candidates on the attached list.

Fortaleza, Brazil, has a hot climate, one railroad, a scheduled airline, a favorable balance of trade, a feudal attitude toward women, considerable unemployment, a low educational level, a low literacy rate, and a strongly nationalistic regime.

The government has ruled that the company must employ Brazilians in all posts except that of manager. It has also installed an official inspector, who will make a monthly report which must be countersigned by the company's representative. None of the company's employees or staff can read or write any language but Portuguese.

There are a number of schools offering degrees in mineralogy, and a passing grade in seismology is essential to qualify for General Membership in the Institute of Mineralogy. The Massachusetts Institute of Sciences requires the following special subjects for graduation: geology, seismology, oceanography, and paleontology.

ENERGY INTERNATIONAL DATA SHEET

Your group is a committee made up of the General Managers of Energy International, a young, medium-sized, growing organization. The prime mission of E.I. is to locate and develop mineral claims (copper, uranium, cobalt, etc.). . . . .

The company's business has grown very rapidly, especially in South America, where your organization has been made welcome by the governments. In a recent meeting, the board of directors decided to develop a new property near Fortaleza, in northeastern Brazil. This operation will include both mining and milling production.

The date is April 1, 1972. You have come from your respective plants in different locations. This is the initial session of your annual meeting. Your first order of business today is to select a new General Manager for the Brazilian plant from among the candidates on the attached list.

Fortaleza, Brazil, has a hot climate, one railroad, a scheduled airline, a favorable balance of trade, a feudal attitude toward women, considerable unemployment, a low educational level, a low literacy rate, and a strongly nationalistic regime.

The government has ruled that the company must employ Brazilians in all posts except that of manager. It has also installed an official inspector, who will make a monthly report to the government which must be countersigned by the company's representative, who must be an American citizen.

Fellowship in the Institute of Mineralogy can be obtained by men over 35 years of age who have otherwise qualified for General Membership in the Institute. St. Francis University, which is not the smallest school, requires the following special courses for graduation: paleontology, geophysics, and oceanography.

ENERGY INTERNATIONAL BRIEFING SHEET

I. Instructions to the Group:
1. You are a committee made up of the General Managers of Energy International.
2. You have just flown into town.
3. This is the first meeting of the group.
4. You have just learned that E.I. will open a new Brazilian plant, and your first job is to select a General Manager from among the seven applicants.
5. Basically, the data you bring with you are in your head.

II. Assumptions Which Need to be Made Explicit:
1. Assume that there is one solution.
2. Assume that all data are correct.
3. You have one hour to work the exercise.
4. Assume that today's date is April 1, 1972.
5. There must be substantial agreement when the problem has been solved.
6. You must work the problem as a group.

ENERGY INTERNATIONAL CANDIDATE SUMMARY SHEET

NAME: R. Illin
DATE OF BIRTH: March 2, 1937
PASSPORT: L3452 — U.S.A.
EDUCATION: N. Y. School of Mines — degree in mineralogy — 1957
EMPLOYMENT: Research Assistant — N. Y. School of Mines — 1958-1960
Lecturer — Mineralogy — Univ. of Bonn — 1966-1970
Manager — Utah Copper Mining Co. Plant — 1970 to date
LANG. COMMAND: English, French, German, Portuguese

NAME: S. Hule
DATE OF BIRTH: May 4, 1929
PASSPORT: H4567 — U.S.A.
EDUCATION: New Mexico Inst. of Earth Sciences — degree in mineralogy — 1955
EMPLOYMENT: Uranium Unlimited — management trainee — 1955-1957
Anaconda Copper Co., Montant area — geology officer — 1958-1965
Manager — Irish Mining Co., Ltd. — 1965 to date
LANG. COMMAND: English, French, Portuguese

NAME: T. Gadolin
DATE OF BIRTH: June 5, 1930
PASSPORT: L7239 — U.S.A.
EDUCATION: New York School of Mines — degree in mineralogy — 1955
EMPLOYMENT: United Kingdom Mining Board — management trainee — 1955-1957
Assistant Manager — N.D.B. Cheshire plant — 1958-1966
Manager — Idaho Cobalt Minerals — 1966 to date
LANG. COMMAND: English, Portuguese

NAME: U. Samar
DATE OF BIRTH: April 6, 1938
PASSPORT: H6259 — U.S.A.
EDUCATION: Mass. Institute of Sciences — degree in mineralogy — 1959
EMPLOYMENT: Jr. Engineer — W. Virginia Mining Research Station — 1959-1968
General Manager — Liberian State Mining Plant — 1968 to date
LANG. COMMAND: English, German, Swahili, Portuguese

NAME: V. Lute
DATE OF BIRTH: August 6, 1935
PASSPORT: K62371 — U.S.A.
EDUCATION: New York School of Miners — degree in mineralogy — 1956
EMPLOYMENT: Jr. Development Mineralogist — Ontario Mining Constr. Ltd. — 1956-1959
Asst. Chief Mineralogy Officer — Canadian Dev. Board — 1960-1963
Plant Manager — Welsh Mining Co., Ltd. — 1964 to date
LANG. COMMAND: English, French, Welsh, Pekingese

```
NAME:                W. Noddy
DATE OF BIRTH:       August 7, 1928
PASSPORT:            H63241 — U.S.A.
EDUCATION:           St. Francis University — degree in mineralogy — 1953
EMPLOYMENT:          Asst. Manager — Societé Debunquant D'ALgerie — 1953-1957
                     Manager — Kemchatka Mining Co. — 1958 to present
LANG. COMMAND:       English, Portuguese, Russian, Arabic


NAME:                X. Lanta
DATE OF BIRTH:       September 8, 1935
PASSPORT:            Q123YB — Canada
EDUCATION:           Univ. of Quebec — Diploma in English — 1955
                     Mass. Institute of Sciences — degree in mineralogy — 1958
EMPLOYMENT:          Tech. Officer, Sardinia Mining Corp. — 1960-1908
                     Manager — Moab Valley Mining Plant — 1968 to date
LANG. COMMAND:       Spanish, English, Portuguese
```

ENERGY INTERNATIONAL PROBLEM SOLUTION

Name	Age	Education	Nationality	Language Spoken	Experience
Illin	35	N.Y. School of Mines	American	Portuguese	*2 years*
Hule	42	*N. Mex. Inst. of Earth Science*	American	Portuguese	7 years
Gadolin	41	N.Y. School of Mines	American	Portuguese	6 years
Samar	33	Mass. Inst. of Sciences	American	Portuguese	5 years
Lute	36	N.Y. School of Mines	American	No Portuguese	9 years
Noddy	43	*St. Francis University*	American	Portuguese	14 years
Lanta	36	Mass. Inst. of Science	*Canadian*	Portuguese	4 years

The New Mexico Institute of Earth Sciences and St. Francis University require three special subjects for graduation and are therefore smaller than the Massachusetts Institute of Sciences or the New York School of Mines. St. Francis is not the smallest; therefore the New Mexico Institute of Earth Sciences must be. This makes N.M.I.E.S. a women's university. Brazilians hold a feudal attitude toward women.

Seismology and paleontology are essential for General Membership. St. Francis does not offer seismology; therefore no graduate of St. Francis can qualify for General Membership.

None of the Brazilian staff understands English, nor do the government inspectors; therefore, before the General Manager can countersign the inspector's report, he must be able to read Portuguese.

Each candidate except Gadolin is disqualified because he lacks the qualifications *outlined*.

81. INTERGROUP MODEL-BUILDING: THE LEGO MAN©

W. Brendan Reddy and Otto Kroeger

Goals

I. To extract the learnings from a competitive teamwork experience, in terms of leadership style, developing alternatives, dominance and submission within teams, and distribution of work and resources.

II. To diagnose the dynamics of an intact group in terms of role-taking.

Group Size

Teams of 8 to 15 participants each.

Time Required

Approximately two hours.

Materials Utilized

I. Sets of special plastic interlocking building blocks of red and white, in the shape of squares, rectangles, and pegs. (*Lego*, by Samsonite. See note below on obtaining sets specially assembled for this structured experience.) Each set of building blocks contains exactly 48 pieces, including 11 red 8's, 12 white 8's, 3 red 6's, 2 white 6's, 6 red 4's, 6 white 4's, 3 red 2's, 3 white 2's 1 red peg, and 1 white peg. Each team will have one set, and one set will be used by the facilitator to construct the model before the experience begins.

II. Lego Man Instructions Sheet for each team.

III. Model Construction Diagram for the facilitator.

IV. Chalkboard or newsprint sheets and felt-tip marker.

V. Scratch paper and pencils if teams wish to use them.

VI. Lego Man Planning and Assembly Table. (Optional.)

VII. Lego Man Planning and Assembly Time Graph. (Optional.)

Physical Setting

I. Large room with a work table for each team placed approximately fifteen feet apart.

II. Table, which displays the model, near the center of the room, also approximately fifteen feet from any team's table.

Process

I. The facilitator assembles the model Lego Man in advance of the experience and places it on the table in the center of the room.

II. If the teams are not intact groups, the facilitator forms teams in any appropriate way. He asks each team to choose an observer. (The facilitator may serve as observer if he desires to and if the number of teams makes this feasible, or he may employ staff observers.)

III. The facilitator asks observers to distribute a set of building blocks among the team members at each table, alloting each member approximately the same number of blocks. He also asks them to give a copy of the Lego Man Instructions Sheet to their teams and to ask team members to wait for further instructions before handling the materials.

IV. The facilitator explains to the observers that they are to monitor team member behavior during the process of planning and assembly of the model. He also explains the task of timing the planning and assembly periods for their individual groups. Both phases will be timed, although the teams will be aware of only the assembly-time factor.

V. The facilitator tells the teams that they will be competing with each other in assembling an exact replica of the model Lego Man on the center table. He explains that they are free to structure their time and resources in any way they find useful. He then reads the Lego Man Instructions Sheet aloud.

VI. When all teams have completed their models, the facilitator announces the winner. He then discusses the times of the individual teams in both the planning phase and assembly phase and reviews representative times of other groups for the teams to use in seeing how they "fit in" with other group norms. The facilitator may put the Lego Man Planning and Assembly Table on a chalkboard or newsprint or distribute copies of the table to the teams.

VII. The facilitator may also wish to incorporate the Lego Man Planning Production Time Graph into the discussion by reproducing the graph as a poster or by distributing copies to the teams. He discusses outcomes of various types of groups, focusing on characteristics of fragmented, smooth, and conflicted groups.

VIII. He then gives a lecturette on the dynamics of problem-solving in terms of interpersonal functioning.

IX. The observers are asked to give their individual teams feedback on how members used resources, how they worked together on an interpersonal basis, what kind of leadership behavior was observed, and what roles were played in an intact group, if applicable. The teams continue to discuss the facilitator's input and the observer's feedback in terms of how they saw their team functioning.

X. The teams are then asked to share their learnings with the group as a whole. (The facilitator may structure the times alloted for IX and X in a way that seems appropriate to the particular group.)

The facilitator may wish to introduce the variable of "outside consultants" by allowing members of the team which have completed assembly of the Lego Man first to offer their services to teams who have not yet completed the task. Observers should be alerted to the possibility of new behaviors when the "outside consultant" is introduced into the on-going efforts of the team.

This structured experience was abstracted from a paper entitled, "An Exercise for the Diagnosis of Team Problem Solving Effectiveness," by W. B. Reddy and Otto Kroeger. Used by permission.

LEGO MAN INSTRUCTIONS SHEET

Each team has a set of 48 Lego Blocks (11 red 8's, 12 white 8's, 3 red 6's, 2 white 6's, 6 red 4's, 6 white 4's, 3 red 2's, 3 white 2's, 1 red peg, 1 white peg).

You are to assemble these pieces *exactly* like the model, which is in the center of the room.

You are to spend whatever time you wish preparing to assemble your pieces. You can work together as a group in any way which you think will be most helpful in preparing to assemble and in assembling the pieces.

There are some ground rules, however:

1. Only one person may leave the table at a time to look at the model. The model may not be handled in any way. The pieces on your model cannot be taken from the table you are working on.

2. Until you are ready to start the assembly, you may not exchange the pieces or put any two pieces together. The pieces must stay in front of each person. They can be handled by that one person, but not fitted together nor lined up in any orderly arrangement.

3. When you are ready to start assembling, you should advise your observer so that he can clock the time.

4. When you are finished assembling, your observer will note the time. He will not tell you the time until all team times are in. You are to bring the assembled man to the center table, where the facilitator will determine whether the assembly has been completed properly.

5. If the facilitator finds an error when the assembly is completed, he will advise the team that the model is not correct, but he will not tell what the error is. The observer will start timing again, adding to the original time.

6. Remember, you can have all the time you want to prepare as a group for the assembly, but let your observer know when you are ready to start assembling.

Lego Man Planning and Assembly Table

In Minutes

Group	Activity	Mean	Standard Deviation
Total (N = 110 groups)	Planning	53.46	28.62
	Assembly	11.04	9.48
Managers (N=14 groups)	Planning	63.28	4.43
	Assembly	6.41	3.59
Teachers (N=11 groups)	Planning	35.06	25.12
	Assembly	17.53	13.01
Administrators (N=11 groups)	Planning	24.72	20.20
	Assembly	27.98	18.01

Record Time: Planning, 93 minutes; Assembly, 38 seconds.

LEGO MAN PLANNING AND ASSEMBLY TIME GRAPH

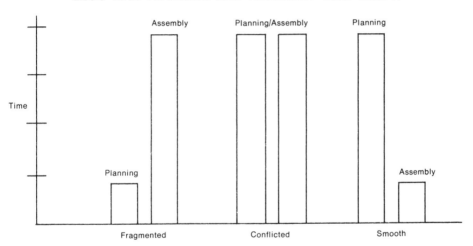

GROUP TYPE

Fragmented groups. Autocratic leadership, subgroupings, and minority pressure forces these groups into making rather quick decisions without considering quality alternatives. Openness is not a norm. They exhibit minimal effort and minimal gain.

Conflicted groups. They are cautious, suspicious, and while they consider many alternate plans, they are not able to move toward consensus. They tend to use majority vote, usually as a desperate move; however, there is little commitment to the plan or outcome. They exhibit maximal effort and minimal gain.

Smoothly functioning groups. They tend to be trusting, cohesive, and exhibit high interaction and sharing. They test for consensus without threatening members and seem committed to the plan and outcome. They are characterized by minimal effort and maximal gain.

LEGO MAN

Top layer, face up.

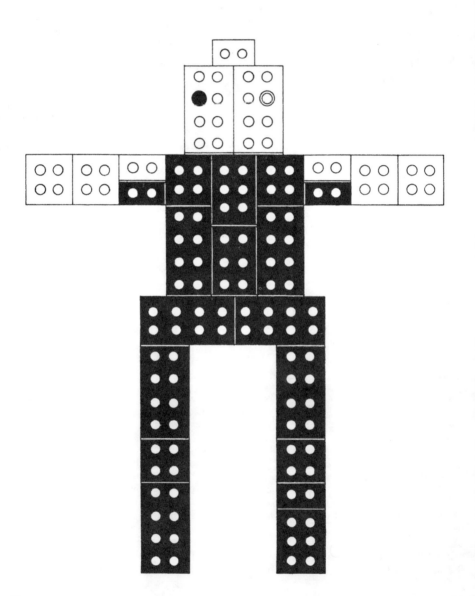

LEGO MAN

Bottom layer, face down

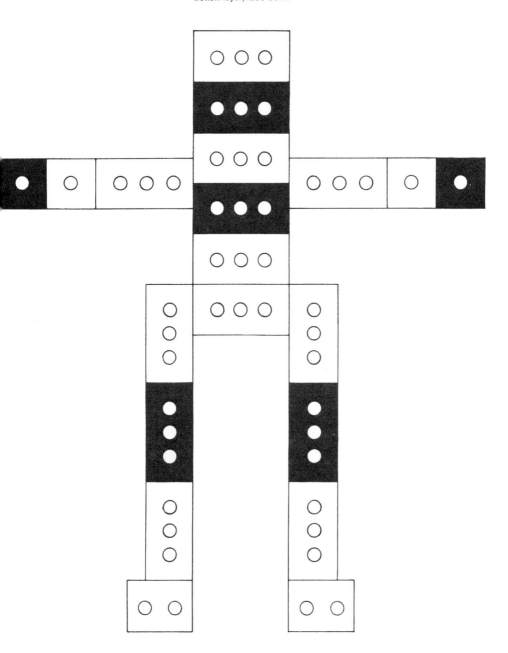

LEGO MAN
Composite view

42

NORMATIVE NOTES

82. GREETING CARDS: AN ORGANIZATION SIMULATION

Goals

I. To observe a group's organizational style and functioning.

II. To gather data on individuals' responses to creating and operating a production-centered organization.

III. To give group members feedback on their organizational behavior.

Group Size

Approximately twenty-four members. Two or more previously designated smaller groups may be joined into one larger group for this task.

Time Required

Three to six hours (one afternoon and/or one evening session, for example).

Materials Utilized

I. Task, Requirements and Attitude Sheet for each member.

II. Product Specifications Sheet for each member.

III. One or two copies of each bulletin from the Acme Brokerage Co. (8:00 p.m., 8:15 p.m., and 8:30 p.m. are the sample times used).

IV. Two copies of the Rating Sheet for each member for pre- and post-testing.

V. Pencil for each member.

VI. Ample supply of 8½"x 11" sheets of paper.

Physical Setting

Large room with movable desks, tables, and chairs to facilitate the group members arranging their own production environment.

Process

I. If the group has not previously met as a whole before, the facilitator may arrange that they have lunch together to become acquainted or he may design some other social interaction with the total group before the task is discussed.

II. The facilitator may wish to briefly outline the task toward the end of this social period so that preliminary discussion of the task may take place.

III. The facilitator will distribute the Task, Requirements and Attitude sheet and the Product Specifications sheet to each member. The group is asked to meet in the room set aside for the production in order to organize itself for the task. A diagram of its organization or plan of operation must be submitted by the group to the facilitator at the end of a specified time period (1-2 hours).

The facilitator asks the group to select two observers who will not participate in any of the interaction from this point on. The observers will take notes on the behavior and interaction of the other group members. They are also reminded to choose one member who will be responsible for getting the market requirements from the Acme Brokerage Co.

The facilitator explains to the group that they may go about the task in any fashion which they choose. He explains that they need not go into actual production until the time indicated on the Task, Requirements and Attitude sheet but that they may wish to have a pilot run to test, in a preliminary fashion, how the organization is working.

IV. At the designated time, the facilitator receives the diagram or plan from the group and administers the Rating Sheet. The group processes the rating data.

V. At the time designated for production, the facilitator gives the first bulletin from the Acme Brokerage Co. to the group member who has been assigned this part of the task. He will continue to distribute a bulletin for each of the next two fifteen-minute segments. After forty-five minutes, he will stop production and ask the group to make its final tabulations. When the task is completed, he administers the Rating Sheet for the second time.

VI. The facilitator asks the group to take a fifteen minute break while the results of the two Rating Sheets are being evaluated.

VII. After the break, the data from the rating sheets will be reviewed and the production figures discussed. The facilitator will then ask the observers to give the group and/or individuals feedback. Finally, he will open the entire task experience for group discussion and evaluation. (The facilitator may design this evaluation period in any way that seems appropriate to the group he is working with, perhaps giving different emphasis to the various aspects of evaluation.

TASK, REQUIREMENTS, AND ATTITUDE SHEET

TASK

The group will create and operate a business organization which will produce a product. The positions in the organization are to be filled by the members of the group.

Be sure your organization can meet emergencies and shifting market demands, since these will be introduced into the exercise.

This exercise is focused primarily on problems of productivity rather than on problems of profitability. Consequently, you do not need to be concerned about problems of capital, retained earnings, balance sheets, pay scales, budget controls, purchasing, etc. Assume that all personnel are adequately paid. Raw materials and floor space will be made available as needed. You will be told what market conditions exist at the time your plant begins operating (8:00 p.m. today).

The products are sheets of paper containing verses of the kind used in greeting cards. Products must conform to the standards outlined on the Product Specifications Sheet. You will need to work out some way of making sure that the specifications are met, and that data are gathered on: 1) *total volume of output*, 2) *proper product mix* (i.e. meeting the market demand for certain kinds of verse), and 3) *percentage of rejects*. Be sure that your records are set up to keep these data current. In determining volume and product mix figures, you can count only finished products in inventory at the end of any production period. Goods in process are *not* to be counted. Thus you will need a place to store finished inventory.

You will not need a sales force, but you will need some person to get market requirements from Acme Brokerage Co. In meeting changes in market requirements, excess finished inventory may be carried over to the next period, but work in process cannot be used this way.

REQUIREMENTS FOR THE ORGANIZATION

1. Produce a large volume of verses that meet specifications and are of the types required to meet market demand.
2. Maximize creativity of all personnel as they do their work.
3. Encourage maximum involvement and self-direction among all personnel.
4. Maintain flexibility needed to deal with changes in market demand or with unexpected internal disturbances of the organization.
5. Provide for assistance and consultation for any personnel who are being blocked or hindered from doing a good job.

ATTITUDE TOWARD THE TASK

Try to be creative in designing the organization rather than using existing organizations as models. You may even wish to use new names for any positions you create. Do not rely on textbook approaches — enjoy yourself!

PRODUCT SPECIFICATIONS SHEET

1. Each 8½"x11" sheet of paper must contain two different two-line verses. Both are about the same occasion, however.
2. The lines of each two-line verse must rhyme, but the two verses on the page need not rhyme with each other.
3. Each sheet must have a title at the top which shows the kind of occasion for which the verses are to be used. For example: New Year's, Mother's Day, Father's Birthday, Get Well, etc.
4. Every sheet must be different; no duplication of verses.
5. Grammar, spelling, punctuation and capitalization must be correct. Lines should have approximately the same meter, but this is not a rigid requirement.
6. Verses may be serious or humorous.

Sample Product

Birthday
I see that you are 82;
The years are sneaking up on you.

———————

I wish you lots of cheer today;
In every friendly sort of way.

GREETING CARD BULLETINS

8:00 p.m. Bulletin

The Acme Brokerage Co. buys all of the cards of your company. The market conditions are such that between 8:00 and 8:15 they will purchase any number of verses in the following percentages:

50% New Year's Day verses

50% Valentine's Day verses

These market conditions may change and the Acme firm is always on the lookout for new markets.

8:15 p.m. Bulletin

The Acme Brokerage Co. now is prepared to purchase verses in the following percentages:

25% New Year's Day verses

25% Wedding Congratulations verses

20% Verses for "sensitivity" cards

30% Verses for Get Well Cards for facilitators

8:30 p.m. Bulletin

The Acme Brokerage Co. announces a change in market requirements. It will now purchase verses in the following percentages:

20% Verses for men who have just become engaged

15% Halloween verses

15% Labor Day Greeting verses

5% St. Patrick's Day verses

20% Get Well Verses for the Boss

25% Verses to develop new markets

GREETING CARD RATING SHEET

1. How strong is(was) your desire to help this organization work effectively?

    (   ) 1. Extremely weak
    (   ) 2. Very weak
    (   ) 3. Weak
    (   ) 4. Neither weak nor strong
    (   ) 5. Strong
    (   ) 6. Very strong
    (   ) 7. Extremely strong

2. How satisfied are you(were you) with your own job assignment in the organization?

    (   ) 1. Completely dissatisfied
    (   ) 2. Very dissatisfied
    (   ) 3. Dissatisfied
    (   ) 4. Neither satisfied nor dissatisfied
    (   ) 5. Satisfied
    (   ) 6. Very satisfied
    (   ) 7. Completely satisfied

3. How free will you be(were you) to use your own initiative and creativity in helping this organization work well?

    (   ) 1. Completely restricted from using initiative and creativity
    (   ) 2. Very restricted
    (   ) 3. Restricted
    (   ) 4. Somewhat restricted, somewhat free
    (   ) 5. Free
    (   ) 6. Very free
    (   ) 7. Extremely free to use initiative and creativity

4. Do you think there is (was) adequate provision for your getting help and consultation when you "get stuck" or have trouble in your work?

    (   ) 1. Completely inadequate
    (   ) 2. Very inadequate
    (   ) 3. Inadequate
    (   ) 4. Somewhat adequate
    (   ) 5. Adequate
    (   ) 6. Very adequate
    (   ) 7. Completely adequate

5. To what extent will you be (were you) feeling bossed, pushed around, over-supervised?

   (   ) 1. A great deal
   (   ) 2. Quite a bit
   (   ) 3. Somewhat
   (   ) 4. A little
   (   ) 5. Not at all

6. How many units of marketable product do you estimate this organization will produce (has produced) per hour?

   Write in number: _____

83. DECISIONS:
AN INTERGROUP NEGOTIATION

Goals

    I. To experience the issues surrounding intergroup trust-building and trust-betrayal.

    II. To explore considerations of intergroup competition versus collaboration.

    III. To examine limited communication under stress.

    IV. To study negotiation and negotiation strategies.

    V. To consider group decision making processes.

Group Size

    Three groups of three to six members each (with more than 18 participants try four groups).

Time Required

    A minimum of four and one-half hours.

Materials Utilized

    I. Participant Instruction Outline sheets.

    II. Decisions Tally Sheets reproduced on newsprint.

    III. Newsprint and felt-tip markers.

    IV. Decision Ballots.

Physical Setting

    Three adjacent rooms. One of the rooms should be large enough for the three groups to meet at the beginning and end of the structured experience. There should also be sufficient space for two pairs of participants to meet separately and simultaneously away from observation by any of the teams (a hallway would suffice).

Process

    I. Three teams of equal size are formed. Then the facilitator distributes one copy of the Participant Instruction Outline to each participant and instructs the participants to take about five minutes to look through the Outline.

    II. The facilitator follows the Participant Instruction Outline as he explains the procedures for the experience. The participants then proceed to their separate rooms.

    III. The Decisions Tally Sheets (if this form is copied on a sheet of newsprint for each group, sharing the results in the discussion following the 10th round is more convenient) and two sets of Decision Ballots are distributed to each group. During the first hour before Round 1 decision is due, each group:

        (1) plans its management philosophy (e.g., The kind of behavior it wishes to exhibit to

produce the desired image, and the way it intends to operate internally during the experience);

(2) determines the percent of the potential market the group wishes to achieve and convert that percentage into a dollar goal (the maximum potential market for the three groups' combined total is $7,425,000; maximum potential for each group is $6,600,000; past experience has yielded actual market totals in the $1,100,000 to $6,900,000 range with a large clustering between $2,800,000 and $5,400,000);

(3) decides upon the 1st decision and projects decisions 2 and 3 for all three groups producing a goal for each of the first 3 rounds.

The management philosophy is recorded on a sheet of newsprint and the market potential, goals, and decisions are recorded on the Decisions Tally Sheet.

The recorder is also chosen by the group during the first hour. The recorder submits all group decisions to the facilitator in order to avoid confusion. The group may change recorders at any time.

IV. At the end of the first hour the facilitator collects from each group recorder two Decision Ballots indicating the group's two Round 1 decisions. The facilitator then sorts the six Decision Ballots for Round 1 and redistributes such that Group A receives the B→A and C→A Ballots, Group B receives the A→B and C→B Ballots, and Group C receives the A→C and B→C Ballots. Each team then records the two decisions received in the appropriate columns on the Decisions Tally Sheet. The result is then computed using the "Summary of Payoffs" table in the Participant Instruction Outline. This payoff is recorded on the Tally Sheet and the cumulative balance is inserted. After this is completed each group should have the first row of the Tally Sheet completely filled in with the group's decision for that round (either "red" or "green") inserted in the "Your decision" column, the group's guess as to the other group's decision for that round in the "Your guess" column, the group's goal for that round (the result of "Your decision" and "Your guess") in the "Goal" column, the other group's actual decision from their Decision Ballot in the "Actual decision" column, the result from the "Summary of Payoffs" table from the combination of "Your decision" and the "Actual decision" in the "Result" column, and the sum of the previous balance and this round's result as the cumulative balance in the "Balance" column.

V. Each group then makes its Round 2 decisions and records them on the Decision Ballots. Ten minutes after the Round 1 decisions were due the facilitator collects the Round 2 decisions, sorts them, and redistributes them as in Round 1. Each team then records the decisions, computes the results, and figures the balance.

VI. At the end of Round 3 the same procedure as in Rounds 1 and 2 is repeated except that the payoff result derived from the payoff table is multiplied by 3. Thus a payoff of plus $25,000 becomes a payoff of plus $75,000 and a payoff of minus $25,000 becomes a payoff of minus $75,000, etc.

VII. After the Round 3 decisions have been redistributed and Round 4 has begun, the facilitator reminds the participants that communication between groups is now possible. If, for example, Group A wishes to communicate with Group B, Group A's recorder informs the facilitator of this desire. The facilitator then goes to Group B and informs its members that Group A wishes to communicate. Group B may agree to communicate at this or a later time or may refuse to communicate. The facilitator returns to Group A with Group B's answer. If Group B has refused to communicate with Group A, Group A may re-request communication with Group B as often and frequently as it wishes. If Group B agrees to communicate, the facilitator instructs each of the two groups to choose one of its members as a representative to the other group. Any member, including the

52

recorder is eligible to be a representative provided that he has not previously been a representative to the third group. When both groups have chosen a representative, the facilitator takes the two representatives to a neutral spot which cannot be observed by any of the three groups (usually a hallway or stairwell suffices). The facilitator remains with the two representatives during their meeting. The meeting ends at the discretion of either representative. The representatives then return to their respective groups. Each time one group wishes to communicate with another group the procedure is repeated.

Round 4 decisions are submitted to the facilitator at the end of the round following the same procedure as the previous rounds.

VIII. At the beginning of Round 5 the facilitator reminds the teams that from this point through the remainder of the experience 15 minute time extensions may be granted. If a group wishes a time extension, that group's recorder informs the facilitator of their desire. The facilitator goes to each of the other two groups separately and informs them that a time extension has been requested. The facilitator does not indicate which group has made the request. If both groups agree to the time extension, the facilitator informs the three groups that a 15 minute time extension has been granted and reminds them of the new time at which this round's decisions are due. If either group refuses to agree to the time extension request, the facilitator informs the other two groups that the time extension has been denied. He does not indicate which group refused to agree to the extension. Round 5 decisions are submitted to the facilitator at the end of the round following the same procedure as in the earlier rounds except that the payoff is multiplied by 5.

IX. The remaining Rounds 6 through 10 are conducted following the same procedure as Rounds 4 and 5. Rounds 6 and 7 contain no payoff multiples. Rounds 8 and 9 use a payoff multiple of 5, and Round 10 has a payoff multiple of 10.

X. After the Round 10 decisions are scored, each group totals its results on the Tally Sheet. The groups are then to reassemble in the central meeting for discussion of the experience.

XI. Discussion of the experience follows focusing on such issues as: the trust which developed or failed to develop between pairs of representatives and groups; the effect of prior judgments or impressions of the members of other teams on trust; the effects of betrayal on later contact between groups; the attitudes exhibited toward competition versus collaboration and their effect on the total dollar market achieved (collaboration usually results in a larger total market than does competition among the three groups); the effectiveness of the communication between representatives; the communication between the representative and his group; negotiation strategies and tactics; decision making in the groups; power and influence among team members; formal and informal leadership styles exhibited.

Suggested Adaptations

This structured experience lends itself to a variety of adaptations depending on the purposes and outcomes desired by the facilitator. Following are a few suggested adaptations. They are by no means intended to be a complete listing.

1. Planning and organizing

   Participants are asked during Round 4 to develop an overall strategy with possible alternative contingencies for the remainder of the experience. This might include negotiation tactics as well as dollar goals for each round. An additional hour time for Round 4 is sufficient for this planning.

2. Problem solving

   Participants are asked during Round 1 and/or Round 4 to use a pre-introduced problem solving model in order to develop the mathematical alternatives for each round's goal. The problem solving input may be used in conjunction with the planning and organizing adaptation.

3. Criteria

   Each group is asked to select one of its members to represent the group on a criteria-setting committee meeting either in Round 4 or at the conclusion of Round 10 (Round 4 is preferable since less justifying of the group's already committed action takes place. Also the first 3 rounds allow the participants to better understand the procedures of the experience.). The committee is then instructed to develop criteria using some previously discussed guidelines for effective criteria, or they are merely told to develop criteria. In order for the entire community of participants to learn from this experience, the remainder of the participants fishbowl the criteria committee (An open chair to allow other participants to move in and out of the committee is very effective.). This type of criteria session usually requires 1½ to 3 hours to do an effective job.

4. Individual values

   The facilitator asks the participants in each group to list adjectives describing the other two groups at various times during the experience. Suggested times are during Round 1, at the beginning of Round 4 before any communication between groups has occurred, before high risk decisions are submitted (especially before the Round 10 decisions are redistributed), after any trust betrayals or "double-crosses," and just before reassembling after Round 10. Putting these on newsprint makes discussion easier.

5. Leadership and group dynamics

   Before reassembling after Round 10, one of the many available group climate or feedback assessment forms are distributed to the participants to complete and then share in each group. Or a facilitator leads an informal discussion in each group concerning the leadership flow, leadership styles exhibited, communication within the group, and/or other aspects of the dynamics which developed during the course of the experience. Whether using an instrument to facilitate the discussion or not, having 3 facilitators, one in each group, is the most effective method for handling this sort of processing.

This structured experience was contributed by Henry I. Feir. Recognition is also given to Richard J. Turner, Robert Cox, Daniel N. Kanouse, and Robert G. Mason, all of RCA Corporation, for their initial development work for this structured experience.

DECISIONS
PARTICIPANT INSTRUCTION OUTLINE

I. Summary of Payoffs

Your Group's Payoff°	Your Group's Decision	Other Group's Decision	Other Group's Payoff°
+ 25	Red	Red	+ 25
− 25	Red	Green	+ 100
+ 100	Green	Red	− 25
+ 5	Green	Green	+ 5

°All plus(+) units represent thousands of dollars of profit
All minus(−) units represent thousands of dollars of loss

Five of the rounds contain multiples which will vary the above payoff summary. The rounds and their multiples are:

Round 3 multiply by 3   Round 9 multiply by 5

Round 5 multiply by 5   Round 10 multiply by 10

Round 8 multiply by 5

II. Initial Assignment

During the first hour each group must:

1. plan its management philosophy (e.g., the kind of behavior it wishes to exhibit to produce the desired image, and the way it intends to operate internally during the experience);

2. determine the per cent of the potential market the group wishes to achieve and convert that percentage into a dollar goal;

3. decide upon the 1st decision and project decisions 2 and 3 for all three groups producing a goal for each of the first 3 rounds.

III. Recorder

Each group chooses one of its members to serve as recorder. In case a decision is not made by the group in the time allowed for the round, the recorder must submit the decision for the group. The group may change recorders at any time.

IV. Communication

No communication between groups is permitted during the first 3 rounds.

Beginning with the 4th round two groups may communicate with each other via 1 representative from each group meeting apart from the other participants in the presence of the facilitator.

The two representatives and the facilitator may freely communicate with each other; however, commitments made during these meetings are not binding upon the group's behavior (e.g., commitments will not be enforced by the facilitator if they are violated). All three groups may not meet together in any one meeting. Thus if Group A wishes to communicate with both Group B and Group C, Group A must send one representative to meet with Group B and a different representative to meet with Group C in a separate meeting.

Each representative may meet with only one group during the course of this structured experience (for instance, if Bill represents Group A in discussions with Group B he can never be a representative to Group C).

The group may change representatives at any time. Groups may communicate as often, as frequently, and as long as time during rounds allows.

V. *Time Schedule*

Round 1 begins at the end of the explanation of procedures for this structured experience. All subsequent rounds begin as soon as the Decision Ballots from the previous round are redistributed to each group. The rounds end when the decisions for that round are due. The time of the 10 rounds is as follows:

Round 1	1 hour	°Round 6	15 minutes
Round 2	10 minutes	Round 7	15 minutes
Round 3	10 minutes	Round 8	15 minutes
Round 4	1 hour	Round 9	15 minutes
Round 5	15 minutes	Round 10	15 minutes

°Rounds 6 through 10 may be extended in 15 minute increments by mutual agreement of all three groups. There is no limit to the number of time extensions allowed.

VI. *Evaluation Criteria*

1. Were your goals reasonable, realistic, and challenging?
2. Was your behavior consistent with your management philosophy?

DECISIONS TALLY SHEET

	A ——→B°								A——→C°°					
Round #	Your dec.	Your guess	Goal	Actual dec.	Result	Bal.		Round #	Your dec.	Your guess	Goal	Actual dec.	Result	Bal.
1								1						
2								2						
3(x3)								3(x3)						
4								4						
5 (x5)								5(x5)						
6								6						
7								7						
8(x5)								8(x5)						
9(x5)								9(x5)						
10(x10)								10(x10)						

A——→B° Total _____

A——→C°° Total _____

A——→B° Total _____

Grand Total _____

Maximum Potential Market _____

% Goal _____

$ Goal _____

_____

°For Team B's Tally Sheet substitute BA
For Team C's Tally Sheet substitute CA

°°For Team B's Tally Sheet substitute BC
For Team C's Tally Sheet substitute CB

DECISION BALLOT°

From Group _____ to Group _____
Round # _____ Decision
        Red   Green   (Circle one)

°The facilitator should prepare 10 copies of each of the following ballots:

From Group A to Group B
From Group A to Group C
From Group B to Group A
From Group B to Group C
From Group C to Group A
From Group C to Group B

84. PSYCHOMAT

Goals

I. To provide an atmosphere in which participants can encounter each other in a variety of ways.

II. To encourage creative, sensitive risk-taking on the part of participants.

III. To explore reactions to a highly unstructured interpersonal situation.

Group Size

Unlimited.

Time Required

All day.

Physical Setting

One room large enough to accommodate a great deal of subgrouping. It is highly desirable that the room be carpeted, so that participants may sit/lie on the floor. Movable furniture (or no furniture) is necessary.

Process

I. Prior to the day of the psychomat, a staff should be assembled and oriented. There should be enough staff for a ratio of 1 to 10 participants. A staff meeting should be held to get acquainted, to sort out roles, and to surface expectations, assumptions, etc.

II. The event is promoted as an exercise in freedom and an opportunity to give and receive feedback. Prospective participants are informed that there will be no planned activities and no rules. They can come and go as they wish and do whatever they are willing to take responsibility for. The orientation might include some examples of things that might occur, such as spontaneous formation of feedback groups, nonverbal exercises, lecturettes, meditation, pairing, etc. It is a self-and-other-oriented "psychological happening."

III. No instructions are given at the beginning of the day or during the course of the event. Facilitators model openness, sensitivity to self and others, positive resolution of conflict, and experimental attitudes. They do what their training, experience, and impulses suggest. They *let* things happen, and they attempt to help participants learn from the experiences.

IV. At the end of the day the staff meets to evaluate the experience, to determine whether any participants need to be followed up, and to discuss their reactions to their roles.

85. GROWTH AND NAME FANTASY

Goal

I. To provide group participants with an opportunity to review, in fantasy, the phases of growth and development they have accomplished.

II. To review their sense of individual identity.

Group Size

Unlimited.

Time Required

Relative to the ongoing process: approximately 45 minutes. The experience is most useful in an introductory period in a laboratory.

Physical Setting

Space enough so that each participant can focus on himself rather than his awareness of others.

Process

I. The facilitator instructs participants to find a comfortable space where they can stretch out, relax, and become aware of themselves.

II. The facilitator spends a short time on suggestions for heightening self awareness: closing eyes, regulating breathing, feeling heartbeat or pulsebeat, becoming aware of body heat, space occupied, etc.

III. The facilitator then begins a slow-paced structured fantasy during which he provides cues for recollections and past memories. He may ask the participants to recall their earliest memory, images of significant others (parents, brothers and sisters) or early childhood experiences. He provides cues for "first" events: the first fistfight, first days of school, or a first pet. He traces a rough chronological order, eliciting memories of school grades, graduations, moves, birthdays, first dates, happy or embarrassing experiences, first job, vocational choice, love relationships, marriage, and so on.

The effectiveness of the fantasy depends on the facilitator's ability to provide concrete memory cues for the participants. Photographs, looking through albums, report cards, diplomas are potent cues for remembering; so are sense experiences, such as smelling home cooking and perfume or tactile experiences such as favorite clothes that were outgrown. Many others will suggest themselves.

IV. After reviewing a life chronology, the facilitator focuses on one aspect of the participant's identity — his name. He asks participants to trace their name with their finger on the rug, to review nicknames, to visualize the name as it has been written in various places:

on a check, at the end of a love letter, on a document, etc. He may suggest visualizing the name in print, in Gothic letters, on a marquee, on the cover of a magazine, in skywriting, etc. Auditory fantasy can be employed; this may include listening to the name as repeated by significant others or by famous voices (Bette Davis, JFK, etc.). He may ask the participants to begin whispering their names and then gradually raising the whisper to a shout.

V. The facilitator begins terminating the fantasy by asking participants to slowly open their eyes, sit up, etc. Processing of the experience can occur in a small group or in dyads or triads.

This structured experience was contributed by Tony Banet.

86. SYMBOLIC CLOSING EXERCISE

Goals

I. To finish a workshop or laboratory with a sense of closure.

II. To re-enact the group process in symbolic nonverbal action.

Group size

Any number.

Time Required

Depends on the area used and number of people. The exercise should be done *slowly*. Approximately ten minutes is an average.

Physical Setting

Preferably to be done outdoors but can be done inside. (If done inside, the center of the room must be clear of furniture.) The space allotted for the experience should have some spot that can be designated as the center. Any object will serve that purpose.

Process

I. The facilitator tells the participants that the closing will be a brief, nonverbal exercise. (If the exercise will be outside, it is advisable to ask participants not to go so far that they cannot hear the facilitator's directions.) He then asks them to follow him in silence to the outside and to continue in silence throughout the exercise.

II. When the participants reach the area designated, the facilitator asks them to spread out into a large circle facing outward so that they cannot see anyone. He asks them to experience the feeling of being by themselves. This should be allotted at least two or three minutes.

III. The facilitator asks the group to slowly turn around and face inward. He then instructs them to slowly move toward the center of the field or room and tells them to get as close as they can to the center so that they bunch together as tightly as possible.

IV. When they have all bunched together, he asks them to take time to experience what it feels like to be a group. Again, allot two or three minutes.

V. The facilitator asks the participants to form a circle shoulder to shoulder, arms entwined. He asks them to look at everyone in this group.

VI. He tells them to drop their arms to their sides and move three steps backward. The facilitator announces that this will be the last opportunity to look at everyone.

VII. Finally, the facilitator asks that the participants face outward once again and move several feet out to where they are by themselves. After about a minute, he announces that the exercise and workshop or laboratory is over.

A. With a group of young people, the center clustering may be a "pile-on," or they may even crawl to the center and pile on. Be careful if the size of the group is more than twenty since there is a danger of crushing someone.

B. At step V above, with a small group of about fifteen, you can designate one person as first and another person at the other end of the group as last. Ask all to hold hands. Have the last person remain stationary and the first person to wind the group around the last one, like a watch spring. The group ends up in a tight cluster. Ask them to experience where they are: in the middle of the group, on the edge, etc. Then reverse the winding so that the first person is in the middle and the last person is on the outside and take a minute for all to experience where they are, the opposite of their original experience in the "spring."

C. When the group has formed a circle in step five, there may be spontaneous dancing, rhythmic swaying, or singing by the group, or the facilitator may suggest it. If they spontaneously begin to talk with one another, allow it to run its course.

D. Generally speaking, there is no need to process this symbolic nonverbal re-enactment of a group coming together and then separating. However, the exercise could be used at the mid-point of a longer lab when there is a day or weekend break. It may be used as the opener of the second half, followed by processing of the dynamics of a group coming together and parting.

Note well: Be sure that you clearly announce that this is the last exercise and the closing of the group and *take your time*. If this is not done slowly, the group may react to what to them seems a very abrupt ending and thus destroy any sense of closure the exercise is trying to achieve.

This structured experience was contributed by Maury Smith.

INTRODUCTION
TO THE
INSTRUMENTATION
SECTION

The purposes of including instruments in the *Annual* are (1) to make available to group facilitators some scales that are useful in research about groups, teaching, training, sensing, etc.; (2) to stimulate the development and adaptation of data-generating devices in the groups field; and (3) to illustrate several approaches for the measurement of variables that facilitators need to observe. This section continues the sharing of instruments which is a feature of the three volumes of the *Handbook of Structured Experiences for Human Relations Training*. Those volumes contain the following instruments:

T-P Leadership Questionnaire (Vol. I, pp. 9-10.)
Opinionnaire on Assumptions About Human Relations Training (Vol. I, pp. 117-120.)
Problem Analysis Questionnaire (Vol. II, pp. 85-89.)
Life Planning Program (Vol. II, pp. 114-126.)
Group Climate Inventory (Vol. III, pp. 29-30.)
Group Growth Evaluation (Vol. III, pp. 31-32.)
Feedback Rating Scale (Vol. III, pp. 33-35.)
Post-Meeting Reactions (Vol. III, p. 36.)
Learning Climate Analysis Form (Vol. III, pp. 42-44.)
Group Behavior Questionnaire (Vol. III, pp. 45-46.)
Intentions and Choice Inventory (Vol. III, p. 47.)
Opionionnaire on Womanhood (Vol. III, p. 67.)

Four additional instruments are included in this section of the *Annual*. The first focuses on measuring the extent to which one's managing style fits the Theory-X — Theory-Y approaches described by McGregor. Hipple devised the IRRS from a broad sampling of goal statements attributed to the intensive small group experience. The Intervention Style Survey is based on the theory of Blake and Mouton and illustrates a measurement approach that is adaptable to other theoretical formulations. Wile developed and validated the GTQ with psychotherapy groups, but the questionnaire has wide utility for facilitators of various types of groups. The GTQ has merit not only for research but also for teaching and providing feedback to facilitators.

The authors of these instruments are interested in feedback on the use of the scales, and facilitators may find mailing addresses in the List of Contributors Section. Norms, summary statistics, study results, and adaptations should be shared directly with these contributors.

Instruments such as those included in this series can be used in a variety of ways by group facilitators. Some purposes served by the use of such devices include the following:

Forming groups, by controlling the homogeneity of their compositions.

Providing instrumented feedback to group members.

Assisting a group in diagnosing its own functioning and development.

Generating sensing data through surveys for organization diagnosis.

Teaching various human relations concepts through self-examination.

Researching outcomes of education/training designs.

These scales are not intended to be used to "fingerprint" individuals, that is, the reliability and validity of such measurement devices often are not sufficient to place high confidence in the accuracy of the responses for a given person. But for use with groups of people, more stable results can be obtained. Individual group members need to be cautioned not to overinterpret their scores.

SUPERVISORY ATTITUDES: THE X-Y SCALE*

The theory underlying this scale is explained briefly in the Theory X-Theory Y lecturette in section III. The intent is to use the X-Y Scale to introduce the McGregor theory by having the respondent think about his own style first.

Five steps can be incorporated into the use of the X-Y Scale:

1. Have trainees complete Part I of the scale.
2. Give a brief lecturette on the Theory X-Theory Y formulation.
3. Have trainees complete Part II.
4. Score Part I and illustrate how trainees locate themselves on the scale using that score.
5. Lead a discussion of the results, comparing discrepancies between self-perception and more specific data at Part I.

Scoring instructions: Items 4 and 10 are worded so that the scoring is reversed from that of the other eight items. For items 1-3 and 5-9 the scoring is done like this:

Do	Tend to do	Tend to Avoid	Avoid
1	2	3	4

The appropriate number is written beside the check mark, and these are summed. (For items 4 and 10 the scale is 4, 3, 2, and 1). This score is located on the scale in Part II and is a crude index of the extent to which the respondent's assumptions match those of the two theories.

---

*The X-Y Scale was adapted from an instrument developed by Robert N. Ford of AT&T for in-house training of supervisors. Ten items were taken from the longer instrument, and the selection was based upon their application to a wide variety of training enterprises.

NORMATIVE NOTES

SUPERVISORY ATTITUDES: THE X-Y SCALE

_____
NAME

_____
GROUP

Part I

Directions: The following are various types of behavior which a supervisor (manager, leader) may engage in in relation to subordinates. Read each item carefully and then put a check mark in one of the columns to indicate what you would do.

If I were the supervisor, I would:	Make a Great Effort to Do This	Tend to Do This	Tend to Avoid Doing This	Make a Great Effort to Avoid This
1. Closely supervise my subordinates in order to get better work from them.				
2. Set the goals and objectives for my subordinates and sell them on the merits of my plans.				
3. Set up controls to assure that my subordinates are getting the job done.				
4. Encourage my subordinates to set their own goals and objectives.				
5. Make sure that my subordinates' work is planned out for them.				
6. Check with my subordinates daily to see if they need any help.				
7. Step in as soon as reports indicate that the job is slipping.				
8. Push my people to meet schedules if necessary.				
9. Have frequent meetings to keep in touch with what is going on.				
10. Allow subordinates to make important decisions.				

Part II

Directions: Read the descriptions of the two theories of leadership below. Think about your own attitudes toward subordinates, and locate on the scale below where you think you are in reference to these sets of assumptions.

THEORY X ASSUMPTIONS

1. The average human being has an inherent dislike of work and will avoid it if he can.
2. Because of this human characteristic of dislike for work, most people must be coerced, controlled, directed, and threatened with punishment to get them to put forth adequate effort toward the achievement of organizational objectives.
3. The average human being prefers to be directed, wishes to avoid responsibility, has relatively little ambition, and wants security above all.

THEORY Y ASSUMPTIONS

1. The expenditure of physical and mental effort in work is as natural as play or rest.
2. External control and the threat of punishment are not the only means of bringing about effort toward organizational objectives. Man will exercise self-direction and self-control in the service of objectives to which he is committed.
3. Commitment to objectives is a function of the rewards associated with their achievement.
4. The average human being learns under proper conditions not only to accept but also to seek responsibility.
5. The capacity to exercise a high degree of imagination, ingenuity and creativity in the solution of organizational problems is widely, not narrowly, distributed in the population.
6. Under the conditions of modern industrial life the intellectual potentialities of the average human being are only partially utilized.

Indicate on the scale below where you would classify your own basic attitudes toward your subordinates in terms of McGregor's Theory X and Theory Y.

| Theory X | | | | Theory Y |
| 10 | 20 | 30 | 40 | |

INTERPERSONAL
RELATIONSHIP
RATING SCALE

John L. Hipple

Development. Measurement of individual and group change in the personal growth area of human relations training is a very difficult task. Many standardized personality instruments are too technical and unwieldy to use in research or training. The Interpersonal Relationship Rating Scale (IRRS) was developed specifically to meet the special needs of human relations training and is designed to test for outcomes in personal growth experiences. In designing the items for the scale, the author considered the following specifications: (1) The content of the items should attempt to measure attitudes and/or behaviors in the individual's relationships with others and how he sees himself. The content of the items must be meaningful to the respondents so that they can respond as accurately as possible. (2) The statements have to be designed to assess observable behaviors and/or attitudes as much as possible. When dealing with interpersonal relationships it is very difficult to be completely objective; consequently many of the items are very subjective. (3) The scale had to examine behavior that would presumably be affected by participation in personal growth experiences of human relations training.

The scale is a self-administered paper and pencil inventory which takes approximately ten minutes to complete. It consists of twenty-four seven-point numerical rating scales, written in such a way that high ratings are "positive" and low ratings are "negative." At this stage in its development, the IRRS is best analyzed in terms of average group ratings on the individual scales, but future research and development is aimed at incorporating an analysis of the total numerical score for the instrument. The instrument is designed so that the participant and/or persons who know him well (significant others) may respond. Data from respondents in the participants' life space can be very valuable in assessing behavioral changes.

The original form of the IRRS was tested on thirty-four participants in a three-day human relations training laboratory. These individuals responded to the IRRS on a pre, post, and seven-week followup schedule. Identified significant others completed the IRRS on a pre and followup basis. Participants described themselves more "positively" after the laboratory experiences, and this "positive" description persisted through the followup period. The pre to post average self-rating increased from 4.61 to 5.16, a statistically reliable result. The significant others did not seem to see as much change in the participants as did the participants themselves. This first form of the IRRS had a confidence factor attached to each item, allowing the respondent to rate the degree of confidence he would assign in regard to the accuracy of each scale response. Both the participants and the significant others were very confident that the ratings they were making were accurate. Due to these high confidence ratings, this aspect of the instrument was deleted from the final form.

The present form of the IRRS was used to evaluate behavioral and attitudinal outcomes for seventy-eight participants and identified significant others in two three-day human relations training laboratories. One control group comprised of members of an educational psychology class and a second control group made up of randomly rejected laboratory applicants were used to evaluate reliability and validity of the instrument.

Reliability. It was important that the IRRS have a reasonable degree of stability, since change was defined as any shift in the value of the scale scores. The stability of the IRRS was studied by means of a test-retest after a one-week interval and a six-week interval, using control group members as subjects. After one week the average of the 24 coefficients was .59, with a range from .29 to .78. The six-week estimate of stability had an average of .51, with a range of .14 to .70. Stability of the IRRS was also studied by computing Spearman rank-order correlations between average profiles. For the educational psychology control group the average profile for a test-retest after a one-week interval a coefficient of .83, while the six-week interval coefficient was .85. The control group composed of rejected applicants had an average profile test-retest rank-order coefficient of .85 at one week and .82 at six weeks. Identified significant others for the rejected applicants had a coefficient of .82 for a six-week test-retest interval. These estimates indicate a high degree of stability for mean profiles for both self-reports and reports of observers. The stability data for the individual scales of the IRRS, however, indicate that use should be restricted to utilization in research and should be employed for use with groups rather than for individuals.

Discerning Change. In the analysis of outcome data for the two three-day laboratories, the IRRS proved to be effective in detecting changes in self-perceptions. The pattern was for participants to describe themselves significantly more positively in the post-testing situation than did nonparticipants. Significant others were also able to observe behavior changes which were in a "positive" direction, but to a lesser degree. By using the IRRS the investigation concluded that participation in human relations training laboratories does seem to have an effect on self-perception and behavior. These changes are more evident to the participant than to persons from his back-home environment who are observing him. The IRRS allows the individual participant and his significant other to assess the effects of the growth experience and to employ new approaches in human interactions in his back-home environment. IRRS results indicate that perceptual changes seem to be more clear-cut than are specific behavioral changes. In other words, the participant believes he has changed and rates the specific scales accordingly, but significant others are frequently not able to see these changes. The versatility of the instrument to tap both self-perceptions and observed behaviors makes it very valuable.

Suggested Uses. Potential uses of the IRRS are many and varied, both as a tool to measure change after group participation and as a device to generate data during the group process. The IRRS could be used in follow-up designs in order that the discrepancy between perception and behavior could be investigated in more depth. The phenomena of "change-back" could be studied with the help of the IRRS. It has been observed that participants in personal growth experiences frequently rate themselves lower or regress toward the mean in follow-up ratings as compared to their immediate post-experience ratings. If facilitators wanted to attempt to reduce the degree of "change-back," the IRRS might provide a tool for evaluation during a series of post-group meetings. Perceptions of actual-self and ideal-self and the usual discrepancy in these self-ratings could be tapped by using the IRRS. This discrepancy data might provide the individual participant or the group with an opportunity to set personal goals, a very important factor in personal growth experiences. Allowing the laboratory participant to see the IRRS ratings submitted by his significant others or the ratings of fellow participants might be very beneficial in starting feedback sessions.

The IRRS can also be useful in other than human relations laboratories. Members of the helping professions, such as teachers, counselors, student personnel workers, clergy, etc., who

70

are taking part in practica might find the IRRS ratings of their clients to be helpful. Also the IRRS ratings of practicum supervisors might provide the student with personal insight. The practicum student himself might fill out the IRRS on a pre- and post-practicum basis. Married couples in a group experience might respond to the IRRS as they see themselves and how they think their spouse sees them. Professionals who have a close working relationship with other professionals (e.g. nurses and doctors, social workers, and professionals in law, criminology and juvenile delinquency) might benefit from sharing the IRRS ratings.

In the realm of further research, the development of more sensitive instrumentation is essential. To improve the sensitivity of the IRRS, a factor analysis approach might add new dimensions in terms of the possible development of a number of general scales that would be more sensitive than the individual scales. Such an analysis might uncover factors having higher stability than the separate items.

At this stage in its development, the IRRS has many positive features. It is quick and easy to give and has adequate stability and face validity. Group leaders will be able to use it both in outcome research and in facilitation of process.

NORMATIVE NOTES

INTERPERSONAL RELATIONSHIP RATING SCALE
John L. Hipple

Participant _____ Observer _____

Complete this form quickly without thinking too much about each item.

For each of the following items, circle the number that best describes the degree to which the statement fits the participant.

Example:

In this example the rater feels that the participant is average in wealth.

A. Wealth of participant.

Very poor — 1 —— 2 —— 3 —— (4) —— 5 —— 6 —— 7 — Very rich

1. Ability to listen to others in an understanding way.

Low — 1 —— 2 —— 3 —— 4 —— 5 —— 6 —— 7 — High

2. Awareness of the feelings of others.

Unaware — 1 —— 2 —— 3 —— 4 —— 5 —— 6 —— 7 — Aware

3. Tolerance of differences in others.

Low — 1 —— 2 —— 3 —— 4 —— 5 —— 6 —— 7 — High

4. Tendency to trust others.

Quite Suspicious — 1 —— 2 —— 3 —— 4 —— 5 —— 6 —— 7 — Very Trusting

5. Tendency to seek close personal relationships with others.

Low — 1 —— 2 —— 3 —— 4 —— 5 —— 6 —— 7 — High

6. Tendency to build on the previous ideas of others.

Infrequent — 1 —— 2 —— 3 —— 4 —— 5 —— 6 —— 7 — Frequent

7. Ability to influence others.

Low — 1 —— 2 —— 3 —— 4 —— 5 —— 6 —— 7 — High

8. Reaction to expression of affection and warmth from others.

Low tolerance — 1 —— 2 —— 3 —— 4 —— 5 —— 6 —— 7 — High tolerance

9. Reaction to the opposing opinions of others.

Low Tolerance — 1 —— 2 —— 3 —— 4 —— 5 —— 6 —— 7 — High tolerance

10. Reaction to conflict and antagonism from others.

Low tolerance — 1 —— 2 —— 3 —— 4 —— 5 —— 6 —— 7 — High tolerance

11. Reaction to others' comments about his behavior.

Reject — 1 —— 2 —— 3 —— 4 —— 5 —— 6 —— 7 — Welcome

12. Willingness to discuss his feelings and emotions with others.

Unwilling — 1 —— 2 —— 3 —— 4 —— 5 —— 6 —— 7 — Willing

13. Level of his self understanding.

Doesn't know self — 1 —— 2 —— 3 —— 4 —— 5 —— 6 —— 7 — Knows self a great deal

14. Level of his self esteem.

Very low — 1 —— 2 —— 3 —— 4 —— 5 —— 6 —— 7 — Very high

15. Level of his giving love.

Cold — 1 —— 2 —— 3 —— 4 —— 5 —— 6 —— 7 — Warm and affectionate

16. Level of his openness.

Reveals little of self — 1 —— 2 —— 3 —— 4 —— 5 —— 6 —— 7 — Reveals much of self

17. **Degree of peace of mind.**
    Restless and Dissatisfied — 1 —— 2 —— 3 —— 4 —— 5 —— 6 —— 7 — At peace with self

18. **Level of his aspiration.**
    Very low — 1 —— 2 —— 3 —— 4 —— 5 —— 6 —— 7 — Very high

19. **Level of his physical energy.**
    Tires easily — 1 —— 2 —— 3 —— 4 —— 5 —— 6 —— 7 — Vital and resilient

20. **Degree of versatility.**
    Can do only a — 1 —— 2 —— 3 —— 4 —— 5 —— 6 —— 7 — Can do many
    few things well   things well

21. **Degree of innovativeness.**
    Likes the status quo — 1 —— 2 —— 3 —— 4 —— 5 —— 6 —— 7 — Very creative
                                                                and inventive

22. **Level of anger expression.**
    Represses it — 1 —— 2 —— 3 —— 4 —— 5 —— 6 —— 7 — Expresses it openly
    Consistently

23. **Clarity in expressing thoughts.**
    Quite vague — 1 —— 2 —— 3 —— 4 —— 5 —— 6 —— 7 — Very clear

24. **Degree of independence.**
    Very little — 1 —— 2 —— 3 —— 4 —— 5 —— 6 —— 7 — A great deal

74

INTERVENTION STYLE SURVEY

B. H. Arbes

The Intervention Style Survey (ISS) was developed to assess how the student personnel administrator responds to his job responsibilities, and to assess how others believe the administrator should respond. Persons such as vice president for student affairs, dean of students, dean of men, dean of women, and their key assistants ordinarily are faced with decisions such as those assessed by the ISS. The National Association of Student Personnel Administrators stated that the highest priority in research should be given to inquiries that clarify and delineate the assumptive basis of the student personnel administrator and the way he responds in fulfilling his responsibilities. This report also stressed the need to be aware of how other members of the academic community think the administrator should respond. An extensive review of the literature revealed a notable lack of studies attempting to assess how the student personnel administrator responds to his responsibilities, and no studies have assessed how others believe the administrator should respond to his responsibilities.

The ISS is based on a model of managerial leadership and change originated by Robert Blake and Jane Mouton. Five definite theories of leadership, with concomitant sets of assumptions and styles of intervention regarding how individuals orient themselves to concern for task and concern for people, are explicated by Blake and Mouton. These five theories, along with Blake and Mouton's numerical designations, are briefly described below:

1. Task leader (9, 1) — Being chiefly concerned with the task and viewing people only in relation to their contribution to the task, this approach defines the change agent's role as planning, directing, and controlling the behavior of those he is trying to change. This approach maintains that people are basically lazy, indifferent and irresponsible.

2. Impoverished leader (1, 1) — This approach emphasizes neither people nor task, and avoids involvement. Since one cannot really change another person, he sees his job as merely telling people the expectations and letting them decide what to do.

3. Country Club leader (1, 9) — With primary emphasis on people and minimal emphasis on task, this leader's main concern is with interpersonal relationships.

4. Middle of the Road leader (5, 5) — This approach emphasizes finding satisfactory and workable solutions through balancing and compromising procedures. This approach values traditions, precedent and social conventions.

5. Team leader (9, 9) — With emphasis on the interdependence of people by involving them and their ideas in determining the strategies and conditions for task achievement, this approach has maximal concern for task and people.

The content of the ISS was based on Hershenson's functional organization of student personnel services: internal coordinating, orienting, supportive and educative. Twelve job situations, three representative of each of Hershenson's four functional areas, were written. The specific situations were selected as typical of those encountered by a student personnel administrator in meeting his usual job responsibilities. All items were submitted to a panel of five judges with the request that they identify the strategy which the various alternatives were supposed to depict. The criterion of agreement chosen for accepting the item was four judges agreeing with the intended key, rewriting those items which did not meet this criterion.

An item analysis of the ISS demonstrated that there is a consistency in the way persons respond to the twelve items. That is, if a respondent ranks a given style high for one student personnel situation, he is more likely to express a high preference for the same intervention style in other situations.

The respondent is presented with a job situation encountered by student personnel administrators, and indicates his personal preference for each of the five alternative responses along a ten-point scale. In so doing, the respondent reveals a preferential ordering of the alternatives and also a scale weight for each alternative, since there are twice as many scale weights as there are response options. By using such a response format in the ISS, the ipsative character of forced-choice items is partially avoided. Ipsative scores lead to problems in statistical analysis, since they are not independent and therefore do not meet a major assumption upon which many statistical procedures are based.

A score for each of the five styles of intervention is obtained by summing the scale weights of the corresponding alternatives for all twelve items. This means that the range of scores for any intervention style is 0 to 108. A computer scoring program is available from the author.

Internal consistency estimates (Cronbach's alpha) and stability estimates of the ISS indicated that the instrument has adequate reliability for group administration and interpretation. However, its utilization for individual interpretation or diagnostic procedures is questionable.

In the study for which the ISS was developed, it was administered to randomized samples of students (STUD), student personnel administrators (SPA), faculty (FAC) and counselors (COUNS) at the three state universities in Iowa. The scores of the 482 respondents on each style of intervention were analyzed by multiple discriminant analysis, simple ANOVA, t-ratios and chi square. The results of the discriminant analysis, using the Mahalanobis D^2, indicated that there are significant differences in the perceptions of student personnel administrators, faculty, students and counselors as to what intervention styles are appropriate in student personnel job situations. While students and counselors' perceptions are comparably close to those of student personnel administrators, faculty are distincly more distant. The "team leader" style had the highest mean response for each group. The differences in the strength of preference which the four groups attached to the 9, 9 style show that the counselors, with the significantly higher scores, believe strongly that the administrator should use the 9, 9 approach, while the faculty hold this view significantly less firmly. The counselors had the most consistent and most homogenous response tendencies, achieving the highest mean response on the team leader and country club leader styles, and the lowest on the other three styles.

The construction of the ISS and its resultant reliability indicate that the instrument is a viable tool for further research in the student services area. Also, it could be utilized as a feedback instrument for student personnel administrators by studying the self-other perceptions of how the student personnel administrator reacts to his job situation. This could easily be accomplished by administering the ISS to an administrator and then having the other members of the staff complete the ISS on the basis of how they see him reacting.

The ISS has value as a training tool for student personnel administrators, not as a specific measuring instrument, but as a means to introduce and study the concepts of change strategies and intervention styles. The Blake-Mouton model of change and intervention seems to be highly relevant for student personnel administrators. Its extensive use in other settings and its theoretical and empirical basis make it a useful model to study and utilize. The ISS assesses the various dimensions of this model in relation to student personnel work. Therefore, its use in teaching styles of intervention and change strategies is very feasible.

The instrument can be adapted for use with other administrators by altering the content to conform to the problems usually encountered in a given managerial situation.

NORMATIVE NOTES

INTERVENTION STYLE SURVEY
B. H. Arbes

_____   _____
           NAME   GROUP

INSTRUCTIONS

Twelve typical situations which a university student personnel dean encounters in his position have been included in this instrument. For each of these situations, five alternate ways of responding have been listed.

Each alternative response is different from the other four. Since you will be asked to differentiate between the five responses, it is necessary that you read all five alternatives before answering.

After reading all five responses, select the response which is most similar to the way you would actually react in that situation, and place the letter corresponding to that response (a, b, c, d, e) somewhere on the "Most Similar" end of the ten-point scale.

Next select the response which is least similar to the way you would actually react, and place the letter corresponding to that response (a, b, c, d, e) toward the "Least Similar" end of the scale. Complete your answer by placing the three remaining letters within this most-least range in terms of how well each response reflects the way you would actually react in that particular situation (see example).

Example: I have just won $5,000 in a magazine publisher's contest. I will probably:

   a. Pay off all outstanding bills and place the remaining amount in a savings account.

   b. Invest the entire amount in sound stock.

   c. Buy a new car.

   d. Take an extensive trip.

   e. Place the entire amount in my savings account.

Most		a	d			c		b	e	Least
Similar	9	8	7	6	5	4	3	2	1	0	Similar

Of the five alternatives, this person chose response "a" as most similar to the way he would respond in this situation, although not giving it a ranking of 10. Response "e" was least similar. He ranked responses "d," "c" and "b" on the most-least continuum, between "a" and "e," response "d" being very similar to the way he would respond and "b" very dissimilar to the way he would respond.

His answer could have been:

Most	b			c	d		a		e		Least
Similar	9	8	7	6	5	4	3	2	1	0	Similar

or

Most				a		e	b	d		c	Least
Similar	9	8	7	6	5	4	3	2	1	0	Similar

There are no right or wrong answers. The "best" response is that one which most accurately reflects the way you would respond in that situation.

In responding to the following twelve items, you are to place yourself in the position of Dean of Students at a large, midwestern, state-supported university. As Dean of Students, you are the chief student personnel administrator at this university and report directly to the president. Included in your division are orientation, placement, alumni relations, counseling, student activities, residence halls and judicial programs and services.

1. One of the associate deans of students has created a stress situation in the office by criticizing many of my decisions to other members of the staff. In discussing this situation with him, I will probably:

   a. Talk as little as possible and wait for him to ask for my opinion or ideas as he feels the need to do so.
   b. Be very active in the discussion so as to clarify for him the reasons underlying my decisions and the position I feel he must adopt.
   c. Allow him to do most of the talking in the interview, and listen in a non-judgmental and accepting manner.
   d. Be as active as he and try to arrive at conclusions which represent our joint points of view.
   e. Try to win his respect and then persuade him to my point of view.

Most											Least
Similar	9	8	7	6	5	4	3	2	1	0	Similar

2. The President has asked me to serve on a committee with various faculty and other deans to devise a proposal for more student participation in campus governance. In these committee meetings, I will probably:

   a. Wait for my opinion to be asked and usually accept the majority opinion.
   b. Assist other members of the committee in clarifying their ideas and emphasize good relations among committee members.
   c. State my ideas and opinions in the context of my contact with student government officers and work toward a feasible, although not perfect, proposal.
   d. Encourage all committee members to actively participate in creating the proposal and emphasize understanding and agreement of a proposal that is satisfactory to all involved.
   e. Try to persuade the committee members to accept my point of view and push for a proposal that can realistically be adopted.

Most											Least
Similar	9	8	7	6	5	4	3	2	1	0	Similar

3. In determining the success of my counseling with a student, I will probably emphasize:

   a. The extent to which his decisions reflect the accepted standard of behavior and the university rules.
   b. The extent to which he follows expected behavior, and the amount of urging necessary on my part to achieve this.
   c. The student's progress toward self-acceptance and personal worth as indications of his ability to live with others.
   d. The value of particular behaviors in relation to the goals he and I have set in the interview.
   e. His loyalty toward and trust in me in the context of our relationship.

Most											Least
Similar	9	8	7	6	5	4	3	2	1	0	Similar

4. I have just been informed about a group of local residents who want me to abolish the new Sensitivity Training Program organized under my office. Five of them have arranged to meet with me next week. In talking with this group, I will probably:

a. Answer their questions directly and courteously but not become involved in an active discussion regarding the purpose and goals of the program.

b. Clarify for them the reasons for the program, the position I and the staff have taken in relation to the program, and my authority in relation to such programs.

c. Listen carefully to their comments and assist them in talking about their concerns without explaining my position or the program in detail.

d. Carefully explain the reason for the program and my position, but also assist them in clarifying both their concerns and ways these concerns can be explored in relation to the program.

e. Listen carefully to their comments, but then gradually attempt to gain their acceptance of my office's position on the new program.

Most										Least
Similar	9	8	7	6	5	4	3	2	1	0	Similar

5. Resident hall assistants have not been attending the weekly in-service training programs carefully planned by myself and other staff members. It was previously decided that these programs were important for the maximum functioning of the assistants, and the assistants were aware of their expected attendance at these programs before accepting their positions. To assure attendance at these programs, I am likely to:

a. Clarify the reasons for the training programs and the consequences of not attending.

b. Arrange a discussion with those not attending and encourage them to explore their personal goals and responsibilities as resident assistants.

c. Carefully outline the reasons for the training program, and the expectation of attendance to all resident assistants.

d. Contact each resident assistant not attending and encourage him to do so.

e. Arrange meetings with all resident assistants to assess why some are not attending the meetings and discuss alternative in-service training formats.

Most										Least
Similar	9	8	7	6	5	4	3	2	1	0	Similar

6. The student-faculty judicial board has asked me to supervise a student placed under strict disciplinary probation for one semester. At the end of this semester, I am to make a recommendation to the board regarding his probationary status based upon my evaluation of his behavior. In working with this student, I will probably:

   a. Meet with the student to review openly our relationship in establishing goals for behavioral change and treat the evaluation as a shared responsibility.
   b. Meet with the student informally and as a friend to share my reactions to his behavior and encourage him to ask questions about a change in his behavior.
   c. Evaluate his behavior for him on the basis of reports, comparing him with others I have supervised, and my understanding of the probationary requirements, and tell him ways in which he can make improvements.
   d. Encourage the student to make his own assessment of his behavior and his places for improvement as he thinks it necessary, and try to stimulate personal commitment and self-confidence on his part.
   e. Develop a rather casual relationship with him, inform him of the probationary requirements, and make a recommendation based upon the expected behavior of students at the university.

Most Similar	9	8	7	6	5	4	3	2	1	0	Least Similar

7. A student has recently been referred to me for counseling by a resident hall director. His behavior in the hall has been marked by numerous child-like responses, and both his fellow residents and resident assistant has talked to the director about him. The student was not told he had to see me, but it was suggested to him that he might want to talk to me about his behavior. To help this student change his present behavior, I will probably:

   a. Encourage him to identify with a student whom he respects and who demonstrates acceptable behavior.
   b. Clearly state a single course of action for the student and the consequences for not following that course.
   c. Assure that the student has a choice between various courses of action and is able to explore these actions before making a decision.
   d. Clarify the need for and direction of a change in behavior, but leave the decision to change or not change up to the student.
   e. Assure that the student has total freedom from others' influence in choosing a course of action and has the support of others once he chooses.

Most Similar	9	8	7	6	5	4	3	2	1	0	Least Similar

8. In establishing a new program with an officer of the alumni organization, I discover that my personal negative feelings toward this individual are interfering with my ability to work with him effectively. In this situation, I am likely to:

   a. Talk to others about their feelings toward this person, and if my feelings are supported, to tell the alumnus about my feelings and what he is doing to hinder our task.
   b. Openly express my feelings to the alumnus and what I think he should do to help the situation.
   c. Openly express my feelings and encourage him to do the same so that personal feelings between us can be cleared up.
   d. Try to better understand his actions and try to overcome my own negative feelings.
   e. Avoid contacts with the alumnus and discuss only necessary agenda with him.

Most Similar	9	8	7	6	5	4	3	2	1	0	Least Similar

9. The Placement Service is a division of my office. As a result of turning down the student government's proposal for a policy change in the Placement Office, I am presently being criticized and challenged to attend a student government meeting to discuss my position. In this meeting, I am likely to:

   a. React more to the way they see the issue than the fact that they are challenging me, and try to re-evaluate their proposal in view of the two positions we are now taking.
   b. Be concerned about my relationship with the student government and inquire about their respect for my judgment.
   c. Discuss and push my position, even if it ultimately means reminding the students of my authority in such policy decisions.
   d. Be concerned but avoid arguing my position and assist the students to clarify their ideas and opinions about the policy.
   e. Simply remind them that I have made the decision and explain the basis of my decision rather than becoming involved in an argument.

Most Similar	9	8	7	6	5	4	3	2	1	0	Least Similar

10. The director of the experimental living-learning center (a member of my staff) and the faculty consultant to the living-learning center are in disagreement about the type of programs to be implemented. Their personal dispute is affecting the other staff members in the living-learning center, and other faculty members are also becoming concerned. I have decided to meet with these two men to discuss the situation. In this meeting, I will probably:

   a. Remain neutral or stay out of the argument.
   b. Try to smooth over the feelings and keep the men working together.
   c. Try to dismiss the conflict and present my views on the disagreement.
   d. Use my position to encourage them to arrive at an equitable solution to the problem situation.
   e. Try to create a situation so the two men can identify reasons for their conflict and explore means to achieve the goals of the living-learning center.

Most Similar	9	8	7	6	5	4	3	2	1	0	Least Similar

11.The new student orientation director and his staff have invited me to discuss my ideas and opinions about orientation programs. In making this presentation, I would probably emphasize:

a. The difference between the high school and college environments and rely on the new students' ability to understand the implications of these differences.
b. The importance of living up to expectations of the college environment and the consequences of not following these expectations.
c. Helping the new student accept himself as a person so that he will have the self-confidence to choose a course of action.
d. A search for facts or information on the part of the new student so that he can evaluate various courses of action in relation to his own goals.
e. Winning the students' respect for the school and then encouraging them to behave so as to win the respect of the school.

Most Similar	9	8	7	6	5	4	3	2	1	0	Least Similar

12. Because of budgetary cutbacks, no new programs or positions can be added to the Division of Student Affairs. In order to meet the continuing and changing demands placed on my staff, an immediate reorganization of the Office is necessary. To assure the staff acceptance of the reorganization, I will:

a. Encourage active participation in the reorganization.
b. Assure that the person who proposes the reorganization is highly respected by staff members.
c. Explain that failure to accept the reorganization will result in a penalty or loss of possible rewards.
d. Emphasize the responsibility for adapting to the reorganization is primarily an "individual" undertaking which will result in some degree of personal satisfaction.
e. Carefully outline both the expectations of and consequences of not accepting the new organization and leave the staff members to their own means.

Most Similar	9	8	7	6	5	4	3	2	1	0	Least Similar

INTERVENTION STYLE SURVEY
SCORING SHEET

Directions: Copy your responses from the items onto this sheet. Be sure to note that the *order* of the letters (a, b, c, d, e) varies for each item. Place the scale value you assigned to the letter "a" on item 1, for example, above the letter "a" on this sheet. Then do the same for all other letters. Your scores for the five theories of leadership are the sums of the five columns on this sheet.

Item

1.
    a   b   c   e   d

2.
    a   e   b   c   d

3.
    a   b   c   e   d

4.
    a   b   c   e   d

5.
    c   a   b   d   e

6.
    e   c   d   b   a

7.
    d   b   e   a   c

8.
    e   b   d   a   c

9.
    e   c   d   b   a

10.
    a   c   b   d   e

11.
    a   b   c   e   d

12.
    e   c   d   b   a

Sums

	(1,1)	(9,1)	(1,9)	(5,5)	(9,9)
Scales	Impoverished Leader	Task Leader	Country Club Leader	Middle-of-the-road Leader	Team Leader

The 1972 Annual Handbook For Group Facilitators

NONRESEARCH USES OF THE GROUP LEADERSHIP QUESTIONNAIRE (GTQ-C)*

Daniel B. Wile

The GTQ-C is an instrument for the measurement of style in group leadership. It presents brief descriptions of group situations and asks the subject to indicate how he would respond if he were the leader in each of these situations. Although originally devised for research purposes, the GTQ-C has proven to have several nonresearch uses. This paper describes these uses, makes reference to related research findings, and includes a sample copy of the instrument along with the answer sheet and scoring system.

The GTQ-C can be used for the following educational purposes: to stimulate discussion in classes devoted to small groups, to evaluate what students have learned from a course in group leadership, to focus attention upon group and leadership processes in an ongoing group, and to aid an individual leader in the examination and study of his own leadership orientation. Since the GTQ-C is a new instrument, backed at present by limited validational evidence, it provides suggestive and tentative rather than definitive information.

The GTQ-C can be used to stimulate discussion of leadership issues in a course on small groups. It can do this because it presents these issues in the intuitively meaningful form of concrete examples. A class discussion of the twenty-one GTQ-C situations typically develops into a series of vigorous and spontaneous debates regarding the relative value of directive vs. nondirective leadership, individual vs. group focus, reassurance vs. confrontation, asking questions vs. making interpretations vs. remaining silent, etc. The GTQ-C thus raises in clear and concrete form the important decisions or choices that anyone who leads a group must make.

Some classes attempt to determine the "correct," "right," or "proper" response for each GTQ-C situation. There is, of course, no such response. Although research results have suggested that some response types tend to be more sophisticated than others (Wile, Bron & Pollack, 1970b; Wile), these results are tentative and, in any event, apply to groups and not to individuals. A response which, in the hands of one leader, is naive, ineffective, and a function of this leader's inexperience, may, because of a difference in the tone and manner in which it is delivered, have a facilitative effect when made by another leader.

---

*The GTQ-C is a revision by the author of a parent form, GTQ-B, which was originally constructed by the author and Gary D. Bron. The GTQ-B was specifically designed for group therapy. The letters — GTQ — stand for "Group Therapy Questionnaire." These letters are maintained in the present form, for the purposes of consistency, despite the fact that the GTQ-C has been broadened to apply, not merely to group therapy, but to group work in general.

The GTQ-C can be used to evaluate what students in a course or training program in group leadership learn from the course. If the GTQ-C is administered at the beginning and again at the end of the course, the changes in score will indicate how the students have been influenced by the program. Different courses appear to teach different things. While one course taught its students to be directive, for example, a second taught its students to be nondirective. Similarly, while one course encouraged students to ask group members more questions, another course encouraged them to ask fewer questions (Wile, Bron & Pollack, 1970b).

I have found this evaluation procedure to be most informative, for the instructor as well as for the student, when the student's pre-course/post-course changes are reported back to him. In fact, the students' GTQ-C changes can be discussed as part of a general evaluation session held at the end of the course. Such an evaluation session can consider both general effects — the systematic effect that a course tends to exert upon all its students — and specific effects — the unique or idiosyncratic manner in which certain individuals respond. For example, one student took advantage of a recent seminar in group leadership to develop his nondirective tendencies while a second student reacted to the same seminar by developing his directive tendencies. Both students showed dramatic GTQ-C changes, although in opposite directions (Wile).

The GTQ-C can be used in an ongoing group to study the leader's style and the manner in which each individual member is reacting to it. This is most appropriate when the group is itself composed of potential or practicing group leaders. Each member fills out the GTQ-C to describe the leader's approach. These protocols can then be compared with each other and with the leader's own GTQ-C responses. This exercise has the advantage of bringing up for group consideration issues which had previously remained unrecognized or concealed. If one member is alone in seeing the leader as directive and attacking, for example, this information can be used to study whether the interaction between the leader and this member has, in fact, been unusually aggressive (and if so, what this might mean), or whether this member's perception is a projection of his own aggressive or competitive feelings toward the leader. Similarly, a member's perception of the leader as extremely reassuring and supportive may reflect this member's fantasy-wish of being nurtured by an unconditionally loving authority or may accurately indicate the existence of a special relationship between the two.

Finally, the GTQ-C can be used as part of the re-examination or re-evaluation in which group leaders engage at various points in their careers. A leader who takes the GTQ-C at systematic intervals can trace the development of his leadership approach (at least within the limits of the reliability and validity of the instrument). The special value of the GTQ-C exists in the manner in which it pins a leader down. Since the GTQ-C asks a leader to specify what he would do in concrete group situations, it helps him discover whether his actual group behavior (as determined by his GTQ-C responses) is consistent with his theoretical views. Leaders are sometimes surprised by the disparity between their theory and their practice. For example, in one case, a leader who was theoretically committed to a nondirective approach to group leadership discovered that he was actually quite directive in his leadership behavior: helping the group over awkward spots, making partly concealed suggestions as to how they might best proceed, and protecting members who were being criticized. Recognizing this, he was then in a position to re-evaluate his leadership orientation and make a conscious and deliberate choice either to become truly nondirective, to continue in his subtly directive style, or possibly, to become even more and unabashedly directive.

Some subjects experience difficulty filling out the GTQ-C, and a few become bored, irritated, and antagonistic. Although these difficulties are often a result of the threatening quality of the questionnaire — e.g., fear about making "wrong" responses, resistance against being pinned down, or discomfort in being faced with one's own uncertainties as a leader — this resistance can also be a reaction to the inherent limitations of the instrument. Since the GTQ-C provides only brief descriptions of each of the twenty-one group situations, it asks respondents to make decisions on partial information. Leaders who are either unwilling or unable to do this, and particularly those who lead groups entirely in terms of their intuitive "feel" for the immediacy of each particular group situation, experience considerable difficulty with this instrument. A subject's negative attitude toward the GTQ-C is, however, itself a valuable piece of data. An exploration of the meaning of his attitude can lead to information which may be useful for him to recognize and consider: for example, a realization of the intuitive nature of his leadership functioning, or his concern about being "found out."

BIBLIOGRAPHY

Wile, D. B. "GTQ-C: An Alternate Form of the Group Therapy Questionnaire." (1970). Unpublished paper available from the author. (Daniel B. Wile, Counseling Services, California State College, Hayward, 25800 Hillary Street, Hayward, California 94542).

Wile, D. B. "What do Trainees Learn from a Group Therapy Workshop?" Submitted for publication.

Wile, D. B. "A Detailed Presentation of the Experiment Summarized in the Paper: 'What do Trainees Learn from a Group Therapy Workshop'?" (1971). Unpublished paper available from the author.

Wile, D. B., Bron, G. D., and Pollack, H. B. "The Group Therapy Questionnaire: An Instrument for the Study of Leadership in Small Groups." *Psychological Reports*, 1970, 27, 263-273. (a).

Wile, D. B., Bron, G. D., and Pollack, H. B. "Preliminary Validational Evidence for the Group Therapy Questionnaire." *Journal of Consulting and Clinical Psychology*, 1970, 34, 3, 367-374. (b).

GROUP LEADERSHIP QUESTIONNAIRE (GTQ-C)*

Daniel B. Wile

This questionnaire presents twenty-one situations which sometimes occur in human interaction groups and asks you to indicate how you would respond if you were the leader in the group. A list of nineteen alternative responses is provided for each situation.

On the separate answer sheet there are three columns to use in recording your preferences. For each situation:

    a. List (in Column 1) the numbers of *all* of the responses among the nineteen that you might consider making if you were the leader faced with this particular situation.

    b. Then, choose from among your selections, the *one* response which you feel is most important to make, and write its number in Column 2.

    c. Record in Column 3 those responses that you might make which have not been included on the list.

*Form C is an experimental modification of Form B of the GTQ, which was originally developed by Daniel B. Wile and Gary D. Bron.

Situation 1: Starting the Group

You are the leader in a group which is meeting today for the first time. All eight members, young adults, are present as you enter the room and sit down. You introduce yourself and the members introduce themselves. Then everyone turns and looks at you expectantly. There is silence. What do you do?

1. Do nothing.
2. Say that the group is theirs to make use of as they wish.
3. Reassure them that a certain amount of tension is typical in the beginning of a group.
4. Break the ice with casual conversation.
5. Describe the purposes and procedures of the group.
6. Say that everyone seems so uptight that you wonder if the group is going to get off the ground.
7. Ask how they feel in this first meeting (about being in the group or about each other).
8. Say how you are feeling (example: tense and expectant).
9. Share an experience in your own life.
10. Ask why everyone is silent.
11. Ask what they think might be going on in the group.
12. Describe how they seem to be expecting you to start things.
13. Suggest that they are wanting you to be an inspirational and protective leader.
14. Describe the silence as an expression of their anxieties about the group.
15. Ask everyone to say why he came to the group.
16. Lead into a discussion of their family relationships and past experiences.
17. Encourage them to discuss their goals in behavioral terms.
18. Use a nonverbal procedure (examples: milling around; focusing on bodily tensions).
19. Use a role-playing or psychodrama procedure (example: encourage a member to act out one of his problems).

Situation 2: Personal Questions

Near the beginning of the first meeting, the members ask you personal questions about your family and background. What do you do?

1. Do nothing.
2. Invite them to say what they think your answers to these questions might be.
3. Say that you can understand why they might be curious about you.
4. Avoid answering the questions without drawing attention to the fact that you are not answering — bring up another issue.
5. Say that you cannot see how this information would be of any use to the group.
6. Say that it is none of their business.
7. Ask how they feel about you and about the way the group has been set up.
8. Say how you are feeling about their questioning (example: uncomfortable).
9. Answer the questions.
10. Ask why they are asking these questions.
11. Ask what they think might be going on in the group at the moment.
12. Describe how the group's attention has become concentrated upon you.
13. Describe these questions as an expression of their concern about what is going to happen between you and them.
14. Suggest that they may be asking about you to avoid talking about their own thoughts and feelings.
15. Encourage them to talk about themselves.
16. Lead into a discussion of their family relationships and past experiences (example: ask if they would like to answer these same questions about themselves).
17. Encourage them to consider behavior they may wish to change.
18. Ask them to express nonverbally how they feel about you and the group.
19. Ask one of the members to role-play your position in the group.

Situation 3: The Chairman

Later in this first session, someone suggests that the group appoint a chairman to conduct the meetings. This idea is received enthusiastically. They explain that this will permit the group to function in a more orderly fashion. Everyone appears to agree with the idea. What do you do?

1. Do nothing.
2. Say that you are willing to go along with whatever the group decides about this.
3. Agree that it is worth a try.
4. Direct attention away from this idea by bringing up another issue.
5. Recommend against the idea.
6. Say, "It's beginning to sound like a PTA meeting in here — I guess no one is really interested in group interaction."
7. Ask how they feel about the way the group has been set up.
8. Say how you are feeling about the discussion.
9. Share a similar experience in your own life.
10. Ask why it is important for the group to function "in an orderly fashion."
11. Say, "What happened that made us decide we need a chairman?"
12. Describe the group's feeling of enthusiasm about the idea.
13. Suggest that their interest in a chairman may be a way of dealing with the ambiguity of the group situation.
14. Interpret their discussion as resistance to becoming involved in the group.
15. Encourage them to talk about themselves.
16. Lead into a discussion of their family relationships and past experiences.
17. Encourage them to consider behavior they may wish to change.
18. Ask them to express nonverbally how they feel about you and the others.
19. Ask them to role-play how the group would be with a chairman.

Situation 4: A Filibuster

The group spends much of the second session talking about politics. No one appears displeased with the discussion, and it looks like it may continue for the remainder of the meeting. What do you do?

1. Do nothing.
2. Ask if they are satisfied with how the group is going today (say, "Is this really the way you want to use the time?").
3. Join in on the discussion.
4. Try to draw them into a more meaningful discussion without criticizing what they were doing.
5. Suggest that they talk about more immediate things.
6. Describe their discussion as cocktail party chatter.
7. Ask how they feel about what has been going on.
8. Say how you are feeling (example: bored).
9. Share an experience in your own life.
10. Ask why they are talking about politics.
11. Ask what they think might be going on in the group today.
12. Describe the group mood of avoidance and withdrawal.
13. Suggest that their interest in politics may have something to do with their concern about the interrelationship — or "politics" — within the group.
14. Suggest that they are discussing politics to avoid talking about more immediate thoughts and feelings.
15. Encourage them to talk about themselves.
16. Lead into a discussion of their family relationships and past experiences.
17. Encourage them to consider behavior they may wish to change.
18. Use a nonverbal procedure to get things going.
19. Use a role-playing or psychodrama procedure.

Situation 5: An Attack Upon the Leader

After spending much of this second meeting talking about dieting and politics, the group suddenly turns on you, accusing you of being uninvolved, distant, and uncaring. What do you do?

1. Do nothing.
2. Say that it is up to them what happens in group, not you.
3. Talk in an approving way about the directness and honesty with which they are able to say how they feel.
4. Direct attention away from their attack by bringing up another issue.
5. Defend yourself — say that you do not see yourself as uninvolved and uncaring.
6. Describe them as a group of whiny complainers.
7. Ask how they feel when they are criticizing you in this way.
8. Say how you are feeling.
9. Share an experience in your own life.
10. Ask why they suddenly became angry at you.
11. Ask what they think might be going on in the group today.
12. Describe the group attitude of dissatisfaction with you.
13. Suggest that they are disappointed that you are not the inspirational and protective leader that they had wanted you to be.
14. Describe how you may be a scapegoat for their dissatisfaction with their own participation in the group.
15. Encourage them to relate this to what is happening in their lives outside the group.
16. Lead into a discussion of their family relationships and past experiences (example: suggest that you may be reminding them of people they have known).
17. Encourage them to use this situation to consider behavior they may wish to change.
18. Use a nonverbal procedure (example: arm wrestling).
19. Suggest that they role-play both how they see you and how they would want you to be.

Situation 6: A Group Silence

The third meeting begins with a silence. Several minutes pass and still no one says anything. It is beginning to look like the silence might continue for some time. What do you do?

1. Do nothing.
2. Ask if they are satisfied with how the group is going today.
3. Say that silences are often productive.
4. Help the group get started without making a special point about their silence (ask questions or bring up things to talk about).
5. Say that they are wasting time.
6. Remark that they look pretty foolish, sitting around waiting for someone else to say something.
7. Ask how they feel when everyone is silent.
8. Say how you are feeling or, possibly, laugh at the absurdity of the situation.
9. Share an experience in your own life.
10. Ask why everyone is silent.
11. Ask what they think might be going on in the group today.
12. Say that it seems that no one wants to talk today.
13. Say that each person appears to have resolved not to be the first to speak.
14. Interpret their silence as an expression of resentment about how the group is going.
15. Encourage them to talk about themselves.
16. Lead into a discussion of their family relationships and past experiences.
17. Encourage them to consider behavior they may wish to change.
18. Encourage them to express themselves nonverbally.
19. Use a role-playing or psychodrama procedure to get things going.

94

Situation 7: A Distressed Woman

Later in this third meeting, one of the women describes how her boyfriend just told her that he wants to break off their relationship. She seems quite upset, skipping from one idea to another, and returning repetitively to the same few despairing thoughts. She has been looking directly at you from the beginning of her remarks, ignoring the rest of the group. When she finishes talking, she asks for your comments. What do you do?

1. Do nothing.
2. Redirect her question to the group (ask how the group might be able to help her).
3. Express interest in her and concern about her difficulties.
4. Try to draw the others into the discussion without making a point of the fact that she had left them out.
5. Suggest that she ask the group rather than you.
6. Accuse her of basking in self pity.
7. Ask the members how they feel about what is going on.
8. Say how you are feeling.
9. Share a similar experience in your own life.
10. Ask why she is asking you.
11. Ask what they think might be going on in the group today.
12. Describe how the group has accepted the role of passive observer.
13. Suggest that her appeal for your undivided attention may be an attempt to regain the feeling of being valued — special — which she lost when her boyfriend rejected her.
14. Suggest that her preoccupation with being rejected is a way of not having to consider her own participation in the breakup.
15. Talk about her problems with her boyfriend, leading perhaps to a general exploration of her problems with intimacy.
16. Encourage her to relate this to her family relationships and past experiences.
17. Encourage her to discuss her problem in behavioral terms.
18. Use a nonverbal procedure to get at her underlying feelings.
19. Use a role-playing or psychodrama procedure to obtain a more here-and-now expression of what happens with her boyfriend.

Situation 8: The Late Arrival

It is the fourth meeting. One woman makes a dramatic entrance fifteen minutes late. Although she has done this before, no one says anything about it. What do you do?

1. Do nothing.
2. Ask why no one says anything about her coming late.
3. Give her attention and express interest in her.
4. Continue as if nothing out of the ordinary were happening.
5. Suggest that she try to get to group on time.
6. Accuse her of acting like a *prima donna* — coming to group late so that she can make a dramatic entrance with everyone watching.
7. Ask her and the rest of the group how they feel about her coming late.
8. Say how you are feeling.
9. Share a similar experience in your own life.
10. Ask her why she comes late.
11. Ask how her coming late might be related to what has been going on in the group as a whole.
12. Mention that she has been late several times.
13. Suggest that her role in the group involves making a grand entrance with everyone watching.
14. Suggest that she comes to group late in order to deny the important role that it plays in her life.
15. Ask if she usually comes late to things (perhaps this is the way she deals with situations).
16. Encourage her to relate this to her family relationships and past experiences.
17. Encourage her to use this situation to consider behavior she may wish to change.
18. Use a nonverbal procedure to get at the underlying feeling.
19. Ask another member to role-play her entrance.

The 1972 Annual Handbook For Group Facilitators 95

Situation 9: The Monopolizer

For several meetings now the conversation has been monopolized by one of the women. Her monologues and interruptions interfere with the development of any kind of meaningful interchange. It is now part way into the fourth meeting. She has had the floor for most of this hour also. What do you do?

1. Do nothing.
2. Ask why they are letting her monopolize.
3. Talk in an approving way about the freedom with which she is able to assert herself in the group.
4. Direct remarks to others in an attempt to increase their participation.
5. Suggest that she limit her comments for awhile to give others a chance.
6. Describe her as a longwinded and insensitive bore who always has to be in the spotlight.
7. Ask how they feel about one person doing most of the talking.
8. Say how you are feeling (example: irritated with her).
9. Share a similar experience in your own life.
10. Ask her why she is monopolizing.
11. Ask how they would describe what has been going on this meeting.
12. Comment on the group's attitude of passive resignation to what is going on.
13. Describe what is going on as a two party interaction where she monopolizes while the others allow and perhaps even encourage her to do it.
14. Describe her need to control as a defense against her fear of being controlled or overwhelmed.
15. Ask if this kind of thing happens with her outside the group.
16. Encourage her to relate this behavior to her family relationships and past experiences.
17. Encourage her and the rest of the group to use this event to consider behavior they may wish to change.
18. Use a nonverbal or gestalt therapy procedure to get beyond her verbal defenses.
19. Ask another member to role-play how she behaves in the group.

Situation 10: The Quiet Member

One of the men has said very little throughout the meetings, although he seems to follow with interest everything that has been happening. It is now the middle of the fourth session and some of the others are finally beginning to question him about his silence. He remains basically uncommunicative, however, and the group seems uncertain how to pursue the matter. What do you do?

1. Do nothing.
2. Even if they look to you for help, leave it to the group to deal with the situation.
3. Say that each person is free to decide when he wants to talk, adding that you would like to hear from him when he does feel like talking.
4. Encourage him to speak but without making a point of his silence (example: ask for his opinion about the group).
5. Tell him that he is not going to get much out of the group if he does not put much into it.
6. Try to get him to react (example: accuse him of being a parasite, sitting back and living off others).
7. Ask how he feels about what the group is saying to him and ask how they feel about his reaction to their remarks.
8. Say how you are feeling.
9. Share a similar experience in your own life.
10. Ask him why he has been silent and ask the others why they object to his silence.
11. Ask how they would describe what has been going on in the group today.
12. Describe how the group seems uncertain about how to discuss this with him.
13. Describe the nonverbal ways in which he interacts with others — eye contact, laughter, attentive expression.
14. Interpret his silence as an expression of tenseness and anxiety about the group.
15. Encourage him to talk about himself (example: ask if he is usually quiet in group situations).
16. Encourage him to relate his behavior to his family relationships and past experiences.
17. Encourage him to use this situation to consider behavior he may wish to change.
18. Encourage him to express himself nonverbally.
19. Ask him to role-play an important situation in his life.

Situation 11: A Threat to Quit

Near the beginning of the fifth meeting, one of the women announces that she is going to quit the group. The others are upset by this and try to talk her out of it. She remains resolute, however, and stands up to leave. She pauses briefly at the door, as if waiting to see if anyone has any final comments. The others just sit there, not knowing what to do. What do you do?

1. Do nothing.
2. Ask what they want to do about the situation.
3. Say that you have enjoyed her being in the group and would be sorry if she left.
4. Draw her into a conversation without making an issue of the fact that she was about to leave.
5. Suggest that she give the group more of a try before making any final decisions.
6. Accuse her of using an obvious play to get the attention of the group.
7. Ask her and the group how they feel about her leaving.
8. Say how you are feeling (example: abandoned).
9. Share a similar experience in your own life.
10. Ask why she wants to leave now, right in the middle of the meeting.
11. Ask how her wanting to leave might be related to what is happening in the group as a whole.
12. Describe how everyone seems confused and uncertain what to do.
13. Interpret their concern and confusion about her leaving as a fear that this may be the beginning of the dissolution of the whole group.
14. Suggest that she wants to stop because she is afraid of becoming involved in the group.
15. Ask if this kind of thing has happened with her before (perhaps quitting is her way of dealing with threatening situations).
16. Encourage her to relate her desire to quit to her family relationships and past experiences (perhaps the group reminds her of her family situation).
17. Encourage her and the others to use this event to consider behavior they may wish to change.
18. Ask her to express nonverbally how she feels toward each member.
19. Use a role-playing or psychodrama procedure.

Situation 12: Marital Problem

Later in this fifth meeting, one of the men talks about his marital problems. The others offer numerous suggestions. He listens to each of them one at a time and then explains why that particular suggestion will not work. What do you do?

1. Do nothing.
2. If they ask your opinion, reflect the question back to the group.
3. Show interest in him and express concern about his difficulties.
4. Seeing the interaction as a stalemate, bring up another issue for discussion.
5. Describe the interaction as a stalemate and suggest that they talk about something else.
6. Criticize him for not seriously considering his problem and wasting the group's time.
7. Ask how he feels about the group response to his problem and ask how they feel about his reaction to their suggestions.
8. Say how you are feeling.
9. Share a similar experience in your own life.
10. Ask him why he rejects all their suggestions and ask them why they are giving so much advice.
11. Ask what they think is going on in the group today.
12. Describe the eagerness with which they are giving him advice.
13. Describe how he asks for help and then rejects all the suggestions.
14. Describe how he is the focus around which all the other members are projecting their own problems — suggest that their advice may have more to do with them than it does with him.
15. Try to help him understand what happens between him and his wife.
16. Encourage him to relate this to his family relationships and past experiences (perhaps his difficulties with his wife have something to do with his feelings toward his mother).
17. Encourage him to talk about the problem in behavioral terms.
18. Use a nonverbal procedure.
19. Use a role-playing or psychodrama procedure to obtain a more here-and-now expression of what happens with his wife.

The 1972 Annual Handbook For Group Facilitators   97

Situation 13: The Return of the Absent Member

A member who had been absent the two previous meetings arrives on time for the sixth meeting. It is now well into this meeting and neither he nor any of the others has mentioned his absences. What do you do?

1. Do nothing.
2. Ask why no one has said anything about his absences.
3. Say that it is good to see him again, that you were concerned when he missed two meetings that he might have dropped out of the group entirely.
4. Seeing his absences as a sign of lack of involvement with the group, try to draw him into the group conversation, but without referring to these absences.
5. Talk about the importance of coming to every meeting.
6. Comment on his halfhearted commitment to the group — say that you doubt that he has ever really been committed to anything.
7. Ask him and the others how they feel about his returning after missing two meetings.
8. Say how you are feeling.
9. Share a similar experience in your own life.
10. Ask him why he missed these two meetings.
11. Ask how his missing two meetings might be related to what has been going on in the group as a whole.
12. Mention that he missed the two previous meetings.
13. Say that there seems to be an unspoken compact among the members not to talk about such events.
14. Interpret his absence as an expression of anxiety about the group.
15. Ask him what is happening in his life which may have caused him to miss those two meetings.
16. Encourage him to relate his absences to his family relationships and past experiences.
17. Encourage him to use this event to consider behavior he may wish to change.
18. Use a nonverbal procedure to get at the underlying feelings.
19. Ask him to role-play an important situation in his life.

Situation 14: A Member Cries

It is the middle of the sixth meeting. A woman who had been unusually silent for the first half of this meeting, makes a brief attempt to fight back tears and then begins to cry. No one says anything about it. What do you do?

1. Do nothing.
2. Ask why no one has said anything about the fact that someone is crying.
3. Express concern and reassurance.
4. Continue as if nothing out of the ordinary were happening.
5. Suggest that it might be more useful for her to talk than just to cry.
6. Accuse her of putting on a show.
7. Ask about feelings (examples: encourage her to give words to her feelings; ask the members how they feel about her crying).
8. Say how you are feeling (examples: moved, embarrassed).
9. Share a similar experience in your own life.
10. Ask her why she is crying (ask what's the matter).
11. Ask them to describe what is happening at that meeting.
12. Say that someone in the group is crying.
13. Describe her crying as an act of involvement in the group and a willingness to share her more private feelings with them.
14. Suggest that she may feel that the only time people are willing to listen and pay attention to her is when she is crying.
15. Encourage her to talk about the events in her life which may be upsetting her.
16. Encourage her to relate what she is feeling to her family relationships and past experiences.
17. Encourage her to talk about her difficulties in behavioral terms.
18. Use a nonverbal procedure to explore the rich emotional experience of crying.
19. Ask her to role-play the situation which her crying is about.

Situation 15: The Grumpy Group

Meeting seven is characterized by a general mood of irritability and negativism. A person can hardly start talking before another interrupts to say that he is bored. No one seems pleased about anything. The warm, involved mood at the end of the previous meeting seems completely forgotten. What do you do?

1. Do nothing.
2. Ask if they are satisfied with how the group is going today.
3. Reassure them that most groups have occasional meetings like this one.
4. Try to emphasize more positive feelings, both in your own remarks and those of others.
5. Suggest that they use the time more constructively.
6. Describe them as a group of irritable old men.
7. Ask how they feel about the meeting.
8. Say how you are feeling.
9. Share a similar experience in your own life.
10. Ask why everyone is being negative.
11. Ask what they think might be going on in the group today.
12. Describe the group's mood of negativism and irritability.
13. Say that there seems to be an unspoken understanding among the members to disagree with everything.
14. Describe their irritability as a reaction to the warm involvement of the previous meeting.
15. Encourage them to relate their grumpy mood to what is happening in their lives outside the group.
16. Encourage them to relate their behavior to their family relationships and past experiences.
17. Encourage them to use this situation to consider behavior they may wish to change.
18. Use a nonverbal procedure to get at the underlying feeling.
19. Use a role-playing or psychodrama procedure.

Situation 16: The Polite Group

The eighth meeting begins in a mood of superficial agreeableness. Everyone is being super-polite. Rambling remarks, evasive comments, behavior which ordinarily would immediately be challenged is being tolerated. It is clear that the group is protecting itself against any possible expression of aggressive feeling. What do you do?

1. Do nothing.
2. Ask if they are satisfied with how the group is going today.
3. Join in on whatever they are discussing.
4. Try to draw them into a more meaningful discussion.
5. Suggest that they get down to real feelings.
6. Be aggressive yourself — criticize the group for pussy-footing around.
7. Ask how they feel about what has been going on.
8. Say how you are feeling.
9. Share similar experiences in your own life.
10. Ask why everyone is being so polite.
11. Ask what they think might be going on in the group today.
12. Describe the group mood of politeness.
13. Say that there seems to be an unspoken agreement among the members to be polite and avoid anything that might rock the boat.
14. Suggest that all this politeness is a reaction against the anger of the previous meeting.
15. Encourage them to relate this to what is happening in their lives outside the group.
16. Lead into a discussion of their family relationships and past experiences.
17. Encourage them to use the situation to consider behavior they may wish to change.
18. Use a nonverbal procedure to get at the underlying feeling.
19. Use a role-playing or psychodrama procedure.

Situation 17: A Group Attack

Throughout the meetings one of the men had been insisting that he has no problems. In the middle of this eighth meeting, the group attacks him for "hiding behind a mask." At the present moment the whole interaction seems to be gaining in intensity — he responds to their accusations by increasing his denial; they respond to his denial by increasing their attack. You are not sure how he is being affected by it. What do you do?

1. Do nothing.
2. Even if they ask for your advice, let whatever happens happen.
3. Say that each person has the right to be the kind of person he wants to be.
4. Direct attention away from their attack by bringing up another issue.
5. Say that he is not going to get anything out of group if he does not put anything into it.
6. Join in on the attack.
7. Ask how he feels about what they are saying and how they feel about what he is saying.
8. Say how you are feeling.
9. Share an experience in your own life.
10. Ask why they are attacking and why he is denying.
11. Ask what they think might be going on in the group today.
12. Comment on the intensity of the argument between him and the rest of the group.
13. Describe the interaction as a standoff — they respond to his intellectualizing with increased attack, and he responds to their attack with increased intellectualizing.
14. Describe his denial as resistance to becoming involved in the group and describe the group's attack as an attempt to force him to become involved.
15. Ask if the kind of thing happening in the group now ever occurs in his life outside the group.
16. Encourage him to relate these group events to his family relationships and past experiences.
17. Encourage him and the others to use this event to consider behavior they may wish to change.
18. Ask him and the others to express nonverbally how they feel toward each other.
19. Suggest that he and another member role-play each other's side in the argument.

Situation 18: A Member Comes Drunk

A man who has been relatively quiet in the two previous meetings comes to session nine drunk. He is mildly disruptive, laughing and singing to himself, and occasionally breaking in when others are talking. What do you do?

1. Do nothing.
2. Ask what they want to do about the situation.
3. Show interest in him and express concern about his difficulties (say that he must have been feeling pretty lonely and depressed).
4. Continue as if nothing out of the ordinary were happening.
5. Ask him to leave and come back when he isn't drunk.
6. Accuse him of behaving like a baby.
7. Ask how they feel about what is happening.
8. Say how you are feeling.
9. Share a similar experience in your own life.
10. Ask him why he came to the meeting drunk.
11. Ask how they would describe what has been going on in the meeting.
12. Describe his effect on the mood of the group.
13. Suggest that he may be trying to tell the group something that he could not say in other ways.
14. Describe his behavior as an expression of anxiety about what has been happening in the group.
15. Encourage him to talk about the events in his life which may be troubling him.
16. Encourage him to relate his behavior to his family relationships and past experiences.
17. Encourage him to talk about his difficulties in behavioral terms.
18. Ask him to express nonverbally how he feels about you and the others.
19. Ask another member to role-play the drunk member's behavior.

100

Situation 19: A Side Conversation

The group had been spending much of this ninth meeting talking about one of the women, when another woman turns to a man sitting next to her and, disregarding the main conversation, starts a competing side conversation. Her talking is a discourtesy and interferes with the main discussion. She continues for several minutes and gives no sign of stopping. What do you do?

1. Do nothing.
2. Ask why no one has said anything about the two conversations.
3. Talk in an approving way about the engaged, intense, and spirited quality of the group interaction.
4. Draw her into the main discussion by inviting her to tell the whole group what she is talking about.
5. Ask that there be only one conversation at a time.
6. Say that it sounds like a nursery school — everyone wants to talk and no one wants to listen.
7. Ask how they feel when there are two conversations going on.
8. Say how you are feeling.
9. Share a similar experience in your own life.
10. Ask her why she is starting a second conversation.
11. Ask how they would describe what has been going on.
12. Say that there are two conversations going on.
13. Describe her side conversation as an expression of jealousy.
14. Describe her interruption as the expression of an underlying fear of being ignored and abandoned.
15. Encourage the interrupting member to talk about herself (perhaps her behavior is a reflection of difficulties she is having in her life outside the group).
16. Encourage her to relate these group events to her family relationships and past experiences (perhaps she felt left out in her family).
17. Encourage her to use this event to consider behavior she may wish to change.
18. Ask her to express nonverbally how she feels toward each person.
19. Ask them to exchange roles and repeat the interaction.

Situation 20: The Fight

Later in this ninth session, two men get into a heated argument over a minor point. The real reason for the argument appears to be their rivalry for the attention of one of the women. Finally one of the men jumps up enraged and threatens to hit the other. What do you do?

1. Do nothing.
2. Ask the members what they want to do about the situation.
3. Comment on the willingness with which these men are able to accept their aggressive feelings.
4. Defuse the situation by redirecting the group's attention to another issue.
5. Say that physical violence is not allowed in group.
6. Tell him to sit down, shut up, and stop acting like a child.
7. Ask about feelings (examples: ask the two men and the woman how they feel about each other; ask the members how they feel about what is going on).
8. Say how you are feeling.
9. Share a similar experience in your own life.
10. Ask the two why they are doing what they are doing.
11. Ask what they think might be going on between these two men.
12. Describe the mood of tension in the group.
13. Attribute the argument to competition between the two men for the attention of this woman.
14. Describe his aggressive behavior as a defense against his more passive and dependent feelings.
15. Encourage the threatening member to talk about himself (perhaps his behavior is a reflection of difficulties he is having in his life outside the group).
16. Encourage him to relate these group events to his family relationships and past experiences.
17. Encourage him and the rest of the group to use this event to consider behavior they may wish to change.
18. Use a nonverbal procedure (example: arm wrestling).
19. Ask other members to role-play the interaction between the two men.

Situation 21: The Sexualized Meeting

The tenth meeting begins in a mood of seductiveness. At the center of the interaction is a girl who, for several meetings now, has repeated a pattern of flirting with a man until he begins to show interest in her. In the present meeting, she has just stopped flirting with one man and has begun with another. Everyone seems to be taking part in the sexual mood, if not as an active participant, at least as a fascinated observer. What do you do?

1. Do nothing.
2. Ask if they are satisfied with how the group is going today.
3. Talk in an approving way about the intensity with which everyone seems to be involved.
4. Seeing the interaction as a stalemate, lead the group in another direction.
5. Suggest that they talk about what is going on rather than simply continuing to do it.
6. Accuse her of being a flirt who is basically afraid of men.
7. Ask about feelings (examples: ask the three major participants how they feel about each other; ask the members how they feel about what is going on).
8. Say how you are feeling (example: fascinated).
9. Share a similar experience in your own life.
10. Ask her why she is flirting the way she is.
11. Ask what they think might be going on among these three.
12. Describe the mood of seductiveness in the group.
13. Describe how the whole group seems to be fascinated by the interaction among the three.
14. Suggest that she flirts with different men because she is afraid of involvement with any one.
15. Ask if this is the way she relates to men outside the group.
16. Encourage her and the others to relate these group events to their family relationships and past experiences.
17. Encourage them to use this event to consider behavior they may wish to change.
18. Ask them to express nonverbally how they feel about each other.
19. Suggest that the three change roles and repeat the interaction.

GROUP LEADERSHIP QUESTIONNAIRE (GTQ-C)
ANSWER SHEET

NAME	DATE	GROUP

Situation	1. *All* of the responses you might consider making as Leader.	2. The *one* response you feel is most important to make.	3. A response you might make that is not included on the list.
1			
2			
3			
4			
5			
6			
7			
8			
9			
10			
11			
12			
13			
14			
15			
16			
17			
18			
19			
20			
21			

GROUP FACILITATOR QUESTIONNAIRE (GTQ-C)
SCORING INSTRUCTIONS AND INTERPRETATION SUGGESTIONS

Scoring: There are nineteen leadership scales in the GTQ-C. The items are arranged so that the nineteen types of response are in the same order for each. On the answer sheet tally the number of times you put the number 1 in Column 1, and record that number below in front of leadership scale 1, Silence. Then count the number of times you have the number 2 in Column 1, and record that number in front of leadership scale 2, Group-Directed. Follow this procedure for each of the other seventeen scales. Then repeat the procedure for Column 2.

1. *All* of the responses you might consider making. Tally	2. The *one* response you feel is most important. Tally	Leadership Scale
_____	_____	1. O Silence
_____	_____	2. GD Group-Directed
_____	_____	3. RA Reassurance-Approval
_____	_____	4. SG Subtle Guidance
_____	_____	5. S Structure
_____	_____	6. A Attack
_____	_____	7. MF Member Feeling
_____	_____	8. LF Leader Feeling
_____	_____	9. LE Leader Experience
_____	_____	10. CQ Clarification-Confrontation Question
_____	_____	11. GQ Group Dynamics Question
_____	_____	12. GA Group Atmosphere Interpretation
_____	_____	13. GI Group Dynamics Interpretation
_____	_____	14. PI Psychodynamic Interpretation
_____	_____	15. PL Personal Life
_____	_____	16. PP Past and Parents
_____	_____	17. BC Behavioral Change
_____	_____	18. NV Nonverbal
_____	_____	19. RP Role-Playing

LEADERSHIP SCALE COMBINATIONS

Potentially Useful Combinations of the Basic Nineteen Leadership Scales

1.	GN Group Initiation	1+2	O+GD
2.	EH Easy Hand	3+4	RA+SG
3.	HH Heavy Hand	5+6	S+A
4.	CF Confront	5+6+10	S+A+CQ
5.	CT Control	4+5+6	SG+S+A
6.	F Feeling	7+8	MF+LF
7.	SD Self Disclosure	8+9	LF+LE
8.	WW What-Why	10+11	CQ+GQ
9.	Q Question	7+10+11	MF+CQ+GQ
10.	GY Group Dynamics	11+12+13	GQ+GA+GI
11.	GC Group Centered	2+11+12+13	GD+GQ+GA+GI
12.	I Interpretation	12+13+14	GA+GI+PI
13.	OG Outside Group	15+16	PL+PP
14.	IC Individual Centered	15+16+17	PL+PP+BC
15.	NS New School	17+18+19	BC+NV+RP
16.	AO Activity Oriented	18+19	NV+RP

Potentially Useful Comparisons Between Scales and Combined Scales

Nondirective-Directive	1+2	: 4+5+6	GN	: SG+S+A
Ask-Tell	7+10+11	: 8+9+12+13+14	Q	: SD+I
	10+11	: 12+13+14	WW	: I
	7	: 8	MF	: LF
Confront-Reassure	5+6+10	: 3	CF	: RA
Group-Individual	2+11+12+13	: 15+16+17	GC	: IC

INTRODUCTION TO
THE LECTURETTES SECTION

This section of the *Annual* is a response to the users of the three-volume *Handbook of Structured Experience for Human Relations Training*. A number of group facilitators indicated an interest in our including more theory and lecture materials for use in training designs. The earlier handbooks are largely atheoretical, but a large body of theory is available to help participants to integrate their learning.

Experience-based learning is not the only strategy available to group facilitators; vicarious learning often is experienced as useful. The lecture method is sometimes the most appropriate way to help participants to learn from their experience, but it can be easily overused. Contrary to some criticisms of the human potential movement, most group facilitators are not anti-intellectual. "Head" learning is just as valuable as "gut-involved" experience.

Facilitators can use these lecture materials as "briefies," short explanations injected into processing sessions or as introductions to particular group events. The facilitator needs to develop a repertoire of interventions, including theory inputs. These materials are better received when they are accompanied by the use of visual media, such as posters, chalkboard diagrams, etc.

The lecturettes in this section are not intended to be technically precise statements of theoretical positions. They are somewhat simplistic in style. Where appropriate, bibliographic references to primary sources are given.

The flow in this section is from five lecturettes focusing primarily on personal growth, through four dealing with persons and tasks, to three concerned with goals and planning.

GUIDELINES
FOR GROUP
MEMBER BEHAVIOR

Over the years, in the process of facilitating beginning human relations training groups, I had created in my mind a list of optimum behaviors for group participants. Unfortunately, it developed that as I began groups I would surface these preferred behaviors — "developing group norms" — in a manner that would reinforce my authority role in the group. I was also finding that as each "norm" emerged I was involving myself in a series of minor confrontations with the participants, centered around my apparent disapprobation of their behavior. My pattern of injecting norms as they occurred, *e.g.*, 1) look at the person you're talking to or 2) speak for yourself, was a rich source of data for the group to process, but it was tending to lock groups into dealing with authority and confrontation as predominate issues.

In looking for a way to avoid this reoccurring phenomenon, it occurred to me that it would make more sense (and be more growth inducing) if I would be "up front" and explicit about my expectations concerning participant behaviors right from the beginning.

I prepared a list of the norms that I had been continually "enforcing," and, as I began a week-long human relations group, I listed these norms on newsprint and posted the list in the group meeting room at the beginning of the first session.

My original list looked like this:

Figure 1.

T-GROUP GROUND RULES

1. Keep in the here and now.
2. Speak only for yourself.
3. Try to maintain eye contact when you are speaking to someone.
4. Minimize head trips.
5. Avoid gunnysacking.
6. Avoid red-crossing.
7. Avoid being judgemental.
8. No dime store psychology.
9. Do not attempt to answer hypothetical questions.
10. We all share the responsibility of avoiding dysfunctional silence.
11. "I feel" does not mean the same as "I think."

Therapy charges:

| Friends | $ .50 | Parents | 2.50 |
| Spice | 1.00 | Other groups | 5.00 |

My approach was to "explain" the jargonistic terms, *e.g.*, redcrossing, gunnysacking, etc., as the opening action of the session.

The two most frequent reactions to this position which have proven to be helpful in getting the group moving are as follows:

1) Occasionally participants challenge the concept of being told "what to do." We deal with this on the spot with the possibility of renegotiating any of the guidelines that are not consistent with the goals of the group.

2) Very frequently, participants who "know the ground rules" will "correct" themselves or other participants (and sometimes, gleefully, the trainers.)

The result of this approach to opening a human relations group has been to free me, as the trainer, from some role restrictions as an enforcer.

"SHOULDISM"

Much of the current thought and practice in the human potential movement (especially the Gestalt approaches) is counter to a series of shoulds (which is what my ground rules list really is). My response to this line of questioning is that shouldism and oughtism *should** be avoided when they attempt to deal with the way people feel as opposed to the way people behave. The group movement (at least to me) is an educational effort which attempts to modify behavior. Therefore, behavioral guidelines seem to me to be not only acceptable but essential.

GOOD VS. FUNCTIONAL

As we work on modifying behavior (growth) in my groups, I try to establish a norm other than the good-bad continuum and replace that concept with a functional-dysfunctional continuum. The measure of the functionality of any given behavior is relative only to the reference group. A value cannot be placed on a behavior in an existential, contextless vacuum. Behaviors which are contrary to the guidelines for group member behavior are neither good nor bad in themselves but may be dysfunctional to the growth of the group members.

BEHAVIOR VS. PERSONAL WORTH

Another key issue centered around the guidelines is that I work to reinforce the concept that I can dislike someone's behavior without disliking the person. We may "be what we eat" but we certainly are not what we do.

My original ground rules are of the Mt. Sinai variety, *i.e.*, thou shalt not's. This is consistent with my personal style, but they are clearly inappropriate for trainers with other styles. Two colleagues of mine** — both of whom have softer interpersonal styles than I do — have modified the ground rules (figure 1) to the following:

---

*There is something slightly paradoxical about a position which says that you *should not* have should nots.
**John Jones and Tony Banet.

Figure 2.

GUIDELINES FOR GROUP SESSIONS

Things to do:

1. Be aware of both your feelings and thoughts.
2. Listen actively to everyone. No person's being heard should get lost.
3. Be as open and honest as you can while being sensitive to the needs of others. Be constructively open.
4. Keep your attention on the "here and now."
5. Whenever possible make statements rather than ask questions.
6. Accept responsibility for your own learning, and collaborate with others in theirs.

Things to avoid:

1. Dime-store psychology. Study the impact of behavior rather than its "causes."
2. Red-crossing. Avoid putting band-aids on persons who are capable of working out their thing. Give support without cutting off learning.
3. "Counseling" that gives nothing.
4. Requiring persons to be like you or to justify their feelings. Accept.
5. Pretending that things aren't the way they are.

Other considerations:

1. Everyone who is here belongs here just because he is here, and for no other reason.
2. For each person what is true is determined by what is in him, what he directly feels and finds making sense in himself, and the way he lives inside himself.
3. Decisions made by the group need everyone taking part in some way.
4. What happens here is confidential to the degree that each person owns his own data.
5. Trainers have trouble following these guidelines, too.

A third list° gives a still milder focus. (Figure 3)

Figure 3.

GROUND RULES FOR GROUP SESSIONS°

1. Everyone who is here belongs here just because he is here, and for no other reason.
2. For each person what is true is determined by what is in him, what he directly feels and finds making sense in himself, and the way he lives inside himself.
3. Our first purpose is to make contact with each other. Everything else we might want or need comes second.
4. We try to be as honest as possible and to express ourselves as we really are and really feel — just as much as we can.
5. We listen for the person inside living and feeling.
6. We listen to everyone.

°Abstracted from E. T. Gendlin and John Beebe III. An experimental approach to group therapy. Journal of Research and Development in Education, 1968, *1*, 19-29.

7. The group leader is responsible for two things only: he protects the belonging of every member, and he protects their being heard if this is getting lost.

8. Realism: If we know things are a certain way, we do not pretend they are not that way.

9. What we say here is "confidential": no one will repeat anything said here outside the group, unless it concerns only himself. This applies not just to obviously private things, but to everything. After all, if the individual concerned wants others to know something, he can always tell them himself.

10. Decisions made by the group need everyone taking part in some way.

EXPLICIT OR IMPLICIT?

I contend that all group facilitators have ground rules or guidelines tucked away in their "trainer heads," e.g., Schutz' list in *Here Comes Everybody*. I believe the issue concerns not whether norms for desirable group behavior exist implicitly within the group setting but whether it is helpful to the group for the facilitator to make his group behavior biases explicit — I contend that it is.

J. William Pfeiffer

RISK-TAKING
AND ERROR
PROTECTION STYLES

There is a statistical concept dealing with the kind of inferences about populations that we make from samples which has some application to styles of human risk-taking. There are basically two types of inferential errors that one may make in drawing generalizations about a population from a sample from that population. These two types of errors are called Type I and Type II. A Type I error is committed when one decides that the population has a certain characteristic when in fact it doesn't. The reverse kind of mistaken inference is a Type II error, deciding that the population does not have certain characteristics when in fact it does. These two types of errors are reciprocal in that protecting against one increases the probability of making the other. That is, if a person sets up his statistical procedure to attempt to diminish the possibility of making errors of the first type, he increases his chances of making the second type of error. He may fail to detect a characteristic that is a real attribute of his target population.

These two types of errors may be graphically illustrated by looking at what might be termed an Inference Window. This is a window with four panes, or a chart with four cells. In the upper left-hand cell are the predicted positive outcomes that actually turn out negatively. We will term these "false positives." In the upper right-hand corner of the window we denote those predicted positive outcomes that actually are affirmed, and we will call those "true positives." In the lower left-hand pane of the window we will indicate predicted negative outcomes that are in fact negative. We will call those "true negatives." Finally, in the lower right-hand part of the window we will denote those predicted negative outcomes that in fact become positive, "false negatives." The upper left- and the lower right-hand portions of the window are false predictions, false positive and false negative. The false positive decisions are Type I errors, and the false negative predictions are Type II errors.

THE INFERENCE WINDOW

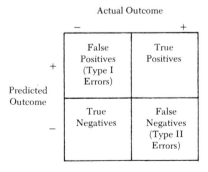

So we can see that there is a possibility of making two basic kinds of mistakes in drawing inferences from samples to populations. To give an example, let us say we wanted to test the hypothesis that happy salesmen make more money. Let us say we took a sample of salesmen by some defensible method, obtained a measure of their happiness and an indication of their earnings, and correlated the two. Now we are going to make a decision about whether in the population of salesmen that we are thinking about there exists some kind of relationship between happiness and earnings. When we apply the statistical test of significance, we determine whether we can have any confidence in generalizing to the population of salesmen about this relationship. If we come up with some statistically significant results, we may conclude that there is a relationship between happiness and earnings among salesmen. If in fact that is wrong, we have made a false positive inference. Let us assume that in our sample we found no relationships between happiness and earnings but, in fact, out there in the real world of millions of salesmen there is some relationship. We have made an error called false negative.

Notice that the window also clearly indicates that the kinds of inferential errors that we make from our observations do not necessarily put us into a double bind. This is not a situation of "damned if you do and damned if you don't." If our observing system is effective, we may, in fact, have a preponderance of true positive decisions and true negative decisions and not make a lot of errors. The errors that we are talking about, the mistakes in judgement that we make, can be considered to be analogous to what some people call sins of omission and sins of commission, that is, failing to act and acting in a way that we should not act.

People can be crudely classified into one of two types also: people whose major decision-making strategies tend to protect against Type I errors ("sins of commission") and persons whose major decision-making styles protect against Type II errors ("sins of omission"). Type I protectors tend to want a lot of data; they often have the attitude that is commonly ascribed to people from Missouri — "Show me." They tend to be low risk-takers and have the general need in decision-making to protect themselves from making public mistakes. They tend to take on easy tasks as opposed to very challenging jobs; they tend to see the world as somewhat dangerous, risky and chancey; their major approach to the world and decision-making is to be careful; their attitude about themselves tends to be, "I may not be able to do it." On the other hand, the person whose major decision-making style is to protect against Type II errors can be characterized as a risk-taker. He is a person whose major approach to choices is to protect against the possibility that he may fail to try something that might work out well. He asks himself, "Let's see if I can do it." He takes on challenges, he tends to see the world in terms of possibilities, chances, and resources, and he tests himself against the world as he sees it.

Len Miller, a rehabilitation counselor educator, draws an analogy between Type I and Type II protection styles and counselor behavior. Rehabilitation counselors have to decide whether to take on particular clients for services. The Type I protectors tend to take only easy cases — people who need eyeglasses or people who may need only minor surgery — and want to protect themselves against taking on people with multiple disabilities, people who are difficult to rehabilitate. On the other hand, Type II protectors tend to take on more difficult cases, be more risk-taking in their relationship with their supervisors, and view the world in terms of what is possible rather than what needs to be prevented. Another illustration may serve to explicate the application of the statistical concept to the way people make ordinary everyday decisions. Imagine a boy and girl sitting in a college classroom together. The boy has been observing her, has some interest in her, would like to ask her for a date, thinks she is good looking, has admired the way she is related to other people in the class, has respect in her contributions to class discussion, and so on. He has several strategies that he can use. He can ask her for a date in such a way that permits her very easily to turn him down; he can fail to ask her for a date when in fact she may be interested in him, and he may never know it if he does not ask her.

114

If he is a Type I protector, he may be very cautious, wait a long time, and try to be very careful in his approach to her. If he is a Type II protector, that is, he doesn't throw away the chance of building happy harmonious relationships that he wants, he may be more aggressive in his approach to her and may test out whether she is in fact interested in spending time with him.

Seeing decision-making in this way implies that the person has some sense of the probabilities of positive and negative outcomes when he commits himself. There are people who protect against very low probability outcomes and are so timorous that they refuse to cross the street under the very small chance that they may be run over and killed. There are other people that don't even look before they walk into the street, figuring that the probability is so low that they are going to be hit, they can take that chance. These extremes illustrate the fact that people differ greatly in terms of subjective probabilities underlying their decision-making. We differ quite a bit in our willingness to take risks. But it is important to consider that the line between risk and folly is very thin. What is needed is a way of managing one's risk-taking. This is perhaps best done by relating one's "stretching" to one's personal growth goals. If a person is in touch with where he wants to go, the kind of person he wants to become, and the kind of life he wants to lead, then his risk-taking takes on significance and direction. If he is not goal-directed, if he is not in touch with some directives in his life, then his risk-taking may, in fact, become foolish. It is important to consider also that one man's risk may be another man's ordinary behavior.

What constitutes a risk for a person depends on whether that is new behavior for him and whether he has a subjective sense of danger involved in the behavior. Let us look at some examples of risks that might be related to one's personal growth goals. One risk that surfaces fairly rapidly in human relations training is the risk to be open with other people. Self-disclosure is one of the most creative and potentially useful risks that a person can engage in. Letting other people know who you are and letting other people know how you relate to them and how they relate to you are risks because they may endanger people's acceptance of you. Being open can be a very chancey thing, but it can also be a very useful productive pattern of behaving if it is done with sensitivity. Another goal is getting involved with people, getting committed to people, linking up with people, being included and including people in one's own activities. These risks of pairing, being with people, are much more difficult for some people than for others. A third risk that is related to human relations training is giving feedback. Some people have great difficulty in giving positive feedback, giving compliments, saying that they love somebody, saying that they are pleased, and so on. Other people have difficulty in giving negative feedback and tend to sit on, or "gunnysack," negative reactions to other people's behavior. The risk to be open about one's reactions to other people can be enormously stimulating to personal growth. Another risk is touching and being touched. For some people this is a big problem, and for other people it's a very pleasant activity. Another risk is becoming intimate with people, becoming close and personal with people. Another risk is confronting conflict. We tend to shy away from conflict, smooth it over in our boss-subordinate relationships, peer relationships, teacher-student relationships, and so on. One risk that might be considered is surfacing conflict and dealing with it in a sensitive but direct way. Conflict can be viewed as useful rather than dysfunctional. Another bag full of risks is trying new ways of behaving toward other people. That may include being quiet, or it may include being more aggressive. This will vary from person to person, and each person defines his own new behavior. Perhaps the biggest risk that a person might take is not to take any risks. As Harvey Cox once remarked, "Not to decide is to decide."

What this lecturette has attempted is the application of a statistical concept to the kinds of decisions that we make in our everyday lives, to take risks in relation to our personal growth goals. If we decide to be risk-takers, what we are doing is deciding to protect against Type II errors, looking at the world in terms of possibilities and trying new things, trying new ways of behaving, testing new approaches to the problems we run into each day, and trying to protect against throwing away opportunities.

SUGGESTED ACTIVITIES

Participants pair off and take turns discussing their personal growth goals. Each of them makes a contract with his partner about a risk that he might take in a specified period of time and about when they will get together again to discuss the outcome of the risk-taking behavor. During the first meeting the partners take each other's personal growth goals and try to sort out the extent to which the planned risk-taking is related to the person's goals and still is sensitive to other people. After the risk-taking period, which may be a day, they meet again to share outcomes of their risk-taking and to give each other support for continued efforts at trying new behavior.

A second activity within a personal growth laboratory is to form what are called N-groups, or "new" groups. The membership in these groups, which will meet only once, cuts across T-groups or other kinds of groups that may constitute a personal growth laboratory experience. The announced purpose of the meeting is to try to behave in the new group meeting in ways that one would like to be able to ordinarily. Each person announces the new behavior that he would like to be able to engage in during the meeting, and individuals get feedback and support for those behaviors during the meeting. Meetings should be planned to last approximately fifteen minutes per participant. That is, with a group of about eight who are going to meet only once, approximately two hours should be scheduled.

John E. Jones

DEFENSE
MECHANISMS
IN GROUPS

Growth through group experience is often painful. Despite the fact that most of us choose to take part in group activities to learn more about ourselves, experiment with new behaviors, and improve interpersonal skills, it can be expected that we will resist the process because it is frightening and demanding. The pressures to engage in self-disclosure, intimacy, and confrontation, may bring about changes in our conceptual framework, precipitate anxiety, shame, guilt and other uncomfortable feelings. There is a natural tendency to avoid such feelings, and each of us has developed his own preferred means. Avoidance behavior or defense mechanisms are usually well-ingrained and unconscious. Each of us brings his own particular set to the group. Because these defenses interfere with individual and group growth, it is important to recognize and deal with them effectively.

Although all defenses are essentially evasive in nature, such maneuvers may be categorized by whether the individual moves toward (fight) or away from (flight) the source of conflict or chooses to manipulate other group members (pairing).

FIGHT DEFENSES: These are based on the premise that "the best defense is a good offense."

Competition with the facilitator: The person who struggles to control the group or "out-do" the trainer may be attempting to prove his group prowess in order to avoid dealing with his own behavior.

Cynicism: This may be manifested by frequent challenging of the group contract and goals, skeptical questioning of genuine behavior, and attacks on stronger, threatening members.

Interrogation: A barrage of proving questions keeps one on the defensive. An individual who habitually cross-examines others in the group under the guise of "gaining helpful information and understanding" may be fighting to keep the spotlight safely away from himself.

FLIGHT DEFENSES: These are the most frequently used means of avoiding honest, feeling-level involvement in group process:

Intellectualization (head trips, dime-store psychology): These are processes by which an individual deals with his emotions in an objective, diagnostic or interpretative manner so that he never comes to grips with his gut-level feelings; e.g., "I guess I'm angry with you because you remind me of my older sister." Even entire groups may resort to becoming involved in apparently worthwhile but evasive, drawn-out discussions of social and general behavior issues.

Generalization: Closely related is the tendency to make general, impersonal statements about group behavior instead of applying them directly to self or specific participants. For example, a tense person states "People can really get anxious when there are long silences" when he really means "I am very uptight with this silence."

Projection: Here the individual attributes to others traits which are unacceptable in himself; e.g., someone competing for attention in the group may attack another person for using more than his share of the group's time.

Rationalization: This is an attempt to justify maladaptive behavior by substituting "good" reasons for real ones; e.g., "I am not getting very much out of this group because there are not enough people my age, and I just can't relate with the group members," or "If only I were in that other group, things would be better."

Withdrawal: This defense may vary in intensity from boredom to actual physical removal of oneself from the group. Consistently silent persons may be passive learners but are not growing interpersonally. Groups which fall silent frequently, especially after dramatic moments, are also in flight. The tendency to deal with past interaction issues instead of the "here and now" is another form of withdrawal.

GROUP MANIPULATION DEFENSES: Participants frequently maneuver other members into specific kinds of relationships in order to protect themselves from deeper involvement or confrontation.

Pairing: Members seek out one or two supporters and form an emotional sub-group alliance in which they protect and support each other.

"Red-Crossing": This may occur both within or outside sub-groups. In conflict or confrontation situations, the member mediates for or defends the person under fire. The assumed contract is "Let's keep it safe; I'll come to your aid if you come to mine."

Focusing on One: An entire group may find itself spending excessive amounts of time and energy on one individual. By keeping the spotlight on a single person for an extended time period, the opportunities increase for large numbers of participants to fall silent or keep the action away from themselves.

Even when recognized, the task of dealing with each of these defenses is not an easy one. Occasionally, an appropriate non-verbal or other structured exercise can be an effective means of uncovering evaded feelings. However, there are no simple, consistently effective methods or responses for dealing with these defenses. Generally, once the evasive maneuver is recognized, the person(s) involved should be confronted, keeping in mind the tenets for effective feedback. As an atmosphere of mutual trust is established, the group participants are apt to lower their defenses and risk experimenting with new growth producing behaviors.

Paul Thoresen

ASSUMPTIONS
ABOUT THE
NATURE OF MAN

Human relationships are based on assumptions about people, what they are like and what their nature is. These assumptions can be either implicit in the way we relate to other people, or they may be explicit. A given person may or may not be able to specify what he believes to be the nature of man. That person who has a coherent point of view about the nature of man is said to have a philosophy. But each of us has in our relations with other people a more or less consistent set of assumptions that we make about other people and about ourselves, and our philosophies may be inferred by observing us relating to other people.

Different assumptions about what other people are like lead to different ways of relating. For example, the person who has the point of view about people that underlies the statement, "People are no damned good," is likely to behave toward people in a suspicious, non-trusting way. On the other hand, the person who assumes that to be loved is a human need relates to people in a fundamentally different manner. Some people emphasize in their assumptions about the nature of man the animalistic side of humanness, and this leads to a different set of behaviors toward other people, particularly of the opposite sex. Persons who hold the assumption that the herd instinct is a part of human nature tend to behave differently than do people who do not have an instinctual basis for their philosophy.

The term "nature" connotes birth, and philosophies about the nature of man have at their roots the assumptions that we make about what people are like without regard for the influence of the environment on them. What is a person like when he is born, is he, in fact, a person? It is important that one be able to assess his assumptions about other people for two reasons. First, to diagnose how he is relating to friends, to co-workers, to other group members. Second, so that he may plan more effectively the interventions that he might make in the human systems of which he is a part. The way one intervenes in human relationships implies a set of assumptions about what people are like.

Gordon Allport specifies three psychological models about the nature of man. The first of Allport's models is that man is a *reactive being*. This model specifies that man essentially reacts to stimuli in his physical environment. He is not *pro*active in the sense that he wills things to happen. He is essentially *re*active, and his behavior is determined by his environment. The second model is man as a *reactive being in depth*. This model specifies that man has an unconscious life, that his behavior is a function of things of which he is not aware. He is reactive to his environment and he is also reactive to drives, instincts, will and other aspects of his personality, which are submerged. The third model is man as *being-in-process-of-becoming*. This model specifies that man is essentially a person who has within himself the capability of becoming good and sufficient, given an environment that nurtures his growth.

These three models subsume most of the schools of psychology that are prevalent today. Allport says that the reactive model takes in naturalism, positivism, behaviorism, operationism, and physicalism. The second subsumes psychoanalysis, psychodynamics, and depth psychology.

The third model contains such trends as holism, orthopsychology, personalistics, and existential psychology.

Each of these three models has different implications for the way we relate to each other. The first, the *reactive* model, implies that we will relate to other people in terms of influence, power, rewards, reinforcement, manipulation, and conditioning. We will relate to each other in ways which cause the other person to react. That is, we become a part of his environment and stimulate him verbally and nonverbally, and we reward his behavior both positively and negatively in order to shape his behavior to our ends. The second model, *reactive being in depth*, implies that we would relate to people in terms of "why." We would try to discover motives, to develop insight. We would in our relations with other people discuss the reasons behind our behaviors, feelings, thoughts, attitudes, and values. The third model, *being-in-process-of-becoming*, implies that we would relate to other people in terms of nurturance and development. We would try to foster climates that would produce growth in each other.

It is important to bear in mind that these models represent different assumptions about the nature of man that are not in the scientific sense verifiable. Nonetheless, they are at the base of all human relations. There is no way to establish the truth about man's nature, but it is worthwhile to make one's own assumptions explicit. E. G. Williamson once said that he didn't like the word truth. He said, "Truth is a shady spot where we sit down to eat our lunch before moving on."

SUGGESTED ACTIVITIES:

1) Participants may be handed 3 x 5 cards or pieces of paper, and on one side they are to write two or three statements which they believe to be true about people and on the reverse side two or three statements which they believe to be not true about people. The group may check their assumptions against the three Allport models to determine the predominance of their agreement with the three different sets of assumptions.

2) Participants may be formed into groups to design advertising campaigns to influence the public to liberate women. They may form three groups, one of which is to design an ad campaign that is based on the reactive model, one to work on the second model, and one to work on the third model.

3) Participants may be guided into a discussion of what classrooms would be like that had teachers espousing the different assumptions about the nature of man. How would the physical environment look, how would the teacher behave, what would be the teacher-pupil relationship, and so on.

The first of these activities could perhaps best be done prior to the lecture.

John E. Jones

Reference: Allport, W. W. Psychological models for guidance. *Harvard Educational Review*. 1962, 32, 373-381.

McGregor's Theory X-Theory Y Model

The first acquaintance with "X" and "Y" for many of us was as unknowns in Algebra I. During the decade of the sixties "X" and "Y" took on some additional meanings for readers in the behavioral sciences and contemporary management thinking.

In 1960, Douglas McGregor published his *The Human Side of Enterprise*. This was to be a major force in the application of behavioral science to management's attempts to improve productivity in organizations. McGregor was trying to stimulate people to examine the reasons underlying the way they tried to influence human activity, particularly at work. He saw management thinking and activity as based on two very different sets of assumptions about people. These sets of assumptions, called X and Y, have come to be applied to management styles; e.g., an individual is a theory X manager or a theory Y manager.

McGregor looked at the various approaches to managing people in organizations — not only industrial organizations but others as well — services, schools, and public agencies and concluded that the styles or approaches to management used by people in positions of authority could be examined and understood in light of those manager's assumptions about people. He suggested that a manager's effectiveness or ineffectiveness lay in the very subtle, frequently unconscious effects of these assumptions on his attempts to manage or influence others.

As he looked at the behaviors, structures, systems, and policies set up in some organizations, he found them contrary to information coming out of research at that time: information about human behavior and the behavior of people at work. It appeared that management was based on ways of looking at people that did not agree with what behavioral scientists knew and were learning about people as they went about their work in some, or perhaps most organizations.

THEORY X

The traditional view of man, widely held, was labeled "X" and seemed to be based on the following set of assumptions:

1. The average human being has an inherent dislike for work and will avoid it if he can.

2. Because of this human characteristic of dislike for work, most people must be coerced, controlled, directed, or threatened with punishment to get them to put forth adequate effort toward the achievement of organizational objectives.

3. The average human being prefers to be directed, wishes to avoid responsibility, has relatively little ambition, and wants security above all.

Of course, these assumptions aren't set out or stated, but if we examine how organizations are structured and policies, procedures, and work rules established, we can see them operating. Job responsibilities are closely spelled out, goals are imposed without individual employee involvement or consideration, reward is contingent on working within the system, and punishment falls on those who deviate from the rules as established. These factors all influence how people respond, but the underlying assumptions or reasons for them are seldom tested or even recognized as assumptions. The fact is that most people act as if their beliefs about human nature were correct and require no study or checking.

This set of assumptions about people may result in very contrasting styles of management. We may see a "hard" or a "soft" approach to managing, but both approaches will be based on these ideas set out above. One theory "X" manager may drive his men at their work because he thinks that they are lazy and that this is the only way to get things done. Another may look at his men in the same way, but he may think the way to get lazy people to work is to be nice to them, to coax productive activity out of them.

This view of man was characteristic of the first half of the twentieth century, which had seen the effects of Frederick Taylor's scientific management school of thought. His focus had been on man as an aspect of the productive cycle much like that of a piece of machinery, and it had allowed for advances in productivity. Yet it was out of this managerial climate that tended to view man as an interchangeable part of a machine—as a machine element that was set in motion by the application of external forces — that the "human relations" view grew and the behavioral science school developed.

I must hasten to add that the application of understandings of human behavior from the behavioral sciences is not an extension of the human relations focus of the 1940's and 1950's. These two grew up separately. One might construe that the human relations view of handling people prevalent at that time was manipulative and merely a "soft" theory "X" approach.

THEORY Y

Another view of man not necessarily the opposite extreme of "X" was called "Y" or theory "Y." This set of assumptions about the nature of man which influenced manager behaviors is set out below.

1. The expenditure of physical and mental effort in work is as natural as play or rest.

2. External control and threat of punishment are not the only means for bringing about effort toward organizational objectives. Man will exercise self-control in the service of objectives to which he is committed.

3. Commitment to objectives is dependent on rewards associated with their achievement. The most important rewards are those that satisfy needs for self-respect and personal improvement.

4. The average human being learns, under proper conditions, not only to accept, but to seek responsibility.

5. The capacity to exercise a relatively high degree of imagination, ingenuity, and creativity in the solution of organizational problems is widely, not narrowly, distributed in the population.

6. Under the conditions of modern industrial life, the intellectual potentialities of the average human being are only partially utilized.

It is important to realize that this is not a soft approach to managing human endeavor. Examined closely it can be seen as a very demanding style: it sets high standards for all and expects people to reach for them. It is not only hard on the employee who may not have had any prior experience with the managerial behaviors resulting from these assumptions, but it also demands a very different way of acting from the supervisor or manager who has grown up under at least some of the theory X influences in our culture. While we can intellectually understand and agree with some of these ideas, it is far more difficult to put them into practice. Risk-taking is necessary on the part of the manager, for he must allow employees or subordinates to experiment

122

with activities for which he may feel they do not presently have the capability. The learning and growth resulting from this opportunity may handsomely reward the risk.

The focus of a Y manager is on man as a growing, developing, learning being, while an X manager views man as static, fully developed, and capable of little change. A theory X manager sets the parameters of his employees' achievements by determining their potentialities in light of negative assumptions. A theory Y manager allows his people to test the limits of their capabilities and uses errors for learning better ways of operating rather than as clubs for forcing submission to the system. He structures work so that an employee can have a sense of accomplishment and personal growth. The motivation comes from the work itself and provides a much more powerful incentive than the "externals" of theory X.

A suggestion for your consideration is to make the same assumptions about others that you make about yourself, and then act in the appropriate manner. You might be pleasantly surprised.

Albert J. Robinson

REFERENCES:

McGregor, Douglas. *The Human Side of Enterprise*. New York: McGraw-Hill, 1961.
McGregor, Douglas. (Edited by Bennis, Warren G. and McGregor, Caroline.) *The Professional Manager*. New York: McGraw-Hill, 1967.

THE MASLOW
NEED HIERARCHY

Abraham Maslow theorized that experienced needs are the primary influences on an individual's behavior. When a particular need emerges, it determines the individual's behavior in terms of motivations, priorities, and action taken. Thus motivated behavior is the result of the tension — either pleasant or unpleasant — experienced when a need presents itself. The goal of the behavior is the reduction of this tension or discomfort, and the behavior, itself, will be appropriate for facilitating the satisfaction of the need. Only unsatisfied needs are prime sources of motivation.

Understanding behaviors and their goals involves gaining insight into presently unsatisfied needs. Maslow developed a method for gaining insight by providing categories of needs in a hierarchical structure. He placed all human needs, from primitive or immature (in terms of the behaviors they foster) to civilized or mature needs, into five need systems. He believed that there is a natural process whereby individuals fulfilled needs in ascending order from most immature to most mature. This progression through the need hierarchy is seen as the climbing of a ladder where the individual must have experienced secure footing on the first rung in order to experience the need to step up to the next higher rung. The awareness of the need to climb further up the ladder is a function of having fulfilled the need of managing the preceding rung, and only satisfactory fulfillment of this need will allow the individual to deal with the new need or rung. Inability to fulfill a lower-order need or difficulty in fulfilling a lower-order need may result in an individual's locking in on immature behavior patterns or may produce a tendency to return to immature behaviors under stress any time an individual feels a lower-order need not fulfilled to his satisfaction. The individual may also revert to behaviors which fulfilled lower-order needs when the satisfaction of higher needs are temporarily blocked. That is not to say that any need is ever completely satisfied; rather, Maslow indicates that there must be at least partial fulfillment before an individual can become aware of the tensions manifested by a higher-order need and have the freedom to pursue its fulfillment.

A HIERARCHY OF NEEDS

The 1972 Annual Handbook For Group Facilitators

The Maslow Need Hierarchy is presented in the illustration above. The Basic level represents needs which reflect physiological and survival goals. At this level are such factors as shelter, clothing, food, sex, and other necessities. In a culture such as ours, where these basic needs are almost automatically met, there is not likely to be any need tension concerning the fulfillment of Basic needs. However, individuals adapt this basic level upward to include such needs as avoidance of physical discomfort, pleasant working environment, or more money for providing creature comforts.

The second level of the hierarchy consists of Safety needs. When the individual has at least partially fulfilled the Basic needs, he will experience the tensions relating to needs of security, orderliness, protective rules, and general risk avoidance. These needs are often satisfied by an adequate salary, insurance policies, a good burglar alarm system for his business, a doorman for his apartment building, etc.

When Safety needs have been met, the individual will become less preoccupied with self and will endeavor to form interpersonal relationships. The relative success of this need for Belongingness will result in his feeling accepted and appreciated by others. Thus the third level needs concern family ties, friendship and group membership.

When an individual feels secure in his relationships with others, he will probably seek to gain special status within the group. His need tension will be associated with ambition and a desire to excel. These Ego-Status needs will motivate the individual to seek out opportunities to display his competence in an effort to gain social and professional rewards.

Because Ego-Status fulfillment is greatly dependent upon the ability of others to respond appropriately to the individual's efforts to perform in a superior way, they are the most difficult to fulfill satisfactorily. However, if the individual has gained satisfaction on level four, he may be able to move up to level five — Self Actualization. At this level, the individual is concerned with personal growth and may fulfill this need by challenging himself to become more creative, demanding greater achievement of himself, and, in general, directing himself to measure up to his own criteria of personal success. Self-Actualizing behaviors must include risk-taking, seeking autonomy, and developing freedom to act.

Sandra L. Pfeiffer

Reference: A. H. Maslow. *Motivation and Personality.* 2nd ed. N.Y.: Harper and Row, 1970.

JOB
ENRICHMENT

The motivation-hygiene theory, underlying what is known as job enrichment, grew out of research on job attitudes conducted by Frederick Herzberg. In establishing his theory, Herzberg draws heavily upon the hierarchy of needs developed by Abraham Maslow. Herzberg stresses that the factors which truly motivate the work are "growth" factors, or those that give the worker a sense of personal accomplishment through the challenge of the job itself. In other words, motivation is in the content of the job, the internal dynamics that the worker experiences in completing his task.

On the other hand, Herzberg maintains that the context, or environmental factors (hygiene), which surround the job cause dissatisfaction when they are in unhealthy condition. These dissatisfiers may be classed as "deficit" needs in that their importance is felt only in their absence. For example, good working conditions rarely motivate workers. However, bad working conditions are frequently cited by workers as sources of dissatisfaction.

MOTIVATION FACTORS (JOB CONTENT)	HYGIENE FACTORS (JOB ENVIRONMENT)
SATISFIERS	DISSATISFIERS
Work Itself	Company Policy & Administration
Achievement	Supervision
Recognition	Working Conditions
Responsibility	Interpersonal Relations
Growth and Advancement	Salary

A simple example might be the telephone installation man who is given the list of places to cover during the day and asked to order them in the way he believes will be most efficient, rather than having been given an itinerary preplanned by the manager who doesn't "know the territory" first-hand the way the installer does.

PRACTICAL APPLICATION

In the years that I have been assisting organizations in the implementation of job enrichment I have witnessed results that are not only dramatic from an economic viewpoint, but, equally important, imply that it has stimulated management awareness, growth and effectiveness. Although not originally designed to fulfill the role, job enrichment has been significantly effective in assisting supervisors to improve their management styles. The organization development applications of job enrichment is popular because 1) it can easily be adapted by all levels of management, 2) payoff (results) can be realized in a relatively short time span and, 3) it can be measured in specific terms.

The primary purpose of this paper is to present an example of a practical model that I have found effective in implementing job enrichment. The model has been utilized in large and small business organizations as well as a medium sized civic organization.

When I first enter the organization or "family" group within an organization, I have two primary objectives in mind. First, I attempt to give a thorough interpretation of job enrichment and my role in it. Secondly, I try to assess the level of management commitment. I point out the possible consequences of inadequate commitment which can affect the supervisor-subordinate relationship in the areas of trust and respect.

After understanding and commitment have been established, management "family" groups attend a two-day job enrichment workshop, preferably removed from the work locale. The workshop is designed to 1) teach the participants the theory behind job enrichment, 2) allow them to witness how others have utilized it, 3) enable the group members to experiment with each other in applying job enrichment and, 4) assist the participants in realizing how the implementation of job enrichment will affect their own jobs as well as the jobs of their subordinates.

Immediately after the workshop, I will either pass out a job reaction survey to everyone in that family organization, management and non-management, or personally interview each person. I receive permission from each person being interviewed to allow me to tape-record the interview for the purpose of playing the tape back to the supervisor. In this manner, the interview feedback has full value in that the supervisor is able to sense the feelings associated with the subject being discussed as the employee describes his reaction to his job. Incidentally, although I prefer the taped interview, it should be noted that it is time-consuming and, therefore, more expensive. It is ideal for small and medium-sized groups. NOTE: In my experience, 75% of those interviewed wanted increased responsibility and autonomy in their job. Their main concern was that their intrinsic talents and interests are not being activated and utilized at work.

The taped interview is played back to the supervisor, and appropriate notes are taken by both of us as we listen. After he has heard all the interviews, he develops a "plan of action" which is a positive reaction to the expressed desires of each individual subordinate. It is essential at this point that the supervisor recognize and accept how the implementation of job enrichment will change the focus of his job and that he begins to deal with new behaviors for himself when interacting with his subordinates.

As soon as possible after hearing the interviews, the supervisor meets with each subordinate separately to mutually decide how best to bring about the changes the subordinate has asked for. This is a key meeting which has the potential for substantially "bridging" the relationship between the two. When handled properly, former "hidden agendas" are surfaced and positively dealt with in a trusting and open discussion.

After this initial stage has been implemented, the supervisor must be on the alert for appropriate opportunities to provide valid, helpful feedback. The amount and appropriateness of feedback will determine how well job enrichment is integrated into the organization. A lack of feedback can be a cause of failure.

From three to five months after the start of the effort, I randomly interview a representative number of employees to determine the degree to which there is a "fit" between how managers are assessing the effort and how subordinates feel about it. Pointing out any differences of opinion is helpful to both. It is also a good opportunity to determine what effects the implementation of job enrichment is having on such areas as the climate of the organization, the management style, other departments, customers, etc.

SOME PAYOFFS

Earlier I alluded to the positive results that I have seen job enrichment bring about. In one clerical office employing a total force of approximately 125 people, turnover was reduced from an average of 14 per month to an average of 4 per month. (This took place prior to the 1969 economic downturn.) The recruiting, training, and production savings in this instance amounted to $141,000.00 annually.

In every successful effort, turnover and absenteeism have been significantly reduced because employees see the job as the vehicle for self-actualization. Union grievances in one organization dropped from four per month to zero. In some cases, suggestions from employees that led to job restructuring resulted in the same production being accomplished by 10% fewer people. The quality of work has improved in all the organizations that I have witnessed that have committed themselves to high effort.

Employees are involved in some interesting experiences as a result of job enrichment. Many of the more capable ones have replaced their supervisors while they were on vacation or at conferences. The "temporary boss" has full responsibility and is paid a differential during the period. Employees are also paid to assist in the training and coaching of new employees and people on new assignments. Where appropriate, employees are given as much freedom and latitude as is possible. External double-checks, such as traditional quality control, are eliminated, and the quality control is internalized within the employee.

The emphasis changes from "management knows best" to the individual himself determining what is best for him in any given situation. The consequences are unlimited. The worker regains the sense of being treated as a unique and talented adult. The supervisor regains the respect of his subordinates. The organization gain is in providing satisfying jobs for employees to increase the organization's effectiveness and health.

Francis V. Jessey

Frederick Herzberg. *Work and the Nature of Man*. Cleveland: World, 1966.

MANAGEMENT
BY OBJECTIVES

Managers have always been challenged to produce results, but the modern manager must produce them in a time of rapid technological and social change. Managers must be able to use this rapid change to produce their results: they must use the change and not be used or swallowed up by it. Both they and the organizations they manage need to anticipate change and set aggressive, forward-looking goals in order that they might ultimately begin to make change occur when and where they want it to and in that way gain greater control of their environment and, in fact, their own destinies.

The most important tool the manager has in setting and achieving forward-looking goals is people, and to achieve results with this tool he must be able first, to instill in his workers a sense of vital commitment and desire to contribute to organizational goals; second, control and coordinate the efforts of his workers toward goal accomplishment; and last, help his subordinates to grow in ability so that they can make ever greater contributions.

In hopes of increasing individual production and contribution, managers have resorted to many different approaches: they have tried to get commitment and hard work through economic pressure and rewards, they have sought greater production by teaching the worker the best or most efficient way to do a job, and they have tried to cajole their employees into a sense of well being hoping that their comfort would produce a desire to contribute. All of these approaches had some success, but none succeeded totally in injecting enough of that element of vitality and adaptability into organizational life to allow it to thrive and remain viable in this age of change and socio/technological turmoil.

DEFINITION

The "Management by Objective" (MBO) approach, in the sense that it requires all managers to set specific objectives to be achieved in the future and encourages them to continually ask what more can be done, is offered as a partial answer to this question of organizational vitality and creativity. As a term, "Management by Objectives" was first used by Peter Drucker in 1954 and as a management approach has been further developed by many management theoreticians among them Douglas McGregor, George Odiorne, and John Humble. Essentially MBO is a process or system designed for managing managers in which a superior and his subordinates sit down and jointly set specific objectives to be accomplished within a set time frame and for which the subordinate is then held directly responsible.

All organizations exist for a purpose, and, to achieve that purpose, top management sets goals and objectives that are common to the whole organization. In organizations not using the MBO approach, most planning and objective setting to achieve these common organizational goals is downward directed. Plans and objectives are passed down from one managerial level to another and subordinates are told what to do and what they will be held responsible for. The MBO

130

approach injects an element of dialogue into the process of passing plans and objectives from one organizational level to another. The superior brings specific goals and measures for his subordinate to a meeting with this subordinate who also brings specific objectives and measures which he sees as appropriate or contributing to better accomplishment of his job. Together they develop a group of specific goals, measures of achievement, and time frames in which the subordinate commits himself to the accomplishment of those goals. The subordinate is then held responsible for the accomplishment of *his* goals. The manager and his subordinate may have occasional progress reviews and re-evaluation meetings, but at the end of the set period of time the subordinate is judged on the results he has achieved. He may be rewarded for his success by promotion or salary increases, or he may be fired or transferred to a job that will give him needed training or supervision. Whatever the outcome, it will be based on his accomplishment of the goals he had some part in setting and committed himself to achieving.

VARIATIONS IN PRACTICE

In practice this MBO approach, of necessity, varies widely, especially in regard to how formalized and structured it is in a given organization and to what degree subordinates are allowed to set their own goals. In some organizations MBO is a very formal management system with precise review scheduling, set evaluation techniques, and specific formats, in which objectives and measures must be presented for review and discussion. In other organizations it may be so informal as to be described simply as, "the way we do things when we get together and decide what we've done and what we're going to do." However, in most organizations MBO takes the form of formal objective setting and appraisal meetings held on a regular basis often quarterly, semi-annually, or annually.

Even more situational than the degree of formality and structure is the degree to which a subordinate is allowed to set his own goals. In this regard the kind of work that an organization does plays a large part in determining how much and on what level a subordinate will be allowed to participate in formulating his own goals. In some organizations a subordinate is almost told what he needs to do and simply asked if he will commit himself to achieve this goal, while in others he is given great latitude and room for innovation. Contrast, for example, the production situation where a superior informs a subordinate that they must make so many widgets over the next six months and simply asks which part of that production burden the subordinate is willing to shoulder, to a university situation where a department head informs a subordinate of the need to develop more community-oriented programs and asks how the subordinate thinks he can contribute to this goal. In the latter circumstance, the subordinate has much more room for innovation and personal contribution as well as a greater part in designing the specifics of a community-centered educational program than did the production worker who was simply asked which part of a very specific activity he cared to commit himself to.

POTENTIAL ADVANTAGES

No matter how the MBO approach looks in a given organization it is, again, essentially a process which helps to (a) direct managers' attention toward results, (b) force members of the organization to commit themselves to specific achievement, and (c) facilitate their thinking in terms of their organization's future needs and setting objectives to meet them. In addition, the MBO approach can supply the manager with greater measures of three of the tools he needs to make the best use of his greatest resource — people. He can:

1. Gain greater commitment and desire to contribute from his subordinates by (a) allowing them to feel that the objectives they are working toward were not just handed to them but rather that they are really theirs because they had a part to play in formulating them, (b) giving the

subordinate a better sense of where he fits into the organization by making clear how the subordinate's objectives fit into the overall picture, and (c) injecting a vitality into organizational life that comes with the energy produced as a worker strives to achieve a goal to which he has taken the psychological and sometimes economic risk to commit himself.

2. Gain better control and coordination toward goal accomplishment by (a) having a clearer picture of who is doing what and how the parts all fit together, (b) having subordinates who are more likely to control and coordinate their own activities because they know what will help and what will hinder their goal achievement, and (c) being able to see which of his subordinates consistently produce and which do not.

3. Gain an increased ability to help his subordinates develop by (a) being better able to see their strengths and weakness in operation on a specific objective and (b) simply using a management approach which teaches his subordinates (and himself for that matter) to think in terms of results in the future: an approach which teaches them to try and anticipate change, define clear and specific objectives, and delineate concrete measures that will tell them when they have achieved their goal.

POTENTIAL FOR MISUSE

However, MBO can easily be misused and often is. What is supposed to be a system that allows for dialogue and growth between boss and subordinate with a view to achieving results, often degenerates into a system where the boss puts constant pressure on the subordinate to produce results and forgets about using MBO for commitment, desire to contribute, and management development. Sometimes even well-intentioned superiors misuse MBO because they do not have the interpersonal skills or knowledge of human needs to keep their appraisal sessions from becoming critical, chewing-out periods. Finally many managers have a tendency to see MBO as a total system which once installed can handle all management problems. This has led to forcing issues on the MBO system which it is not equipped to handle and thereby frustrating whatever good effects it might have on the issues with which it is designed to deal.

Thomas M. Thomson

KEY REFERENCES

Drucker, Peter, *The Practice of Management,* New York, Harper Row, 1954
Humble, John, *Improving Business Results,* London, McGraw-Hill, 1968
Humble, John, *Management by Objectives in Action,* London, McGraw-Hill, 1970
McGregor, Douglas, *Leadership and Motivation,* Cambridge, The M.I.T. Press, 1966
Odiorne, George, *Management by Objectives,* New York, Pitman Publishing Corp., 1970
Reddin, William J., *Managerial Effectiveness,* London, McGraw-Hill, 1971

CRITERIA
OF EFFECTIVE
GOAL-SETTING:
THE SPIRO MODEL

Personal growth goals and achievement goals in business and in school are more useful and effective if they are made explicit rather than remaining implicit in one's behavior. Thinking which is purposive is more effective than thinking which is random, jerky, or disjointed. Goal-directed behavior is more efficient and more effective than the behavior which is completely spontaneous, unplanned, and unorganized. The alternative to being goal-directed is to drift, to float, to achieve in a random manner. Establishing goals explicitly has a great deal of utility. For one thing, planning the next step is much easier if goals are explicit. The management of personal, social, intellectual, and economic development is easier if goals are attainable and have some directional quality to them. Having explicit goals also helps a person in developing a sense of accomplishment. Another benefit to objective goal-setting is that a person is far more likely to inventory the resources available to him and to utilize those resources, if his goals are clear. That is not to say that there is no room for serendipity and spontaneity in one's development. In fact, some of the most significant scientific achievements have been made by people who were working toward goals and discovered side effects or observed phenomena that they were not looking for.

The purpose of this lecturette is to provide some criteria for judging or critiquing statements of personal goals. Five criteria will be discussed. These five criteria, taken together, constitute the SPIRO model. The five criteria are: Specificity, Performance, Involvement, Realism and Observability. Applying these five criteria to personal goals can result in more effective goal-setting and more efficient planning.

Specificity. General goals are less useful than specific ones because the specific ones imply next steps or imply behaviors that need to be changed. An example of a non-specific goal would be, to improve my sales record next year. An example of a specific goal statement would be, to produce five percent more sales volume in the next year.

The second criterion is *Performance.* "What will I be doing?" Performance-oriented goal statements are more effective in guiding what the person is going to do rather than some non-performance statements. An example of a non-performance goal would be, to gain the respect of fellow class members. An example of a performance goal might be, to make at least one point in each seminar meeting.

The third criterion is *Involvement;* that is, the extent to which the person himself is involved in the objective. An example of a non-involving goal might be, to get the boss to accept criticism. An example of a goal that meets the criterion of involvement might be, to give negative feedback to the boss in private and to check whether he hears it accurately.

The fourth criterion of effective goal-setting is *Realism;* that is, the attainability of the goal. An example of an unrealistic goal might be, to change the attitudes of the teaching staff to accepting minority group students. An example of a realistic goal related to that concern might be, to acquaint teachers with the value orientations of parents of minority group students.

The fifth criterion in the SPIRO Model is *Observability.* This has to do with whether other people can see the result, whether it is obvious that the criterion has been met, or whether the results are covert. An example of a non-observable goal might be, to build more self confidence.

A corresponding goal that meets the standard of observability might be, to reduce the frequency with which I began declarative statements with the phrase, "I guess."

Applying these five criteria to one's own personal growth goals should result in greater understanding of where one is going. It helps if one's goals are made public, if one confides them to another person or publishes them in some way. To commit oneself publicly to growth goals is a way of using one's environment for support to try new behaviors. It is also helpful if goals are time-bound; that is, if there are some deadlines involved in the attainment of the objectives. It also helps if one's goals are planned in such a way that there is a good likelihood that there will be some reward from the environment for trying the attainment of that goal.

One idea related to goal-setting is contracting. One may write his personal goals, critique them himself, critique them with the help of another person, and develop a contract with the other person that by a certain time he will have accomplished his goal or a certain consequence will take place. For example, a professor may contract with his wife that he will get three journal articles written in the next six months, and if he does not, she will mail his personal check for $50 to the Ku Klux Klan. That is a kind of avoidance training.

Goal-setting is a continuous activity and is a core behavior in a continuous stream of effort that is coming to be called, in the human potential movement, Life Planning. What happens in life planning is that a person stops every now and again to reassess his goals, to apply criteria such as the SPIRO model to them, and to restate them as he improves in his understanding of himself. There are basically four core questions that are useful to ask oneself over and over again in life planning. One of those questions, which is perhaps the most difficult, is, "Who am I?" It sounds like a very simple question, but it is exceedingly complex and difficult question to answer cogently. The second question, of almost equal importance, is, "What am I up to?" That is, what is going on with me right now, what am I trying to get done right now, and what are my motives right now? The third question is, "Where am I going?" That question relates directly to effective goal-setting. The fourth question, which perhaps overarches all the other three, is, "What difference does it make, anyhow?" If one recycles these questions through his consciousness from time to time and applies hard standards to himself in terms of his personal objectives, his life management is much more likely to be effective and satisfying.

The motto of the state of South Carolina is a Latin phrase, "Dum spiro spero." Translated, that means, "While I breathe, I hope." Goals represent hopes while we're alive and being spirited, and those goals which are objective and explicit are more attainable and are more likely to help us realize our hopes than are those that are less obvious.

SUGGESTED ACTIVITIES

Participants may spend some time (thirty minutes or so) writing down their personal growth goals, critiquing them against these criteria, pairing off with a partner to critique each other's goals, and rewriting goals in terms of the SPIRO criteria. It is sometimes helpful in a personal growth laboratory for these helping pairs to meet several times, so that the person can have continuous checks on the extent to which his personal growth goals are being met by his behavior in the laboratory experience.

A second activity might be to help participants at the end of a personal-growth-laboratory experience to establish definite, written contracts with each other for follow-through and for application of laboratory learning to their back-home environments. The SPIRO criteria can be applied to the specific plans that one makes for reentering the back-home environment.

A third activity is to have pairs of people who ordinarily work together critique their production goals, and apply the criteria to their performance objectives on the job. For example, divisonal goals, departmental goals, or unit goals, can be evaluated by teams in a team-building session.

John E. Jones

AN INTRODUCTION
TO PERT ... OR ...

NOW THAT WE'VE ALL FINALLY AGREED ON WHERE WE WANT TO GO, HOW
DO WE ARRANGE TO GET THERE FROM HERE.

Suppose you wake up on Saturday morning and decide to take the family on a picnic.

Going through your head is a jumble of activities and tasks that need doing in order to get
the picnic organized. "Coffee. Is the thermos clean? Remember this time to take some fly-spray.
Do we have any beer? What kind of sandwiches would everyone like? "

How to accomplish all the preparations? Obviously, you need the help of the rest of the
family. But if everybody is involved in the task, how will it be coordinated? How avoid two
people getting the napkins and nobody remembering to get the first-aid box? How to assign
responsibility for the can-opener? And how to decide what must be done first, and what can be
done at any time?

These kinds of questions *could* be all answered by one person, who would assign tasks and
maintain supervision, settle disputes and respond to the inevitable complaints about work-loads,
tasks neglected, and so forth.

Or there could be a non-directed kind of process in which the family periodically stops what
it is doing to argue about everything from where we want to go down to which kind of olives
to take.

But there is a planning method that permits a group to ...

Be mutually aware of the process and sub-goals. Contribute to and share in the decisions
made about how, when and by whom activities are done

Make more efficient use of resources by concentrating effort and time on the *critical tasks*
rather than devoting time to sub-tasks while tasks of greater priority lack hands.

Re-evaluate the project while it is underway, and re-allocate resources to cope with
unexpected blocks to task accomplishment, or to take advantage of unanticipated
success in meeting some sub-goal.

This planning method is called PERT, one of those acronyms to be sure, but no less valuable
for that. It stands for Program Evaluation and Review Technique, and it has saved government
and industry many millions of man-hours and dollars. A variation of PERT is known as CPM, or
the Critical Path Method, a name that expresses something about how the thing is done. In this
brief paper, we can only glimpse the bare outlines of PERT/CPM. Please consult the references
for more detailed discussions.

PERT is a group analysis and flow-charting procedure that begins with identifying the
sequences of dependent activities.

One begins, in true Lewis Carrol fashion, at the end.

Before we can arrive at the picnic grounds, we must travel there in the car. Before we can
travel in the car, we must fill up with gas and check the oil. Before we can do that, we must
have traveled to the service station. Before we can start out for the service station, we must
have loaded all the supplies in the car ... except ice, which we can get at the gas station.

So we draw a network of *activities*, each of which ends in an *event*, in this manner:

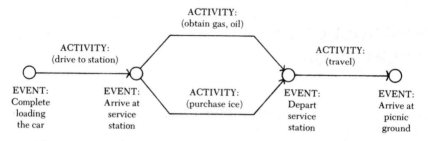

Just to keep it from looking as trivial as you probably think it is, we have shown the purchase of ice as a parallel activity, beginning and ending in the same events as the obtaining of gas and oil.

Now, suppose that you know that you need to arrive at the picnic ground no later than 11:00 am. When will you need to start from home?

Just like the radio or television producer, you now must *back-time* each activity. Estimate its duration as well as you can, and label each activity.

Travel to the picnic ground: 60 minutes.

Obtain gas and oil: 10 minutes.

Purchase ice: 15 minutes (You must also open the ice chest and pack the food and drinks.)

Drive to service station: 10 minutes.

ADD UP THE SEQUENCE OF ACTIVITIES THAT WILL TAKE THE MOST TIME. You discover that you don't need to add the time spent gassing the car; the obtaining of ice will require five more minutes than that.

You have determined that purchasing ice is on the CRITICAL PATH and gassing the car is not.

You have also discovered that it will take you an hour and twenty-five minutes to reach the picnic ground. If you must arrive there at 11:00 am. you must leave no later than 9:35.

What if you cannot leave by then?

You must shorten the time required to accomplish one or several of the activities in the CRITICAL PATH or else revise your plans drastically.

At this point, your oldest boy suggests that the time required to purchase ice could be shortened if he opened the ice chest and partially unpacked the food while his younger brother got the ice bag out of the freezer and little sister gave the attendant fifty cents.

This did not come from you as a command or directive. It came from one of the other planners in response to a perceived need to increase the efficiency of some activity leading to a common goal. And while there may be some squabbling among the children about which child gets to pay the attendant and which gets to carry the ice, there is no cavilling at the division of tasks or the necessity for all to share.

Moreover, every party to the enterprise has a means of evaluating how well the timetable is being met, and of revising the group performance to meet needs that arise unexpectedly.

Each is able to contribute not merely his labor, but his knowledge of the special task he individually performs as it relates to the overall effort.

As boss of the family, you might have been able to come up with the idea of dividing up the task of ice purchase . . . or you might not. And if you had thought of it, the family members might not have performed it as ably under your directive as they would have if it had been their own idea.

136

The example we have given is thus seen to be trivial, indeed, but at the same time a paradigm of the planning process.

PERT is seen to be a tool of communication, and not just an abstract exercise performed only by the staff planners, thereafter executed under duress by the grumbling line.

PERT is a method that permits revision of the plan when things don't work out like the original plan said they should.

Plans never work out right.

But *the planning process is indispensable*.

D. E. Yoes

H. F. Evarts. *Introduction to PERT*. Dallas: Allyn and Bacon, 1964. (An excellent, short, non-technical introduction.)

R. C. Levin. *Planning and Control with PERT/CPM*. N.Y.: McGraw-Hill, 1966. (More like a textbook, concentrating on industrial management.)

J. J. Moder. *Project Management with CPM and PERT*. N.Y.: Reinhold, 1964. (Develops the mathematics of the process, focusing more on systems development than on industrial management.)

J. D. Wiest and F. K. Levy. *A Management Guide to PERT/CPM*, Englewood Cliffs, N.J.: Prentice-Hall, 1969. (A simplified text for management, but concerned with organizational planning as well as industrial management.)

INTRODUCTION TO
THE THEORY AND
PRACTICE SECTION

In this section of the *Annual* there are three major types of papers. The first three papers, on the IAASS, types of growth groups, and organizational development are primarily informational in character. That is, they are not designed to result in particular types of action on the part of the facilitator. We invited Benne and Ruma to write the paper on the International Association of Applied Social Scientists because we believe that this association will become enormously important in the human potential movement in the next few years. We feel that it will be the one association to which all group facilitators will wish to belong. There is considerable confusion within the human relations training field about terminology, and Jones' paper on types of growth groups is an attempt to clarify some distinctions between the broad types of groups that are commonly found in the field. Sherwood's paper represents an attempt to explicate what is organization development as opposed to other innovations within human systems.

The second part of this section on theory and practice includes three papers that are basically expositions of the theoretical positions held by their authors. The TORI theory developed by the Gibbs over the last few years has received wide application in the human relations field, and this paper is a summary of the highlights of that theory of human growth. Olmsk's paper on change strategies grew out of his experience in consulting with a variety of organizations and represents a way of codifying the multiple change designs that are available to organization development personnel, both internal and external.

Pfeiffer's paper on transcendence theory attempts to spell out a way of thinking about human growth that explodes the myth that independence is a valuable end.

The final selection of papers in this section consists of five applications of human relations theories to the practice of group facilitators. Egan is best known for his book, *Encounter*, which is reviewed in the final section of this annual. His paper represents a very practical approach to developing contracts with group participants. Pfeiffer and Jones have explored the use of openness and have drawn implications for the practicing group facilitator. Middleman and Goldberg have done considerable work on nonverbal methods of working with groups, and their paper is addressed to the effects of structure on group interaction. Herman explains in a unique way some applications of Gestalt theory to organizational development. His statement is a very personal one, as indicated by his inclusion of some of his poetry.

Levin's paper represents his point of view about how human relations training theory can be adapted to the training of clinicians and to clinical setting.

This section of papers, then, moves from information through theory to application. Each of the authors has been requested to write to an audience of practitioners rather than researchers and theoriticians, and it is hoped that these papers will result in innovative activity on the part of the users of this handbook.

These papers may be reproduced for use as handouts in education/training settings. It is not required that facilitators obtain special permission to employ them in this way, but the following reference should be used to acknowledge their source:

THE INTERNATIONAL ASSOCIATION
OF APPLIED
SOCIAL SCIENTISTS

Kenneth D. Benne and Steven J. Ruma

The International Association of Applied Social Scientists is a professional association, incorporated under the laws of the District of Columbia in June, 1971. The persons it seeks to bring into associational membership are practitioners of an emerging profession, not clearly demarcated from other helping professions at the present time. The bylaws of the Association recognize two principal foci of effort within this emerging profession:

a) Persons who work with small groups to facilitate re-education and learning of members through the use of collaborative and scientific methods; and,

b) Persons who intervene in larger social systems to facilitate system changes through the use of collaborative and scientific methods.

No doubt further differentiations and refinements of these broad categories will occur as the profession and the Association develop over time.

Members of the Association will, therefore, be made up of practitioners who work with human systems of various magnitudes and who draw with varying emphases upon the disciplines of the social and behavioral sciences and the established professions in their work with clients. Association members will, in many cases, have collateral memberships in the disciplinary associations of psychology, sociology, anthropology, political science, and economics; in the professional organizations of psychiatry, medicine, education, counseling, training, consultation, social work, public health, organizational management, and environmental planning, as well as in various groupings of those in the humanities — philosophy, linguistics, and religion. The Association will seek thus to be cross-disciplinary in its membership and its concerns.

Its members will, of course, have important things in common. All will be engaged for some substantial part of their time in direct work with clients, whether in educational-training, consultative, or applied research relationships. All will be committed to collaborative ways of working with clients in facilitating personal and/or social change. All will be concerned with the utilization and application of knowledge and methodology from the social and behavioral sciences in practice settings. It is hoped that persons with various ideological orientations, consistent with these general commitments, as well as persons committed to the development of various techniques of practice will find their way into membership in the Association.

Although the Association is incorporated in America, it is hoped that it will develop as an international organization in actuality as well as in name. Efforts are being made to include qualified professionals from Europe, Latin America, Canada, Asia, and Australasia in the charter membership of the Association.

One of the important functions of the Association initially will be to develop standards of competence for professional practitioners of applied social science. It will emphasize performance criteria and de-emphasize academic credentials in developing standards. It will work out equitable procedures for applying these standards to applicants for admission to accredited membership in the Association.

The Association recognizes the earlier and current efforts of various associations and institutions to establish and apply standards of competence in accrediting practitioners in the profession it is seeking to demarcate and develop. It will try to learn from these previous and continuing efforts in approaching its own tasks. The Association recognizes that there are various associations with a legitimate interest in accrediting applied social and/or behavioral scientists. Some of these are concerned with accreditation of professionals for work in a particular institutional setting, for example, the Association of Religion and Applied Behavioral Science. Others are concerned with accrediting professionals for work in a particular geographic region, for example, the European Institute of Trainers. Still other efforts to set standards are made by established disciplinary or professional associations with a relatively large number of the "new professionals" in their membership, for example, the American Psychological Association. The Association hopes to cooperate with various agencies with a legitimate interest in accrediting applied social scientists, to the mutual benefit of its work and the work of the other agencies as well. It is the firm policy of the Association not to "grandfather" those on the accredited list of any other organization into its own membership. The selected international list of about 150 outstanding practitioners who are currently being invited to charter membership in the Association will be required to submit evidence of their qualifications and experience. Applicants for membership, after the charter list is complete, will, in addition to submitting written evidence of qualifications and experience, be examined orally by a panel of Association members. Working criteria and procedures for examination of applicants will be developed before the end of 1971.

The Association hopes to serve a double purpose through the development, publicizing, and utilization of standards of professional competence. One purpose is to protect the public and potential clients from the depredations of incompetent, self-accredited practitioners. The Association will seek to educate the public concerning the proper uses and the abuses of applied social science. The other is to protect qualified professional practitioners in the practice and improvement of their professions.

The Association recognizes that standards of ethical practice are needed by the profession, in addition to standards of technical competence. It will develop ethical standards inductively, using the collaboration and experience of its members and the relevant experience of other helping professions in the process of developing criteria of ethical practice.

The Association will encourage self-improvement and self-discipline on the part of its members. It will re-enforce self-discipline through the development of ways of investigating and adjudicating charges of incompetence or of malpractice brought against any member of the Association. These processes will be designed both to protect members from irresponsible and unsubstantial charges and to discipline members where charges are found to be substantial.

The standing committees of the Association are designed to implement the purposes and function already discussed. These are a Committee on Standards and Admissions, a Committee on Ethics, and a Committee on Discipline.

Governance of the Association is vested in a Board of Trustees. At present there are seven members of the Board, although the By-laws of the Association authorize a membership of nine. The initial Board members are: Kenneth D. Benne, Board Chairman, Center for Applied Social Science, Boston University; Cynthia Wedel, Board Secretary-Treasurer, President, National Council of Churches; Warren G. Bennis, President, University of Cincinnati; John Glidewell, University of Chicago; Henry Riecken, President, Social Science Research Council; and Orian

Worden, Oakland University. The paid executive of the Association, its President, is Steven J. Ruma, who is *ex officio* a member of the Board of Trustees.

Dr. Ruma has established the headquarters of the Association at 1755 Massachusetts Ave., N.W., Suite 300, Washington, D.C. 20036. The initial Board membership is, in effect, self-appointed. The By-laws provide for participation by members in nominating and electing replacements of members of the Board and in influencing the policies of the Association in other ways.

In addition to the functions already discussed, the Association will develop a program of professional services for its members, as needs for service are identified by the membership, always, of course, within the limits of the resources of the Association.

Inquiries and suggestions concerning policies and procedures for membership application or concerning other aspects of the Association's program should be addressed to Dr. Steven J. Ruma at the headquarters address.

TYPES OF
GROWTH GROUPS

John E. Jones

In the field of human relations training there is considerable confusion over terminology among both professionals and the public. The most obvious example of a failure to use a common language is the term, "sensitivity training." To some persons that term connotes brainwashing, manipulation, and a host of other horrid activities. To others the term refers to a technology of helping people to grow in self-understanding from analyzing their experience in social situations. To others the term carries the meaning, "feel and reveal." There are many other connotations attached to the term sensitivity training, and, because it has such surplus meaning, it is for all practical purposes a garbage term. There is a need for consumers of groups — that is, prospective participants and persons who hire group consultants — to have realistic expectations when they elect to invest in the group approach. There are important differences among various categories of groups commonly found in the human potential movement, and it is very useful for the public to understand what those differences are.

A major reason why making distinctions among the various types of groups can be useful is that the various group strategies are not equally appropriate in all learning situations. The counseling group can be highly appropriate as an intervention in the lives of young people in school, where the emphasis is on their personal development; whereas, a more therapy-oriented approach may place too great an emphasis on personal deficiencies, or may be inappropriate for a variety of other reasons. There are also political reasons why distinctions among different types of groups are important. The counselor in the school is taking a large risk if he describes his counseling groups as T-groups, since most parents are not equipped to understand the distinction and may have been propagandized by the mass media to think negatively of the T-group experience.

Some of the distinctions among the more common types of groups found in the human potential movement today are very real in practice, and some have an aura of arbitrariness about them; that is, the distinctions are in terms of degree rather than kind. An analogy may help. There are two times during the day when we cannot say for sure whether it is day or night: at dawn and during the twilight hours we cannot say with complete confidence that it is day or that it is night. Nevertheless, we find the two terms, day and night, to be enormously useful. While there are rather large commonalities among T-groups, counseling groups and other kinds of groups, there are some differences that are useful to explore. These very often represent differences in the degree of emphasis on a particular method or a particular learning goal, and often different types of groups look similar and are experienced very much alike.

The dimensions that will be considered to differentiate the selected types of groups are goals, time orientation, the settings in which they are found, the roles of facilitators, and the usual clientele to whom the group experience is offered. The major types of groups which have been selected for analysis are the T-group (training group), the encounter group, the marathon group, the therapy group, and the counseling group. The accompanying chart represents a summary of the major distinctions between these types of groups. There is no attempt to make exhaustive lists of the variety of types of groups that are available in the human potential movement today, such as developmental groups, emergent groups, transactional analysis groups, etc.

TYPES OF GROWTH GROUPS

GROUP TYPE DIMENSION	TRAINING	ENCOUNTER	MARATHON	THERAPY	COUNSELING
GOALS	To Develop Awareness and Skill-Bldg.	To Develop Awareness and Genuineness	To Break Down Defenses	To Increase Coping	To Develop Effective Planning Skills
TIME ORIENTATION	Here and Now	Here and Now Plus	Here and Now Plus	Past and Present	Present and Future
SETTING	Education, Business	All over	All over	Clinical	Educational
ROLE OF FACILITATOR	Model and Scan	Model and Confront	Confront Aggressively	Treat	Facilitate group helpfulness
CLIENTELE	"Normals"	Anyone	Anyone	Persons deficient in coping	"Normals"

TRAINING GROUPS

The major objectives of a T- or training group are awareness and skill building. The objectives center around helping the individual participant to grow in increased awareness of his feeling experience, of his reaction to other people, of his impact on other people, of how they impact him, and in his awareness of how people interrelate and of how groups operate. In terms of skills, the objectives are to improve his ability to listen to people, to understand them empathically (to put himself in their shoes, so to speak), to be more effective in expressing what is going on with him, and to improve his skill in responding to other people when he is attempting to give them feedback. The major goals, then, are increased awareness and increased skills in interpersonal relations. The goals also include understanding group process, i.e., becoming more cognizant of trends, unacknowledged relations and communications, functional roles, and so on. There are two major types of T-group trainers: those who emphasize the personal growth of the individual participant in terms of awareness and skills and those who take as their primary objective helping people to learn about how groups operate, how societies form, and how communities develop.

In terms of time orientation, the T-group is distinguished from all the rest of the types that will be discussed in this paper by a rather rigid adherence to what is called the "here and now." There is no history-taking, no story-telling, and no future-planning activity. The entire energy of the group is focused on the immediate present, trying to find that reality and discussing it openly with each other.

T-groups are most commonly found in educational and business settings. The educational settings are usually in teacher training, in-service education, and in higher education. Very little T-group work is done, as such, with elementary and secondary school students. In fact, it can be argued that the T-group is largely an inappropriate intervention into the lives of children and early and middle adolescents. It is generally felt that the giving and receiving of open, honest feedback about feeling reactions to one's behavior requires that the participant have a certain amount of ego strength and stability in his view of himself. T-groups have long been a part of managerial training; however, in recent years there has been a retrenchment from wide (occasionally indiscriminate) use of T-groups in industries. Managers and other people in business and industry experienced subtle coercion into participating in T-groups, and the effects of T-groups on managerial development were sometimes negative, or at least not positive. The development of a set of theories and strategies called organization development has largely supplanted the misuse of T-groups in business and industry; however, the appropriate use of them can be found as a part of the repertoire of organization development specialists and consultants in the business and industrial arena.

The role of the facilitator in a T-group is to participate and to provide some leadership in helping people to get in touch with themselves and to share openly with each other. Two major approaches that T-group trainers use are modeling and scanning. These ideas are described most aptly by Schein and Bennis (1965). The T-group trainer who models is a person who tries to be as open as he can be, gives feedback, and solicits feedback; he tries to be, in short, an ideal participant. He does not run things; he simply attempts to be as open and sensitive as he can. The T-group trainer who adopts the role of scanner is a person who participates less as a person and more as a professional. He is the person who monitors the dynamics of the group's development and comments on the processes that he sees. He is more aloof from the interaction, more authoritative in his approach, and is likely to be a person whose major interest is more in getting people to learn some model of social interaction than in getting people to be more open and sensitive. Both modeling and scanning are necessary to group training to various degrees depending upon the needs of the individual group, and many T-group trainers assume both roles with varying emphasis during the life of the group.

The clientele for T-groups is that broad range of people who are colloquially called "normal." Egan describes some of the psychopathology of being normal in *Encounter*. For purposes of this discussion, the term "normal" describes that person who gets along in his everyday existence without significant assistance from other people. His level of coping is sufficient for him to accomplish his objectives. In addition, he is a person who does not ordinarily distort the reality of the situations in which he finds himself. There is no precise technical definition of normality that has been agreed upon by those in the helping professions. What we are concerned with in the T-group are people who encounter and respond appropriately to everyday concerns. The T-group is not a place for a person who is under a great deal of psychological stress or who is incapable of understanding reality the way most people do.

The T-group, then, functions primarily toward the individual's development and awareness of interpersonal skills and is restricted to the immediate present. It is found primarily in educational and business settings. Facilitators tend to be a part of the process as people and focus by modeling and scanning on interpersonal issues and group development. The T-group experience is designed primarily for the broad range of people called normal. It consists of 10-15 people who begin work for about 20-30 hours in a highly unstructured way, usually with no ground rules. They develop and discuss a structure as it emerges in the group. The kinds of interactions that take place are encounters between people and the sharing of feeling reactions to the interpersonal behavior that occurs. The attempt is to get people to try new behavior, to try new ways of relating to each other, and to share emotional reactions to the behavior that spontaneously occurs in the group setting. The technology that is often used consists of lectures, skill-building games such as listening exercises, process observation experiences, games, simulations, and other structured experiences. But the core of the learning experience is the unstructured T-group meeting, in which members take responsibility for their own learning and participate in a free, give–and–take of feeling reactions to each other's behavior. There is little or no attempt to try to discover why people behave the way they do; rather the emphasis is on studying the effects of behavior and exploring alternative behaviors that might be more effective.

A major distinction is made within T-groups between content and process: what is *talked about* and what *happens* in the group. Another major distinction that is drawn within T-groups is between thinking and feeling. Participants learn that what they think and what they feel may not be highly correlated. The major effort of the T-group is to help people share their feeling experience of each other.

Incidentally, the intent of the T-group is diametrically opposed to the intent of brainwashing in that the T-group is an exercise in democratic interpersonal relating, in which people become more free as a result of becoming more aware of what they do to each other on an impact level. The intent is not to get people to conform, to cry, or to feel alike, but to increase a person's freedom of choice and freedom of behavior by giving him an accurate reading on the way he comes across to other people and what other people do to him. The emphasis is on his learning in order for him to run his own life more effectively.

ENCOUNTER GROUPS

The major goals of the encounter group are awareness and genuineness. The encounter group differs from the T-group in that it has a relatively high emphasis on helping the person to have a real experience of other people. The flavor is existential, that is, the concern is not so much with the application of the learning as it is with the realness of the encounter between people. The major objectives are to help a person get in touch with himself more fully, more authentically, to help him relate that to other people more openly, and to help him be with other people in the world. Being-together-in-the-world in a very open, level way is presumed to have a justification of its own. There is relatively less emphasis than in the T-group on skill-building and back-home application.

In terms of time orientation, the encounter group may be described as "here and now plus." A great deal of attention is spent looking at the immediate reality, but there is some story-telling. There is some sharing of one's psychological development. It is permissible in the usual encounter group to talk about people who aren't there; ordinarily in the T-group that becomes forbidden. In the encounter group the major emphasis is on the present, but one may look at the past and the future.

Encounter groups can be found almost anywhere. They are used in business, industry, schools, a variety of clinical settings, in teacher training, in parent effectiveness training, and are independently offered by growth centers and others as isolated personal experiences.

The facilitator's role in the encounter group is to model and to confront. He engineers confrontations in the sense that he encourages people to be more open than they ordinarily would be, more genuine, and more level in looking directly at the interpersonal reality that emerges. He also participates in the interchange, giving and receiving feedback.

The usual encounter group facilitator would exclude no type of person arbitrarily. All sorts and conditions of men can be found in encounter groups, from "normals" to therapy patients. Sometimes encounter facilitators will require therapy patients to obtain prior permission from their therapists, but generally that is for legal protection rather than because of any design for the kind of interaction that will take place.

The encounter group meeting tends to be emotionally charged. There is perhaps more attention given to extreme feelings of loving and aggression in the encounter group than in the

148

T-group. The technology of the encounter group tends to be more in the area of dyadic confrontation, touching, and nonverbal communication than in the T-group. Encounter group facilitators very often eschew T-group games and lecturettes and tend to use a wide variety of nonverbal and fantasy techniques to generate the interpersonal confrontation data.

MARATHON GROUPS

The major goal of the marathon group, as opposed to the major goals of either the T- or encounter group, is to deliberately strip away from the person his ordinary defensive behavior so that he is able to look at himself more genuinely than he might ordinarily.

The time orientation could be described in a manner similar to that of the encounter group, i.e., "here and now plus." A good bit of attention is placed on looking at the participant as he interacts with other people in the marathon setting, but the participants often develop histories of their psychological development and explore those with each other. The major distinguishing feature of the marathon group is the time that the group consumes. Marathon groups take place in uninterrupted meetings generally of 20 or more hours. Some facilitators conduct marathons of less than 20 hours, but ordinarily at least 20 hours of continuous interaction is planned. The rationale behind the marathon is that fatigue can serve to lower one's need for defensiveness and that genuine, real behavior is more possible if one is able to stick with the task over a long period of time. Meals are brought in, people excuse themselves to go to the bathroom, sometimes the facilitator reserves the right to take a break himself for brief periods of rest, but the participants stay with the group throughout the time that the group is together in continuous meeting.

Marathon groups can be found in a variety of settings and are often not a separate group experience but rather one phase of a total training design. Sometimes a marathon group is an intervention in a school, in a hospital, or with a therapy group. Some facilitators like to begin groups with a marathon session, and some teachers begin a course the same way. There is almost no limit on the portability of the idea.

The facilitator takes a slightly different role in a marathon group than he does in a T-group or encounter group. He is more likely in a marathon group to engage in direct confrontation. Depending on his theoretical persuasion, he may also interpret some of the behavior of the participants in an analytical way. At any rate, his major style tends to be to use direct, sometimes aggressive confrontation.

The clientele of marathon groups can be almost anyone since they may be integrated into designs for other types of growth groups. The marathon group can be used as a very powerful intervention for therapeutic purposes, or it may be used to enhance the growth of essentially normal people. Sometimes groups are made up of combinations of people who are psychotherapy patients and people who are there primarily for their own personal growth and not for "treatment."

THERAPY GROUPS

There are endless varieties of approaches to group therapy, but there are some major distinctions between group therapy and other groups that have been discussed. One major distinction is that the goals of therapy groups generally focus on the increased coping ability of members. That is, the person is led in a therapy group to explore himself in ways that will permit him to be more effective in his daily living, so that he will be less anxious, more capable of making decisions, more capable of accepting responsibility for his behavior, less depressed, etc.

The time orientation of the therapy group differs from the three groups that have been discussed in that in a therapy group a great deal of life history data is discussed. The time orientation of the therapy group is primarily past and present. People talk through unresolved difficulties in their pasts and talk about their lives in the present because the goals of the therapy group is typically to improve the life situation of a person in the immediate present.

Therapy groups are most commonly found in clinical settings, i.e., in hospitals, mental health centers, medical clinics, student health centers, etc.

Ordinarily the therapy group is conducted by a doctoral-level therapist whose role is to *treat* the participants or patients. The usual interaction that takes place in the therapy group is for the therapist to treat people one at a time, with other group participants watching and helping. Some group psychotherapists function differently by using group process observations and interventions as a treatment strategy, but the usual procedure is individual treatment in a group session.

The clientele of therapy groups could be considered those people who are significantly below par in their level of ordinary, everyday coping. These people would be considered non-normal in the sense that they require significant assistance from other people for them to solve their everyday problems.

COUNSELING GROUPS

There must be as much variety among counselors as there is among group psychotherapists in the approaches that are used in their groups, but some broad differences exist between counseling and any of the other four types of groups that have been discussed. On the dimension of goals the counseling group is usually distinguished by its emphasis on effective planning. The counseling group has as its major objective helping people to learn to manage their lives more effectively. Members develop increased awareness of who they are, awareness of what opportunities are available to them, and increased ability to make decisions in planning their own development.

The time orientation of the counseling group is generally present and future. Persons talk through their normal development problems, but a great deal of attention in counseling groups is placed on, "Where do we go from here?"

Counseling groups most commonly are found in educational settings from the elementary school through higher education. The facilitator in the counseling groups has the job of helping group members to learn how to be helpful to each other. He perhaps does more teaching of effective group membership than do facilitators in other types of groups. He may also inject into counseling groups a great deal of educational and vocational information. His job as an intervener in group meetings is to help people to accept responsibility for helping their peers. Counseling groups are designed to facilitate the orderly development of normal people who are experiencing the same kinds of problems that most people do.

NEW DEVELOPMENTS

These broad distinctions among the most common types of growth groups are not intended to be precise but to be illustrative of trends in the human potential movement. It is significant that there is overlap among such groups. Such commonalities stem in large part from the major commitment among group facilitators to find new ways to enhance the personal growth of the general populace.

Four streams of activity are taking place in the human potential movement. A number of persons are doing some highly creative work in developing group approaches that will facilitate sensory awakening, sensory awareness, and self-expression on the part of people whose adult life situations do not permit them the freedom of learning about themselves and being genuine with each other. A second stream is in education — both within institutions and in the free education movement — to find new ways of using group approaches to get away from teacher-centered, highly structured classroom interaction. A third area of considerable activity is in finding new ways of working with clinical populations, those people who are hospitalized, those who are out-patients in various clinics, and so on. A number of people are working on ways of borrowing from education models and from the experimental work that is being done in growth centers ideas that may be useful in accelerating the treatment of persons who need interpersonal assistance to develop effective coping. A fourth stream of activity that is a vital part of the human potential scene is the infusion of all these activities into organization development and into working with people within their work settings. A number of business and industrial officials are now coming to see that there are responsibilities on the part of the corporations for the personal development of employees, and a number of corporations are experimenting with life planning laboratories, counseling, career development, T-groups, encounter groups, and so on, with people in their natural work environments, with the people that they interact with day by day.

There will be a continuation of confusion within the human potential movement as new group models are developed, but the person who is thinking about participating in a group or hiring people who work in groups as consultants can make some order out of what appears to be chaos by taking into account the dimensions that have been stressed in this paper. Of those dimensions the single most important is goals. The consumer of groups needs to have a good sense of what the learning goals are of the group he is contemplating. The technologies of groups are nothing but means toward ends. The ends, or goals, do vary depending on the facilitator and the type of group he is working.

Perhaps the most significant commonality among the types of groups that are being experimented with today is that they are all designed to be helpful to participants. It may be that we are on the verge of redeveloping the culture in a way that permits groups of people to be supportive of each other.

REFERENCES

EGAN, G., Encounter: Group Processes for Interpersonal Growth. Belmont, Calif.: Brooks/Cole, 1970.
SCHEIN, E. H., and W. G. BENNIS, Personal and Organizational Change Through Group Methods. N.Y.: Wiley, 1965.

AN INTRODUCTION
TO ORGANIZATION
DEVELOPMENT*

John J. Sherwood

Organization development is an educational process by which human resources are continuously identified, allocated, and expanded in ways that make these resources more available to the organization, and therefore, improve the organization's problem-solving capabilities.

The most general objective of organizational development — OD — is to develop self-renewing, self-correcting systems of people who learn to organize themselves in a variety of ways according to the nature of their tasks, and who continue to expand the choices available to the organization as it copes with the changing demands of a changing environment. OD stands for a new way of looking at the human side of organizational life.

What is OD?

(a) A long-range effort to introduce planned change based on a diagnosis which is shared by the members of an organization.

(b) An OD program involves an entire organization, or a coherent "system" or part thereof.

(c) Its goal is to increase organizational effectiveness and enhance organizational choice and self-renewal.

(d) The major strategy of OD is to intervene in the ongoing activities of the organization to facilitate learning and to make choices about alternative ways to proceed.

*Copyright© 1971 by the American Psychological Association, Inc., Washington, D.C. All rights reserved. The Experimental Publication System, Issue No. 11, and used by permission.

This statement liberally uses material from "What is OD?" *News and Reports from the NTL Institute for Applied Behavioral Science*, Vol. 2 (June), 1968; Wendell L. French, "Organization Development Objectives, Assumptions, and Strategies," *California Management Review*, Vol. XII (Winter), 1969; Richard Beckhard, *Organization Development: Strategies and Models*. Reading, Mass.: Addison-Wesley, 1969; John W. Gardner, "How to Prevent Organizational Dry Rot," *Harper's*, October, 1965; Thomas A. Wickes, "Organizational Development Technology," unpublished manuscript, TRW Systems, October, 1968; Warren G. Bennis, *Organization Development: Its Nature, Origins, and Prospects*. Reading, Mass.: Addison-Wesley, 1969; and Douglas McGregor, *The Human Side of Enterprise*. New York: McGraw-Hill, 1960.

I appreciate the comments on an earlier version of this paper by Richard E. Byrd, Donald C. King, Philip J. Runkel, and William J. Underwood.

Objectives of Typical OD programs. Although the specific objectives of an OD effort vary according to the diagnosis of organizational problems, a number of objectives typically emerge. These objectives reflect problems which are common in organizations and which prevent the creative release of human potential within organizations:

(1) To build trust among individuals and groups throughout the organization, and up-and-down the hierarchy.

(2) To create an open, problem-solving climate throughout the organization — where problems are confronted and differences are clarified, both within groups and between groups, in contrast to "sweeping problems under the rug" or "smoothing things over."

(3) To locate decision-making and problem-solving responsibilities as close to the information sources and the relevant resources as possible, rather than in a particular role or level of the hierarchy.

(4) To increase the sense of "ownership" of organizational goals and objectives throughout the membership of the organization.

(5) To move toward more collaboration between interdependent persons and interdependent groups within the organization. Where relationships are clearly competitive, e.g., limited resources, then it is important that competition be open and be managed so the organization might benefit from the advantages of open competition and avoid suffering from the destructive consequences of subversive rivalry.

(6) To increase awareness of group "process" and its consequences for performance — that is, to help persons become aware of what is happening between and to group members while the group is working on the task, e.g., communication, influence, feelings, leadership styles and struggles, relationships between groups, how conflict is managed, etc.

The objectives of organizational development efforts are achieved through planned interventions based on research findings and theoretical hypotheses of the behavioral sciences. The organization is helped to examine its present ways of work, its norms and values, and to generate and evaluate alternative ways of working, or relating, or rewarding members of the system.

Some Assumptions Underlying the Concept of OD. Using knowledge and techniques from the behavioral sciences, organization development attempts to integrate organizational goals with the needs for growth of individual members in order to design a more effective and fully functioning organization, in which the potential of members is more fully realized. Some of the basic assumptions underlying the concept of OD are as follows:

(1) The attitudes most members of organizations hold toward work and their resultant work habits are usually more *reactions to* their work environment and how they are treated by the organization, than they are intrinsic characteristics of an individual's personality. Therefore, efforts to change attitudes toward work and toward the organization should be directed more toward changing how the person is treated than toward attempting to change the person.

(2) Work which is organized to meet people's needs as well as to achieve organizational requirements tends to produce the highest productivity and quality of production.

(3) Most members of organizations are not motivated primarily by an avoidance of work for which tight controls and threats of punishment are necessary — but rather, most individuals seek challenging work and desire responsibility for accomplishing organizational objectives to which they are committed.

(4) The basic building blocks of organizations are groups of people; therefore, the basic units of change are also groups, not simply individuals.

(5) The culture of most organizations tends to suppress the open expression of feelings which people have about each other and about where they and their organization are heading. The difficulty is that the suppression of feelings adversely affects problem-solving, personal growth, and satisfaction with one's work. The expression of feelings is an important part of becoming committed to a decision or a task.

(6) Groups which learn to work in a constructively open way by providing feedback for members become more able to profit from their own experience and become more able to fully utilize their resources on the task. Furthermore, the growth of individual members is facilitated by relationships which are open, supportive, and trusting.

(7) There is an important difference between *agreement* and *commitment*. People are committed to and care about that which they help create. Where change is introduced, it will be most effectively implemented if the groups and individuals involved have a sense of ownership in the process. Commitment is most assuredly attained where there is active participation in the planning and conduct of the change. Agreement is simpler to achieve and results in a simpler outcome — people do what they are told, or something sufficient or similar.

(8) The basic value underlying all OD theory and practice is that of *choice*. Through the collection and feedback of relevant date — made available by trust, openness, and risk — more choice becomes available to the organization, and to the individual, and hence better decisions can be made.

Organization Development Technology. Basic to all OD efforts is an attempt to make the human resources of the organization optimally available. Outside consultants often share the responsibility for this process, but they also work toward increasing the organization's own capacity to understand and manage its own growth.

In contrast to management development which is oriented toward the individual manager, OD focuses on groups and changing relations between people. The system — be it a unit of the organization, or the entire organization — is the object of an OD effort.

A frequent strategy in OD programs is the use of an *action-research* model of intervention. There are three processes in an action-research approach, all of which involve extensive collaboration between a consultant and the organization: data gathering from individuals and groups; feedback to key client or client group in the organization; and joint action planning based on the feedback. Action-research is designed to make data available from the entire system and then to use that information to make plans about the future of that system.

Some OD interventions or building blocks of an OD program are the following:

(1) *Team building:* focus is on early identification and solution of the work group's problems, particularly interpersonal and organizational roadblocks which stand in the way of the team's collaborative, cooperative, creative, competent functioning.

A group's work procedures can be made more effective by using different decision-making procedures for different tasks and learning to treat leadership as a function to be performed by members of the group, not just as a role or as a characteristic of an individual's personality.

The interpersonal relationships within a team can be improved by working on communication skills and patterns; skills in openness and expression of what one thinks and feels; the degree of understanding and acceptance among team members; authority and hierarchical problems; trust and respect; and skills in conflict management.

(2) *Intergroup problem solving:* groups are brought together for the purpose of reducing unhealthy competitiveness between the groups or to resolve intergroup conflicts over such things as overlapping responsibilities or confused lines of authority, and to enhance interdependence when it appropriately exists.

Intergroup problems sometimes exist between different functional groups which must work together, e.g., sales and engineering; or between line and staff; or labor and management; or between separate organizations involved in a merger.

(3) *Confrontation meeting:* is a problem solving mechanism when problems are known to exist. An action-research format is used. The entire management group of an organization is brought together, problems and attitudes are collected and shared, priorities are established, commitments to action are made through setting targets and assigning task forces.

(4) *Goal-setting and planning:* supervisor-subordinate pairs and teams throughout the organization engage in systematic performance improvement and target-setting with mutual commitment and review. Goal setting becomes a way of life for the organization.

(5) *Third party facilitation:* involves the use of a skilled third person to help in the diagnosis, understanding, and resolution of difficult human problems — e.g., difficult one-to-one relationships between two persons or two groups.

(6) *Consulting pairs:* often a manager can benefit from a close and continuing relationship with someone outside his own organization (a consultant, either internal or external to the organization), with whom he can share problems early.

In an effective OD effort each member of the organization begins to see himself as a resource to others and becomes willing to provide help to others when asked to do so. Such attitudes become norms or shared expectations. Once such a norm is established, members of the organization become potential consultants for one another, and the dependence of the organization on outside resources becomes less and less.

A major characteristic of organization development is that it relies heavily on an educational strategy emphasizing *experience-based learning* and on the skills such a procedure develops. Thus, the data feedback of the action-research model and the confrontation meeting are examples of how the experiences people have with each other and with the organization are shared and become the basis upon which learning occurs and upon which planning and action proceed. To be sure, OD is not simply human relations training (nor is it sensitivity training) however, openness about one's own experiences — including feelings, reactions, and perceptions — represents a cornerstone of many organizational development efforts. Furthermore, laboratory training experiences are often used to help members of the organization develop more interpersonal competence, including communication skills, ability to better manage conflict, and insights into oneself and into groups and how they form and function. Laboratory training programs are, therefore, a good preliminary step to an organization development effort.

TORI THEORY
AND PRACTICE

Jack R. Gibb

TORI theory is a general, unitary theory that applies to all formal and informal social systems (3, 6). It is structured in such a fashion as to be particularly adapted to the engineering of system change: learning communities (8), therapeutic communities (4, 9), management systems (1, 3, 7), change-inductive small groups (2, 5, 8, 10, 11), and organizations (3, 12).

Several assumptions of the theory are directly relevant to the work of leaders, trainers, and consultants in small groups.

1. Any social system — a group, person, community, nation, or organization — is best understood and improved most effectively by focusing upon system characteristics of a living, growing organism.

2. The primary and leverage variables in organic growth are the antithetical processes of fear and trust and their correlates.

3. Growth occurs as a movement from fear towards increasing trust. The primary correlates of this central process are the following four: movement from depersonalization and role towards greater personalization, from a closed system towards a more open system, from impositional motivation towards greater self determination, and from dependency towards greater interdependence (2, 8, 12). TORI is a convenient acronym for these four factors in the organic growth of living systems: trust, openness, realization, and interdependence.

4. Fear-defense levels are thus manifested in systems in four ways: depersonalization and role living, facade building and covert strategies, impositions and persuasions, and high control and dependency (2, 3).

5. Trust and low defense levels are manifested in systems in four ways: personal, intimate and non-role behavior; open and transparent behavior; self-determining, assertive, and actualizing behavior; and reciprocally-fulfilling, interdependent, and "with" behavior.

6. An efficient and powerful way of optimizing growth and the trust factors in growth is to focus upon the environmental forces that impinge upon participants in the system. This environment may then nurture and sustain growth behaviors which are associated with classic and desired group outcomes: creativity, high learning, group productivity, personal growth, and group vitality (7, 12). This is true of training and therapy groups as well as "natural" teams in industry, volunteer organizations, and educational systems.

TORI theory implies a theory of learning which is inextricable from the main body of the theory. Growth occurs when a person, on his own steam, on his own impetus, does things that reinforce desired physical responses and behavior patterns. Changed behavior results from showing feelings rather than from talking about them, from doing things rather than thinking about or observing them, from letting one's self happen rather than examining one's motives, and from physically carrying out an impulse or making a choice. After growth people look different. Growth is its own reward. The kind of sustained learning and growth that makes possible living in trust comes from self-sustained and self-directed changes in life style and behavior patterns.

The primary condition of learning is not diagnostic sensitivity but the process of trying out things that a person deeply wants to do and then experiencing the effects of the behavior upon the self and upon others. Permanent and genuine growth comes from a person finding out what he is and what he deeply wants to do, getting in touch with what his body tells him, and then doing things that integrate self-body at all levels of experience and awareness. Deep learning is not a remedial or corrective process but an inner emergence, a building upon organic strengths, and an increasing trust in self.

PERVASIVE ASSUMPTIONS

There are several assumptions in the TORI system which are immediately pertinent to the leadership style of the trainer, leader or consultant:

1. A group leader is most effective when he is as personal, open, allowing, and interdependent as it is possible for him to be within the limits of his own defense level.

2. A system such as a small group "learns" actualizing styles of coping when the environment is low-defense. The group itself develops a norm system which implements its actualizing style. The most effective leader is one who "flows" with the organic growth of the group norm system, becomes an active, assertive member of the group, but does not attempt to place himself out of the group system as a "role" or as a "leader" in the classic sense.

3. Functional behaviors or styles (personal, open, self-determining, and interdependent behavior) are intrinsically rewarding and self-perpetuating if the immediate system environment is a high-trust and low-defense environment. The group leader "trusts the process" to develop and does not feel the need to teach, train, persuade, or model behavior for others.

4. Groups tend towards entropy when group styles are predominantly impersonal and in-role, strategic and closed, persuasive and coercive, and dependent-controlling. Groups tend towards self-sustaining growth when system styles are predominantly personal, open, allowing, and interdependent.

5. The flow of perceptual and feeling data in high-defense groups is so low that raising these data to visibility in the group is a powerful force in creating more functional styles of coping and relating. Functional feedback is apparently a powerful variable, as is indicated in a number of recent studies.

USES OF TORI THEORY IN THE LEADERSHIP OF GROUPS

The following table gives a checklist for persons who would try to apply this theory to a practical setting, either in therapy or training groups, or in team training in an organizational setting.

The primary leverage principle is that the TORI leader makes a series of trust assumptions about the world. He is predisposed to trust his impulses, his inner self, the motivations of others, the health-directed processes of group interaction, the general non-malevolence of nature and persons, his own abilities and capacities, the capacities of persons to assume responsibility for their own lives, and the world in general. When the leader is fearful he tends to be impersonal, closed, non-allowing, and controlling. He recognizes these tendencies and their genesis in his non-trust. Predisposed to recognize his fears, he is able to reduce his tendency to "act them out." Experience with groups and group phenomena enables the TORI leader to trust himself to show his fears when he recognizes them, to trust enough to show his distrusts, to share with others in a joint quest for a more trusting relationship in and out of the group.

CHECKLIST FOR GROUP LEADERS USING TORI THEORY

Leader moves away from:

1. Being impersonal, "in role"
2. Selecting my behaviors because they are helpful or therapeutic (a role prescription)
3. Focus upon relations between role and role (leader and member; member and member)
4. Responding to what patients or members seem to need (programming)
5. Screening my responses and modeling appropriate, relevant, helpful, role, or professional aspects of self
6. Responding to the other as a client, patient, member, or person needing help
7. Concern for changing, curing, or remedying the deficient individual
8. Being consistent with my theory of action, training, therapy or group growth
9. Focus upon motives, interpretations, and other derivative, inferential, or role concepts
10. Focus upon separate, autonomous individuals or entities, as entities
11. Focus on abstraction, generality, or principle
12. Focus upon evaluative or moral judgments
13. Focus on and concern for *then* (other relationships in the past or future and on the past history of members)
14. Focus on and concern for *there* (data from other relationships and contexts)
15. Focus upon description of the passive self as a static being
16. Focus upon limitations of the person
17. Focus upon punishment and rewards
18. Focus upon legality, "contracts," norms, controls
19. Focus upon the terminology of fear, risk, caution, and conservation
20. Focus upon words, semantics, and speech

Leader moves toward:

1. Being personal, non-role
2. Responding to my current feelings and perceptions (showing my self)
3. Focus upon relations between persons and persons
4. Responding to how I see and feel about my relationships now (being spontaneous)
5. Minimal screening but sharing all areas of self, however relevant or professional they may seem to me to be
6. Responding to the other as a unique person, *qua* person
7. Concern for growth and development of each of us in all of our relationships
8. Focus upon intuition, "gut feel" of what to do: following impulse
9. Focus upon more available, direct, experienced and visible behavior
10. Focus on *relationships* (on how it is now between or among us)
11. Focus on concrete, primitive and elemental feelings and perceptions
12. Focus on descriptive statements about feelings and perceptions
13. Focus on and concern for *now* (how each of us feels and sees things at this moment)
14. Focus on and concern for *here* (feelings and perceptions visible and available to all)
15. Focus upon description of the dynamic, in-process, becoming organism/person
16. Focus upon strengths and growing edges of the person
17. Focus upon flowing behaviors and feelings
18. Focus upon flow, fluidity of temporary, self-sustaining systems
19. Focus upon trust, venture, impulse, and liberation
20. Focus upon non-verbal and body flow and organic integration

Fears become less frightening as they become more familiar, as their effects become better known, and as one learns that the fears will dissipate with openness and interaction. In order to become truly personal in a group, a leader must become very familiar with his fears and the fears of others and be able to deal with these verbally and nonverbally in the continuing feedback of the group interaction.

The inexperienced leader has many fears: fear of letting things get out of control, fear of being seen as incompetent or unprofessional, fear that persons in the group will be hurt or damaged, fear that he will not be perceptive enough to see what is going on under the surface of things, fear that he will not live up to the expectations of group members, fear that he will lose his objectivity as a professional observer, fear that members might see others in the group as more competent or helpful than the appointed leader, and fear that he will not be able to invent or provide a method for resolving a conflict or crisis in the group. Only when the leader sees himself as a role, tries to live up to role expectations, and protects himself from personal relations does he have these kinds of fears. As he comes to see himself as a person and accept his personal relationships with others he finds that these fears come to dissipate.

The leader who comes through theory-motivated and theory-guided experiences in "leaderless" (person-full) groups to gain trust of group processes is increasingly able to enter the group as a person. He is able to ignore the initial role demands of inexperienced group members and to enter into personal relationships. He gains his satisfactions from his own growth, from genuine interdependence, from depth relationships with other persons, from the exchange of human emotions with others, from his growing congruence, and from his growing freedom from the crippling feelings of responsibility for the lives and learnings of others. These are health-giving satisfactions, intrinsic rewards, and freedom-giving behaviors (11).

The central concepts in the leader style described are freedom from role (11), taking responsibility for self and giving others responsibility for themselves (6), giving self the freedom to follow impulses and one's own spontaneity (12), giving primacy to interdependent and with-relations (6), the focus upon emergent strengths rather than upon remedial processes (5), the focus upon organic flow rather than upon "contracts" or role obligations (8), the focus upon ecological engineering rather than upon leader behavior for group improvement (5), and the focus upon bodily and non-verbal processes rather than upon verbal relationships. The TORI theory relies upon a set of general assumptions and experiences and a general world or person viewpoint or set, rather than upon a methodology or a technique. TORI is a life style, a way of living, an organic integration and not a tool or a method. The orientation comes both from a person-oriented theory of life and from a set of experiences that create a trusting stance toward persons and groups. One can learn to be more trusting. The general trust theory outlined above emerges in individuals who have trust-inductive experiences. Trust is a master variable. As a person becomes more trusting he becomes more personal, open, allowing, and with others. He inevitably becomes less role-locked, closed, manipulative, and dependent-controlling. *One can choose to be* less controlling or more open. This choice-directed behavior, if theory-directed and if satisfying to the learner, is self-fulfilling. That is, such experiments with self can reduce fears and increase trusts. The experimenter finds, for instance, that allowing and non-manipulative behavior is more satisfying to him and to others and the allowing behavior can become ascendent as an emerging life style.

Proficiency in the use of TORI theory and practice as a life style and as a way of working with training groups and natural groups can come in one of several ways. Reading the theory as outlined in the sampling of references listed at the end of this essay may be helpful. Performing miniature experiments upon oneself in trying out a role-free style in a series of group experiences is helpful in getting oneself in tune with his capacities to be personal, communicate in depth, join in shared search, and live interdependently. In my experience I have seldom seen a person who makes a genuine and sustained effort to be role-free revert to role behavior. Role-free behavior is more organically rewarding to all relatively non-defensive people than is role behavior. Role behavior is rewarding only in defensive climates, in formal structures, and in controlled or dependent relationships. Non-role behavior is organically suited to the actualization of man. Another route to learning a TORI personal style is to work closely with a person who is using TORI theory in practice. There is obviously no single path to personness.

The TORI group leader, when he has developed a congruent life style, acts in the same way in the group when he is the announced leader or trainer as he does if he were a member of the group. He uses the same "theory" in all situations. His behavior as a therapist, an administrator, a trainer, a parent, a teacher, a counselor, a manager, or a friend is essentially the same. He does not have a special theory to fit a special situation. He does not "choose a leader style." He is as much a person in all situations as it is possible for him to be. He does not "take the role" of parent or therapist. Being present as a full person in the here and now and responding with minimal screening to himself and to others has growth-giving effects. In being a full person in all situations he gives and receives life, warmth, love, with-ness and humanness. He thus, as serendipity, meets his role obligations as a parent, a therapist, a teacher, or a minister. That is, people around him grow, learn, get healthier, and become more creative and enriched. People may model after him if they wish, as all persons in some ways model after many others. He *does not set himself up as a model* or consciously intend his behavior to be a model. His life is a continuing quest for richer interdependence. Interdependence is the direction of the growth. Openness, congruence, self-actualization, and role-freedom are means, are steps along the way, and paths toward more full interdependence.

TORI-STYLED LEADERSHIP IN ORGANIZATIONS

The TORI style of leading a group is appropriate to the most functional leadership within the organization. When persons take or are given "managing" positions in groups or organizations (parents, teachers, administrators, managers) they often attempt to manage the warmth, the communications, the motivations, and the structure of the system (3). They inherit from conventional theory and prevalent practice a series of distrust assumptions about the nature of men and organizations. Based upon these assumptions they institute a series of counter-growth and self-defeating programs: praise and punishment, performance appraisal, merit badges and merit pay, competition, quality control, and arbitrary rules. The critical dynamics of the system are so masked that leaders continue to get falsely confirming data. The systems seem, on the surface, to be effective, but they exacerbate latent and cumulative counter-growth forces: depersonalization, role behavior and fear; strategic distortion and circumvention; persuasion-passivity; and dependence-hostility (1, 3, 7).

More functional behavior for the parent, teacher, group leader, or manager is to "go with the flow" and contribute directly to the emergence and growth of the system. When this happens persons and organizations grow, emerge, and become. There is movement toward primary and stated aims: productivity in the company, spirituality in the church, socialization in the home, learning in the school, and psychological health in the clinic. Movement and growth are toward the health and fulfillment of members: the essence of effectiveness of any social system. Growing — personal, open, realizing, and interdependent behaviors — is highly correlated with each of the organizational outcomes stated above.

It is my observation, both in research and consulting, that the most direct, economical and powerful way for the manager, group leader, or therapist to enhance these organizational outcomes is to direct attention to increasing the trust level. He optimizes growth and reduces defense levels by being personal, open, self-determining and interdependent, and fostering these behaviors in others.

This is not to say that the manager or group leader becomes passive, non-directive, "permissive," impotent, encaptured by forces he cannot understand or control, an observer, or even a servant. Rather, the high-trust TORI leader becomes a full person. He is assertive, warm, open, active, demanding to be heard, expressive of his own feelings and needs, and very much involved in decisions and processes in the group and in its creativity and productivity: just as are all the other growing members of the group or the organization.

The leader does not assume responsibility for the group or the organization. Taking responsibility for someone else feeds the counter-growth forces of role taking, filtering, passivity, and dependency that we see in low-trust groups, teams, and organizations.

Any change in a person or group or organization, however significantly it may relieve symptoms of distress, is dysfunctional if it does not move in the direction of increasing the trust level and optimization of the four variables of personalization, openness, self-determination, and interdependence.

REFERENCES

1. Gibb, J. R. Defensive communication. *The Journal of Communication,* 1961, 11 (3), 141-148.
2. Gibb, J. R. Climate for trust formation. In L. P. Bradford, J. R. Gibb & K. D. Benne (Eds.), *T group theory and laboratory method.* New York: Wiley, 1964.
3. Gibb, J. R. Fear and facade: defensive management. In R. E. Farson (Ed.), *Science and human affairs.* Palo Alto: Science and Behavior Books, Inc., 1965.
4. Gibb, J. R. The counselor as a role-free person. In C. A. Parker (Ed.), *Counseling theories and counselor education.* New York: Houghton Mifflin, 1968.
5. Gibb, J. R. Group experiences and human possibilities. In H. A. Otto (Ed.), *Human potentialities.* St. Louis: W. H. Green, 1968.
6. Gibb, J. R. Search for with-ness: a new look at interdependence. In W. G. Dyer (Ed.), *New dimensions in group training.* New York: Van Nostrand, 1971, in press.
7. Gibb,. J. R. Managing for creativity in the organization. In C. W. Taylor (Ed.), *Climate for creativity.* New York: Pergamon Publishing Co., 1971.
8. Gibb, J. R., & Gibb, L. M. Humanistic elements in group growth. In J. F. T. Bugental (Ed.), *Challenges of humanistic psychology.* New York: McGraw-Hill, 1967.
9. Gibb, J. R., & Gibb, L. M. Emergence therapy: the TORI process in an emergent group. In G.M. Gazda (Ed.), *Innovations to group psychotherapy.* Springfield, Ill.: Thomas, 1968.
10. Gibb, J. R., & Gibb, L. M. Leaderless groups: growth-centered values and potentials. In H. A. Otto & J. Mann (Eds.), *Ways of growth: approaches to expanding awareness.* New York: Grossman, 1968.
11. Gibb, J. R., & Gibb, L. M. Role freedom in a TORI group. In A. Burton (Ed.), *Encounter: the theory and practice of encounter groups.* San Francisco: Jossey-Bass, 1969.
12. Gibb, J. R., & Gibb, L. M. The process of group actualization. In J. Akin, A. Goldberg, G. Myers, & J. Stewart (Eds.), *Language behavior: readings in communication.* The Hague, The Netherlands: Mouton & Co., 1971.

SEVEN
PURE
STRATEGIES
OF CHANGE

Kurt E. Olmosk

In recent months I have become increasingly aware that various individuals and groups approach the problem of change in various ways. There tends, however, to be a certain amount of consistency in the strategies employed within one group or by one individual over time.

This paper is an attempt to describe the various approaches I see being used most often. It is by no means an all inclusive list of strategies currently in use or theoretically possible. It is an attempt, however, to describe some of the more prevalent strategies in some detail.

I first began thinking about the various strategies used to bring about change, while working with a group in Kansas City. This particular group described their purpose as an attempt to increase contact between blacks and whites and to increase awareness of the racial problems facing the city and country. This was to be done through reading, study, and discussion in an atmosphere which would encourage frank and open examination of feelings and prejudices as well as facts. As I worked with this group, it became clear that they were following a strategy similar to that used by many churches and other volunteer organizations. I call this approach the Fellowship Strategy.

This strategy, and seven others, are described on the following pages. They are summarized in the table at the end of this article. The order in which they are presented is not meant to signify either their relative importance or frequency of use.

FELLOWSHIP STRATEGY

Simply stated, the assumption underlying this model seems to be, "If we have good, warm interpersonal relations, all other problems will be minor." Great emphasis is placed on getting to know and like each other. For this reason, it is not unusual for groups using this model to sponsor discussion groups, group dinners, card parties, and other social events which will bring everyone together.

This strategy places strong emphasis on treating everyone equally. This is often interpreted as needing to treat everyone the same way. Everyone must be accepted into membership, no one is turned away. When questions of choice or decision-making must be faced, everyone is allowed to have his say and all opinions are to be weighed equally. No fact, feeling, opinion, or theory is to be considered inherently superior to any other. Arguments are few and confusing since conflict is generally suppressed and avoided.

Groups which tend to use this strategy also tend to be composed of individuals who have emotional needs for warmth, love, and trust in their fellow man. Much of this strategy is geared to satisfying these needs. Most of the discussions, dinners, and parties are light and pleasant with a minimum of conflict. They are designed to foster feelings of warmth and goodwill among the participants.

Groups which use this approach are fairly successful in gaining members initially and often they are able to mobilize a great deal of initial energy. They give people something to belong to. For many people, this is extremely valuable and may sustain a group for some time even though its goals are unclear and its concrete accomplishments are few. In fact, this initial mobilization of energy and commitment is what the fellowship strategy seems to do best.

However, groups which employ the Fellowship approach as a primary strategy tend to face some chronic problems. Since much of the initial commitment is to individuals, rather than to ideas or projects, the group often begins to feel directionless. It has trouble stating what it is really trying to do. With the added strong emphasis on warm feelings and treating everyone equally, it often becomes virtually impossible to set priorities. There is bound to be someone who does not entirely agree with any decision which is made. And, since everyone must be heard and no one must be unhappy, one person can immobilize the whole group.

For these same reasons, the group often has trouble implementing any decisions it is able to make. The trouble may take several forms. Being unable to face conflict, the group often makes unrealistic plans. Because the emphasis is primarily on keeping everyone happy, questions of economics, politics, or engineering feasibility are often minimized. An example of this is the fact that many churches have difficulty remaining financially solvent. Yet unless this is done, plans may have to be changed or the church dissolved.

As plans are ignored or changed, it becomes increasingly difficult for groups using this strategy to maintain the commitment of their members. The feeling begins to grow that the group is floundering, that it isn't doing anything, and that it is a waste of time. At this point, old members begin to leave and the group can only survive by finding new members who need to belong to something.

As I have implied above, groups using this strategy tend to suppress certain questions from their members. These are questions of individual competence and of individual difference which would threaten the norm that all people are equal and that they should all be treated in the same way. They also suppress the question, "What's in it for me?" This last question is often interpreted as "You don't trust us (the group)." If the group cannot find a way to face these questions, it is usually short lived.

In my experience, the Fellowship strategy is most often used by churches and other voluntary groups which have few financial or physical resources with which to reward or punish behavior of members.

POLITICAL STRATEGY

The assumption underlying this approach can be stated as follows, "If all the 'really' influential people agree that something should be done, it will be done." Emphasis is placed on finding and understanding the power structure that must be dealt with. This power structure usually includes not only the formal, recognized leaders, but the informal unofficial leaders as well. Much of the work done using this strategy is done informally on the basis of one-to-one relationships among these leaders.

This strategy emphasizes the identification and influencing of those individuals who seem to be most able to make decisions and have them carried out. It generally focuses on those men who are the most respected and have the largest constituency in a given area. Within this strategy, influence is based on the level and breadth of one's perceived power and on one's

164

ability to bargain or work with other influential people to achieve goals valued by one's constituency.

The groups which use the political approach as a primary strategy seldom believe that all men are really equal or the same. They often view individual differences as unimportant unless these differences relate directly to power. The primary emotional needs of these groups seems to be for control and attention. Much of the effort expended in these groups goes toward seeing that decisions which are made are favorable to them, and that people know they were influential in making the decision.

Groups which use this approach are often fairly good at getting decisions implemented once they are made. Because so much energy is expended on getting influential people involved initially, once a decision is made it is often simply a matter of carrying it out. This mobilization of power and the implementation of decisions is the area in which this approach seems to work best.

However, over time, groups which rely primarily on the political strategy face a variety of chronic problems. Since influence is defined as being able to get decisions made which are beneficial to one's-self and one's constituency, a few adverse decisions may severely limit one's influence and completely change the power structure. It is often a fairly unstable system with a continual shifting of positions.

This shifting of positions leads to another and related problem, that of maintaining credibility. With the constant bargaining and compromising which this approach requires, it is often difficult to remain consistent in one's actions and to fulfill all of the promises made to one's constituency. Over time this can lead to a loss of faith by one's constituency and a corresponding loss of power and influence for the leader.

Finally, this approach often leads to backlash by the wider public and by individuals with opposing constituencies. Any decision is bound to be unpopular with some people and if enough decisions are made which they don't like they may organize their own power group to counter those making unpopular decisions.

People using this strategy often have trouble dealing with questions concerning value systems and loyalty. When compromise is called for, it is often hard to draw the line between decisions which are within the bounds of acceptability to one's own value system and to one's constituency, and decisions which are the result of short term pressures.

ECONOMIC STRATEGY

The underlying assumption for this approach is "If we have enough money or material wealth, we can buy anything or any change we want." The emphasis in this approach is on acquiring, or at least having influence over, all forms of material goods. These might include money, land, stocks, bonds, or any other tradeable commodity. This strategy is widely used in the United States and the Western World.

Inclusion into a group using this approach is usually based upon possession or control of marketable resources. Influence within the group is based on perceived wealth. The more money you have, the more people are willing to listen to you.

Most of the decisions made by the group are heavily, if not completely, influenced by questions of profitability as measured by an increase in tangible assets. The approach is highly rational and all people are assumed to behave more or less rationally from economic motives. Groups using this strategy often evidence strong emotional needs for control and rationality in all of their dealings.

The economic strategy works well in the United States. With the Puritan ethic still strongly held by many people, material wealth is not only a means of making life more comfortable, but is also a positive sign of talent and being one of the chosen. As long as the money holds out, this strategy is usually able to get decisions implemented once they are made.

This strategy does have some drawbacks, however. As Herzberg (1966) pointed out, money and material rewards are only temporary satisfiers. When people have been paid to make changes, they are satisfied for a while, but sooner or later they want more rewards. In order to maintain a change, it may be necessary to keep paying for it indefinitely.

This is related to a second problem in using this strategy. Few individuals or groups have unlimited resources. Some things or changes may simply be too expensive to buy given the resources available. There is often no way to significantly increase the available resources in the short run.

As with all other strategies, this one suppresses certain questions in its pure form. The most significant of these is "Is the practice ethical?" Since this is a somewhat emotional and philosophical question, it can not be answered within a strictly logical economic framework. This strategy also suppresses or ignores all questions which can not be answered in terms of profit or loss. These include most questions dealing with feelings of people.

As might be guessed, this strategy is most often used by corporations or the very rich. It is, however, beginning to be used by other groups such as the poor in Operation Breadbasket.

ACADEMIC STRATEGY

The academic strategy makes the assumption that "People are rational. If you present enough facts to enough people, people will make the changes required." To this end, individuals and groups adopting this strategy undertake an unending series of studies and produce thousands of pages of written reports each year.

Membership in groups using this strategy is based primarily on the possession of knowledge in a given area, or the desire to acquire such knowledge. Leadership and influence within the group is generally dependent upon the degree to which the individual is perceived to possess specialized knowledge, i. e., the degree to which he is seen as being an expert. The newcomer to the field is generally considered to have little to contribute to the group while the man with a Ph.D. or many years of specialized study is listened to closely.

People using this strategy tend to approach most problems, and the world in general, in a detached, analytical way. Their primary emotional needs appear to be for rationality and autonomy. People using this approach as a primary strategy often pride themselves on being disinterested observers or researchers of the world around them.

This approach is very useful in some cases. It often produces much relevant information and makes it available to people considering change. It may point out opportunities or consequences of action which would not be considered otherwise. It may also point out the cause of problems so that they may be corrected.

The academic strategy does not, however, have a very good record when it comes to actually bringing about change. There are several reasons for this. Because this approach emphasizes detached and disinterested study, it is often difficult to get people interested in the findings later. Only the researcher has been involved in the study during most of the time prior to publication so only he feels committed to the findings. The time and effort required to read and digest a complex report just does not seem worth it to most people. Without reading the complete report most people have trouble interpreting or believing the results of the study.

The emphasis on being a disinterested observer also makes it very difficult for the researcher to mobilize the energy and resources to implement the findings. For many academically oriented people, the emphasis on being a disinterested observer makes it hard to take an advocacy position on almost anything. Therefore, unless someone else becomes interested in the results of a study, no action will be taken on the findings.

There is one further problem with using the academic strategy to solve most problems, it is time consuming. It takes time to do studies and to write reports. Unless the problem being studied is fairly stable, the situation which faces the decision maker when the report is finished, may not be the same one that existed when the study began. This is sometimes the excuse given for not implementing findings, occasionally with justification.

The emphasis on rationality and being a disinterested observer which this strategy requires, makes it very difficult for people using it to answer several questions. One of the most prominent of these is "How should the results be used?" Most academically oriented individuals feel this question is up to other people to answer.

A second but related question that often goes unanswered by the researcher is, "How do I feel about the results?" The emphasis on rationality blocks direct examination of this question.

My experience would indicate that this strategy is likely to be used by people in some positions more often than by people in others. This approach to change is often used by people who are outside the system they hope to effect. For instance, this approach is particularly popular with many consultants and people in staff positions (as opposed to line positions).

ENGINEERING STRATEGY

This strategy is particularly interesting because it tries to bring about change in individual behavior without dealing with people directly. The apparent underlying assumption can be stated as "If the environment or surroundings change enough, people will have to change also." For this reason, much time may be spent studying the work situation, the classroom, or the ghetto street from the standpoint of physical layout, required or permitted interaction patterns, and role descriptions.

Groups which approach change in this way often recruit their members on the basis of the technical skills the individual possesses. The group may look for a systems analyst, an engineer, or a management specialist in order to grow. Group needs are often defined in terms of technical skills and these are considered more important than interpersonal style.

Within the group, influence is based on the perceived level of the particular technical skills required at the time. Outside the group, however, influence is exerted primarily by changing the structure or the environment of given tasks or individuals. For example, the assembly line may be speeded up in order to get workers to produce more. Or, departments may be reorganized and tasks redefined in order to break up troublesome cliques.

Basic to this strategy is the need for rationality. The emotional side of human beings gets in the way and is suppressed whenever possible. Within this focus on rationality, there is a strong emphasis on task relevance. Data and decisions are evaluated primarily on the basis of these criteria. If the information or decision does not help to get the task done, it is irrelevant.

Because of its strong emphasis on being aware of the structural aspects of problems, this approach often leads to considerable awareness of the environment in which a group works. This may be particularly helpful in highly unstable situations, since new developments and information are discovered quickly. Because many management problems are problems of information flow, this approach may also produce results when reorganization and redefinition of tasks results in new and shorter communication links.

Although this strategy does get results in some situations, it also runs into some typical problems. Management literature is full of studies and articles concerning ways to get people to accept change. Since people are often treated like objects or machines when problems are being analyzed, they are often resistant to changes this approach would indicate as desirable. The people most directly effected often do not feel committed to the change or do not understand it. Since people are assumed to be totally rational, their feelings are being ignored, and thus can not be talked about.

There are several other problems which are often encountered by groups using this strategy. First, it is often time consuming. While changes in the surrounding world may be detected quickly, analysis and decisions based on these changes take time to implement. Second, structural or environmental changes often produce unexpected results. A department which is reorganized in order to break up troublesome cliques may also lose the close working relationships which made it reasonably efficient. Third, in most organizations, there are very few people who have a broad enough perspective and enough power and influence to bring about widespread structural change. For this reason, this strategy is most often used by fairly high level management in an organization.

The question most often ignored or suppressed by groups using this strategy is "How will people feel about the change?" Because of the emphasis on rationality and efficiency which is inherent in this strategy, this question is usually considered to be of little importance.

MILITARY STRATEGY

This approach to change is based on the use of physical force to change behavior. The name Military has been given this approach because it seemed to convey the right connotation to most people, not because the military is the sole user of this approach. In various forms, this approach is also used by many police departments, 'revolutionary' student groups, and some teachers.

The basic assumption behind this approach can be stated as "People react to real threats. If we possess enough physical force, we can make people do anything." To this end, considerable time is spent in learning to use weapons and to fight. Priorities may also be given to physical conditioning, strength, and agility.

Membership in groups using this approach is often determined on the basis of the possession of physical power, and willingness to submit to discipline. Both within the group, and in its dealings with the surrounding world, influence is exerted primarily through the fear of authority and the threat of punishment. Even though the iron fist is hidden in a velvet glove, there is never any doubt that the iron fist exists and can be used.

Much of the perceptual approach used by groups using this strategy is determined by the emotional needs of the members for control, status, and security. Out of these needs often grows a tendency to see most problems and relationships in terms of power, authority, threat, and exploitation.

One of the main strengths of this approach is that it is often good at keeping order. If the threats are severe enough, most people are reluctant to misbehave and will try to find ways of getting what they want within the existing system.

One of the most severe handicaps of this approach is that once resorted to, the 'enforcer' can never relax. As soon as he does, the change that is being imposed will disappear.

A second problem is that force is often met with force. Resorting to the use of force often starts an ever escalating cycle of violence. People resist having change imposed on them and whenever possible will rebel.

When this approach is used, many moral questions tend to be ignored by most of the group. The average member seldom asks who should "really" make decisions. He 'knows' that the answer is "Those in authority". Questions of right and wrong are also difficult to face since in a very real sense "Might makes right" within this approach.

CONFRONTATION STRATEGY

This approach to change is based on the assumption that if you can mobilize enough anger in enough people and force them to look at the problems around them the required changes will be made. From this basic assumption, it is clear that this strategy is a high conflict strategy.

However, as it is being thought of here, the strategy stresses non-violent argument as opposed to the actual use of physical force.

Membership in groups using this approach to change is often based on one's ability to deal with and use conflict in ways that further the goals of the group. Influence both within and outside the group is based primarily on one's ability to argue one's point and to deal with conflict short of coming to blows. Most of the early civil rights groups and student groups made heavy use of this approach to bring about change.

As I think of the groups that use this approach, it appears that they base much of their argument on a very narrow definition of the "Truth". Much of their perceptual approach is in terms of highly idealized moral arguments. Out of this idealized morality often come strong emotional needs to express one's anger, sense of indignation, and sense of self. It is out of these needs that the confrontation with other "offending" groups is generated.

This approach to change has several strengths. When a group adopts this approach it is usually fairly clear to the "opponents" that they will need to make some kind of answer before the confronting group will go away. To this extent, this approach often does get people to look at problems they would rather not acknowledge. Secondly, and sometimes more importantly, this approach gains attention and publicity in the larger community. It is very hard to ignore a thousand people marching down Main Street. If the cause for which these people are marching catches on, the increased pressure on the decision makers to do something may bring about changes where all other approaches have failed.

This approach to change also has several major drawbacks. While it often does gain attention and point out problems, this approach, when used exclusively, often fails to suggest solutions. Because many of the people using this approach have little power to make changes themselves, and because people join the protest movements for such a wide variety of reasons, it is often difficult to get any agreement on alternatives or solutions to the problems.

Secondly, because this approach is based on the use of conflict, it often polarizes people and creates considerable backlash. When students stage a sit-in in the dean's office, he often becomes determined not to give in to this type of pressure. If this is the second or third group of students who has tried to use this strategy, he may feel he has no choice but to call in the police. When this happens, even students with legitimate complaints may have trouble getting a hearing.

As the confrontation approach to change escalates, one question tends to get suppressed. "Is there anything in the opponent's argument that is worthwhile?" To suggest that the opponents might be right about some things is often close to heresy and the person who makes that kind of suggestion is often treated accordingly.

This approach to change has most often been used by students and the poor. These groups often feel that they have no other way to make themselves heard.

APPLIED BEHAVIORAL SCIENCE MODEL

In recent years many people have been increasingly vocal in their assertion that most problems are extremely complex. This is the basic assumption in the Applied Behavioral Science Model. Simply stated, this assumption is "Most problems are complex and overdetermined. A combination of approaches is usually required to achieve a solution."

Groups using this approach usually argue that inclusion into membership should be based on the effect the issues under consideration will have on people. As many people as possible, who will be effected by the decision, should be included in making the decision. Within the group, influence is based on knowledge and the degree to which the decision will effect the individual. Ideally, the individual with the most knowledge about a given problem and/or the person most effected by the decision should have the most influence in the group when the decision is being considered. Given this outlook, it also follows that leadership of the group should change as the problem being considered changes.

The perceptual approach to the world by groups using this approach is often very eclectic. Any information or theory which will help to understand the situation and reach a decision is used. In its purest form, the emotional needs of members seem to be primarily for emotional and intellectual integration. Attempts are made to keep from fragmenting one's life and approach to problems.

This broad based approach to problems, along with a situation centered focus, is the major strength of this model. Very often more information is considered and utilized in reaching decisions by groups employing this approach, than by groups using most of the other approaches.

This approach does have some drawbacks, however. One of the biggest is simply making itself understood. Because it is so eclectic and situation centered, people using it often have difficulty answering what appear to be simple questions. When considering the question of how to motivate workers, for instance, the work situation, task requirements, social needs of workers, value systems of everyone involved, work precedents and many other factors need to be looked at. Any answer which considers all these factors is likely to be long, complex, and somewhat confusing.

Second, because each situation is somewhat different than every other, people using this approach may appear to be somewhat inconsistent. A slight change in one of the variables under consideration, may change the recommended solution completely. To the outsider, it may appear that the question is the same but only the answer has changed.

The question that is most often suppressed or ignored by people using this approach is "How should I 'really' do it?" This question just can not be answered within this approach since the assumption is made that there is no one best way to solve any problem.

SUMMARY

In the preceding pages, I have tried to describe several of the strategies I have seen used most often by groups and individuals to bring about change. I have described each of these as a pure strategy. In practice, these are seldom used as pure approaches. Rather, one strategy may predominate with modifications based on one or two of the other approaches.

My main purpose here has been to describe each strategy in as much detail as possible with the hope that if people can recognize the strategy being used, and the underlying assumptions, approaches which are appropriate to the situation can be chosen.

All of the strategies described in the preceding pages are summarized in the following table.

Frederick Herzberg. *Work and the Nature of Man.* Cleveland: World, 1966.

	FELLOWSHIP	POLITICAL
Basic Assumption	If we have good warm interpersonal relations, all other problems will be minor	If all the really influential people agree to do something, it will be done
Inclusion	Get everybody in	Get everyone in who possesses power
Influence	Everybody equal	Based on level and breadth of perceived power
Perceptual Approach	Accepts all. Shuts out none	Stereotype. Ignore individual differences unless they relate to power
Emotional Needs	Warmth, love and trust	Control and attention
Good at	Mobilizing initial energy	Mobilizing power. Implementing decisions once made
Chronic Problems	Financial support. Actual implementation of decisions. Maintaining long run commitment	Maintaining credibility. Fighting backlash
Questions suppressed	What's in it for me? Competence. Individual difference.	Is my action consistent with my value system?
Most often used by	Churches. Volunteer organizations. Groups with limited power.	Those already in power

	ECONOMIC	ACADEMIC
Basic Assumption	If we have enough money or material wealth, we can buy anything or any change we want.	People are rational. If you present enough facts to people, they will change
Inclusion	Based on possession of marketable resources	Based on possession of knowledge and facts
Influence	Based on perceived wealth	Based on specialized knowledge and expertise
Perceptual Approach	Materialistic	Analytical and detached
Emotional Needs	Control and rationality	Autonomy and rationality
Good at	Implementing decisions once made	Finding causes. Presenting relevant information
Chronic problems	Maintaining change and/or satisfaction. Few people or groups have unlimited resources	Implementing findings. Mobilizing energy. Getting people to pay attention or read reports. Time consuming.
Questions suppressed	Is it ethical? Most feelings	How do I feel about results? How should results be used?
Most often used by	Corporations. The very wealthy	Outsiders. People in staff positions.

	ENGINEERING	CONFRONTATION
Basic assumptions	If the environment or surroundings change, people have to change	If we can mobilize enough anger and force people to look at problems around us, the required changes will be made
Inclusion	Based on possession of technical skills	Based on ability to deal with and use conflict
Influence	By changing structure or task environment	By non-violent argument
Perceptual approach	Task relevance and rationality	Narrow belief in "Truth"
Emotional needs	Rationality, clarity and structure	Expression of anger. Expression of self
Good at	Being aware of surroundings and/or environment	Forcing people to look at issues they may not want to acknowledge. Gaining attention and publicity
Chronic problems	Gaining acceptance for change. Dealing with unexpected consequences. Time consuming. Few people can control structure.	Finding alternatives. Dealing with backlash
Questions suppressed	How will people feel about it?	Is anything in opponents argument worthwhile?
Most often used by	Top management	Revolutionary students. The poor Unions.

	MILITARY	APPLIED BEHAVIORAL SCIENCE
Basic assumption	If we possess enough physical force, we can make people do anything.	Most problems are complex and overdetermined. A combination of approaches is usually required.
Inclusion	Based on possession of physical power	Based on including as many of those effected as possible
Influence	By fear of authority and threat of punishment	Based on knowledge and the degree to which the decisions will effect them
Perceptual approach	Exploit for use of power structure	Ecclectic but situation centered
Emotional needs	Control, status and security	Emotional and intellectual integration
Good at	Keeping order	Using as much information as possible
Chronic problems	Rebellion. Can never relax.	Making itself understood. Not appearing "wishy-washy".
Question suppressed	Who should "really" make decisions? Is it "right"?	How should I "really" do it? Do you really know what you are doing?
Most often used by	Military. Police. "Weathermen"	Human relations consultants, organization development consultants

COMMUNICATION MODES: AN EXPERIENTIAL LECTURE

John E. Jones

When we are attempting to transfer our meaning to another person, we use three different modes, methods, or channels to carry our intentions. We use these modes to tell people who we are, how we experience the world, and the meaning we attach to our experience. We communicate symbolically, verbally, and nonverbally. This discussion centers around the definition of each of these modes and includes some suggested activities designed to look at the implications of these modes for improving one's communication with others. The intent is to explore the implications of the mixed signals which one often emits in attempting to share a meaning with another person.

When two persons, A and B, are attempting to communicate with each other, their communication is distorted by their personalities, attitudes, values, belief systems, biases, the assumptions they are making about each other, their experience background, and so on. A's communication to B flows through A's screen and through B's screen. When B responds to A, B is responding to what he heard rather than what A might have intended. He shoots his message back to B through his own screen of attitudes, values, and so on, through A's screen. What is often not understood is that the way we get messages through our screens and through another person's screen often is confusing and distorting in and of itself. We add to what we hear, we fail to hear, and we distort messages according to the modes that are used to convey messages.

SYMBOLIC COMMUNICATION

We say a great deal to each other about who we are and how we experience each other and the rest of the world through symbolic means. The symbolic communication mode is essentially passive, and messages emitted in this way are very easily misinterpreted.

What are some of the symbols that we use? First, our choice of clothes can tell a great deal about who we are, what our values are, what our status is, how conservative or liberal we are. We associate differences in occupational status with different uniforms. The banker wears a suit, the hod carrier wears overalls, and so on. The radical student wears colorful, loose clothing, the so-called "straight" professor wears a tattersall vest. The second set of symbols with which we often associate meaning is hair. Bearded people are presumed to be more liberal than unbearded people, and people with long hair are presumed to have different political, economic, social philosophies than people who do not have long hair. We stereotype people who have crewcuts. The type of hairdo's and our facial hair, say a great deal about who we are. These signals are often highly ambiguous, however. A third symbolic form is jewelry. Married people often wear wedding rings, some people wear beads, some people wear highly expensive jewelry, and so on. These are passive messages that are given out continuously to other people. A flag in the lapel, a peace symbol around the neck, an earring in one ear say many things to other people. A fourth form of symbolic communication to other people is cosmetics, or makeup. We associate meanings with different ways women apply makeup to their bodies. The prostitute usually has heavier makeup than other women. The man who uses a great many cosmetics is giving out a symbolic message about the meaning that his world has for him. A fifth symbolic mode is the choice of automobiles. The business executive who drives a sports car is giving out a different set of messages to the world than his colleague who drives an ordinary family car. A sixth symbolic mode is the choice and location of our houses. Social status is directly related to the type of dwelling one lives in and its location. Seventh, the geography of our living spaces is a form of symbolic communication. If you sit behind your desk in your office interviewing somebody who is on the other side of the desk, you are giving out a fundamentally different set of messages than if the two of you sit face to face with no intervening furniture.

So we are giving out a continuous stream of signals about our meaning to other people through the symbols that we choose to surround ourselves and invest ourselves with. These symbols are essentially passive. They are, however, a real part of our communication. When we are talking, when we are not talking, and when we are sleeping, we emit passive symbolic signals.

SYMBOLIC ACTIVITIES

For the symbolic mode, participants can pair off and take turns interpreting all of the symbols about each other and to share experiences in having their own symbols misinterpreted in their past. An alternative activity might be the statue game. Participants pair off and take turns being "It." The person who is "It" imagines that he is a statue in an art gallery. The other person's job is to examine the statue very closely, to try to be alert to all the details of that person, to try to memorize these details so that he can tell a third person what he saw to help to make a decision as to whether he wants to buy the statue. After the partners have taken turns and inspected each other as statues, then they interpret as much of what they saw in terms of the kind of person each is.

VERBAL COMMUNICATION

The communication mode which we rely on most often to carry meaning from one person to another is the verbal mode. Everyone who has ever thought about it has come to the insight, however, that there are enormous difficulties in sole reliance on this mode of communication. History is replete with examples of misunderstandings among people who were relying on words to carry meaning. Perhaps the most significant learning that has come out of this experience has been that words themselves do not have meaning. *People* have meaning, and words are simply tools that we use for trying to convey meaning that is idiosyncratic to one person into the idiosyncratic meaning system of the other person. One of the difficulties with words is that we attach to them different experiential and emotional connotations. Words are not always associated with similar experiences or similar feelings on the part of the listener and speaker. Other difficulties encountered in using the verbal mode include the use of jargon, the use of cliches, and the use of specialized vocabularies. It is often said that words have meaning only in context; it can be better said that words only have meaning when they are associated with people in context.

It is not uncommon to observe people attempting to find the right words to say what they mean. There is a myth afoot in the land that there is a way to "say it right." If we can extrapolate from that phenomenon, it is easy to hypothesize that there are some people who, instead of experiencing feelings and sensations, more often experience language: that is, their experience parameters are defined by their vocabularies and their articulateness. The psychologist, Piaget, describing cognitive development in children, says that we go through three phases: concrete, imagic, and abstract. When the little baby first experiences the world, he is incapable of a highly differentiated emotional or sensational experience. He experiences only distress or delight, and his major inputs are concrete, that is, he touches things, he tastes things, he sees things, he hears things, he smells things. As it becomes necessary for him to interact with the world and significant others in his environment in order to have his needs met, he develops a fantasy life, an imagic experience. He can imagine mother when mother is not concretely present. That fantasy life can remain throughout his life. As he develops verbal fluency, he begins to abstract, from physical stimuli which bombard him and from the images that are triggered by those stimuli, meanings which he attaches to his experiences. This abstract experience is a translation of sense data into a meaning system. The difficulty with adults, of course, is that very often we do not let into awareness the physical sensations which we experience. We often mistrust our fantasy lives and tend to be afraid to permit ourselves to dream. We experience the world, then, in an abstract way rather than in a concrete and imagic way. The meanings that we permit ourselves to be aware of are verbal and abstract. What we abstract from the physical stimuli which we experience is dependent on our vocabularies and our reasoning abilities. But those three layers of experience — concrete, imagic and abstract — are going on continuously. People experience concretely, people experience imagically, and people experience the abstracting process which they do when they are awake and attributing meaning to what they see, hear, feel, taste, touch. Not all of these meanings can be carried from one person to another through the verbal mode only.

VERBAL ACTIVITIES

Suggested activities for exploring the verbal mode include the following: Participants form triads and talk for three or four minutes using as many cliches as they can remember. Then each triad is instructed to attempt to come to some agreement on definition of several words, such as uptight, heavy, straight, and funky. Members of the triads are encouraged as a third activity to try to express verbally their here-and-now feeling experience of each other and of themselves. A fourth activity might be to get the members of the triads to attempt to agree on the percentage of time that they think about when they use the word, "usually." Once the triads have reached some consensus on the percentage of time associated with that word, these can be posted on a chalk board or flip chart to illustrate the range of experience that we connote with the word. Similar tasks can be to ask the triads to attempt to come to some agreement on which is wetter, damp or moist. After three or four minutes of discussion the triads can report in a voting manner which of those words connotes the most wetness.

NONVERBAL COMMUNICATION

Recently a number of psychologists and people in the human potential movement have turned their attention to the nonverbal ways in which we share meaning with each other. The science of nonverbal communication is called kinesis. One's nonverbal communication, or body language, is usually involuntary, and the nonverbal signals that one emits often are a more valid source of gleaning information than are the signals which are expressed verbally and symbolically.

There are a number of forms of body language. *Ambulation* is a first form. How one carries his body, whether he swishes or stomps, tells a great deal about who he is and how he is experiencing his environment. We associate different meanings to different ways people carry their bodies from one place to another. *Touching* is perhaps the most powerful nonverbal communication form. We can communicate anger, interest, trust, tenderness, warmth, and a variety of other emotions very potently through touching. People differ, however, in their willingness to touch and be touched. Some people give out nonverbal body signals that say that they do not want to be touched, and there are other people who describe themselves and are described by others as "touchy feely." There are many taboos associated with this form of communication. Persons can learn about their own personalities and self concepts through exploring their reactions to touching and being touched. The skin is the body's largest organ, and through the skin we take in a variety of stimuli. *Eye contact* is a third form of nonverbal communication. We tend to size each other up in terms of trustworthiness through reactions to each other's eye contact. Try a little experiment with yourself. Remember the last time you were driving down the road and passed a hitch-hiker. The odds are very high that you did not look him in the eye if you passed him up. Con men and salesmen understand the power of eye contact and use it to good advantage. Counselors understand that eye contact is a very powerful way of communicating understanding and acceptance. Speakers understand that eye contact is important in keeping an audience interested in one's subject. *Posturing* is a fourth form of nonverbal communication. How one postures the body when seated or standing constitutes a set of potential signals that may communicate how one is experiencing his environment. A person who folds his arms and legs is often said to be defensive. It is sometimes observed that a person under severe psychological threat will assume the body position of a fetus. The seductive person opens his body to other people and postures himself so that his entire body is exposed to the other person. *Tics* constitute a fifth form of nonverbal communication. The involuntary nervous spasms of the body can be a key to one's being threatened. A number of people stammer or jerk when they are being threatened. But these mannerisms can be easily misinterpreted. *Subvocals* constitute a sixth form of nonverbal communication. We say uh, uh, uh, when we are trying to find a word. We say a lot of non-word things in order to carry meaning to another person. We hum, we grunt, we groan and so on. These subvocal noises are not words, but they do carry meaning. *Distancing* is a seventh form of nonverbal communication. Each person is said to have a psychological space around him. If another person invades that space, he may become somewhat tense, alert, or jammed up. We tend to place distance between ourselves and others according to the kinds of relationships that we have and what our motives are toward each other. These reasons for establishing distances are often not displayed openly, but the behavior is, nevertheless, interpreted. *Gesturing* is an eighth form of nonverbal communication. It is said that if we tie a Frenchman's hands, he is mute. We carry a great deal of meaning between each other through the use of gestures. But gestures do not mean the same thing to all people. Sometimes people attach a different emphasis or meaning to the hand signals that we give out. For example, the A-OK sign, a circle formed by the thumb and the first forefinger, is considered very obscene in some other countries. The "We're number one signal" is also considered obscene in some cultures. We give emphasis to our words and we attempt to clarify our meaning through the use of gestures. *Vocalism* constitutes a ninth form of nonverbal communication. As an example, take the sentence, "I love my children." That sentence is meaningless unless it is pronounced. The way that that sentence is packaged vocally determines the signal that it gives to another person. For example, if the emphasis is on the first word, "*I* love my children," the implication is somebody else doesn't. If the emphasis is on the second word, "I *love* my children," a different implication is given, perhaps that some of their behavior gets on my nerves. If the emphasis is placed on the third word, "I love *my* children," the implication is that someone else's children do not receive the same affection. If the emphasis is placed on the final word, "I love my *children*," a fourth implication may be drawn, that is, that there are other people whom I do not love. So the way we carry our words vocally often determines the meaning that another person is likely to infer from our message.

NONVERBAL ACTIVITIES

There is a wide variety of activities that can be used to study nonverbal communication. Suggested for use with this lecture might be nonverbal milling about the room, encountering people in whatever way a person feels comfortable with, pairing off to do a trust walk, forming small groups to do a fantasy object game and so on.

SUMMARY AND IMPLICATIONS

These three modes of communication — symbolic, verbal and nonverbal — are used by every person when he is awake and talking. Symbolic and nonverbal signals are continuous, just as are our experiences of the world in concrete and imagic ways. A steady stream of symbolic signals is being emitted from us to other people. Our bodies, voluntarily or involuntarily, also give out a continuous stream of messages to other people. Those messages, of course, may be different from what we intend. There is also the possibility that our intentions are not highly correlated with our actual gut-level experience. When we are awake and talking with each other, we are giving out three sets of signals. These signals may not be correlated with each other. Our tongues may be saying one thing, our bodies saying another thing, and our symbols may be saying a third thing. True communication results when people share a common meaning experience. If there is a consistency among the modes that one is using to share meaning, then communication is much more likely to occur. When one is whistling in the dark (saying one thing and experiencing another), he is giving out confusing, mixed signals that can be very misleading to another person.

The implications are clear. For communication to occur, there must be a two-way interchange of feelings, ideals, and values. One-way communication is highly inefficient in that there is no way to determine whether what is heard is what is intended. The office memo is a form of one-way communication which is perhaps the least effective medium for transmitting meaning. A second implication is that for true communication to be experienced, it is necessary that there be a feedback process inherent in the communication effort. There needs to be a continuous flow back and forth among the people attempting to communicate, sharing what they heard from each other. The third implication is that the individual person needs to become acutely aware of the range of signals which he is emitting at any given moment. He can learn that by soliciting feedback from the people with whom he is attempting to share meaning.

TRANSCENDENCE THEORY

J. William Pfeiffer

One of the most significant ways in which individuals differ is in their means of managing the dissonance that inevitably occurs in their lives, *i.e.*, an individual's emotional system functions smoothly until such factors as conflict, thwarting of expectations, threats to self esteem, and being confronted with the hostility of others create emotional disharmony. This paper attempts to explore responses to dissonance and to suggest a model for conceptualizing growthful and life-enriching functional accommodations to that inevitable dissonance.

Conflict-engendered dissonance, probably the most prevalent type, is the least easily managed. The Judeo-Christian ethic fosters a pattern of passive-aggressive responses by promoting "turning-the-other-cheek," conflict avoidance, and an attempt to deny the emotional reality of the dissonance. In fact, Western culture engenders guilt in individuals who are unable to manage conflict in the "Christian" manner. It places a potent moral value on pseudo-acceptance rather than open manifestation of hostility. This adjustment, which appears on the surface to be accepting, is, in fact, a system-exhausting suppression of hostility. For the purposes of the transcendence model, this state of passive-aggressive response to dissonance is labeled Level I.

It is at this level of accommodation that most individuals enter a human relations training group. Frequently, the goal of the group is centered around freeing members from the constrictions of their Level I responses in order that they may learn the ability to express hostility overtly. For most group members, this is a difficult step and a true achievement if they find that they are able to respond openly to conflict. For most individuals it means overcoming an ingrained behavior pattern and frequently produces an exhilirating sense of freedom. Much of the euphoria experienced by individuals in their first human relations growth group is a result of the release from the discomfort of suppressed hostility.

It is appropriate that this goal of open expression of emotion should be sought after in the human relations training group, and the trainer who focuses on helping individuals move to Level II responses — overt expression of hostility — is facilitating the growth process. However, the ability to express overt hostility is too often seen as an end product rather than as a means to an end. Progressing from a Level I response to a Level II response is a meaningful and necessary step in an individual opening himself to more self-actualizing behavior. The immediate response to conflict, even though it may only take the form of a cathartic release of emotional toxin, is growthful. There is, however, the potential for an individual to transcend to a more constructive response pattern, Level III — introspective sharing.

To illustrate the three levels of response, we will examine a situation which has high potential for conflict-engendered dissonance: a circumstance involving a lack of punctuality. If I make an appointment with someone for three o'clock and he arrives at three-thirty, I have, according to the transcendence model, three response choices. The conventional response, definitely Level I, is for me to attempt not to show my anger. I may even enter into the "excuse" interaction by being supportive, *e.g.*, reassuring the late comer that I "understand" that "those things" happen or that I have had the same experience myself. However, the hostility which was building up from 3:01 until 3:29 cannot be dissipated by "forgiving" the lateness. It is, at best, suppressed. If I respond to the situation at Level II, I will be openly angry, vent my feelings, and clear my system of the hostility. However, my Level II response does not take the other person's needs into account, and it does not help me understand why the lack of punctuality has upset me so much. My system can be emptied of anger, but I have nothing positive with which to replace it. Moreover, I have probably made the person who has come late angry and/or defensive. He must in turn choose a response. His choice may be Level I, to suppress his anger, in which case it will be difficult for him to function smoothly with me. He may also choose to vent his hostility. What can result is that a potentially important issue for the parties involved will be reduced to "blowing off steam."

Anger is a secondary emotion; it is impotent in that it can supply no data other than the empirical fact of emotional upset. It is imperative that the anger be "turned over" to reveal the primary emotion behind it. In order to find the real issues and deal with them in a productive way, I need to respond on Level III — introspective sharing. If I can keep from suppressing my hostility and can further resist the temptation to dissipate my hostility by becoming openly angry, then, by sharing the fact that I am upset, we can explore together what my concerns really are. What may be revealed by our exchange is that I interpret the other person's lateness as a message from him that I am not a valuable person, not worthwhile and not important. For me, this is a highly threatening implication which may be alleviated by sharing my concerns about my relative worth. The result may be more than just a resolution of the conflict; it may be a growthful resolution.

If I can begin to respond to dissonance with introspective sharing, then I am no longer limited to Level I responses. Revelation of hostile feelings is no longer guilt-inducing or threatening to me. Furthermore, I have transcended the need for Level II responses, although I have learned that I need no longer fear releasing the natural hostility I feel from conflict-engendered dissonance. More importantly, I know that I am no longer uncomfortable about telling others "where I am" emotionally when I am feeling hostile. However, I cannot go from responding at Level I to responding at Level III without first developing the ability to respond at Level II. A Level I person is not able to reveal to another that the hostile feelings exist. He may, in fact, not be able to admit their existence to himself; therefore, there is no way to share feelings which, in one way or another, are being denied.

The weakness of the existing model of human relations group experience results from the too frequent assumption that to master the ability to overtly express feeling data (hostility in particular) is "to arrive" in human potential sense. This goal is desirable but is only the second of three possible levels of response. Only by learning the intermediate ability are we able to transcend to the more constructive level of response as indicated in Figure 1.

Figure 1

ACCOMMODATION OF DISSONANCE

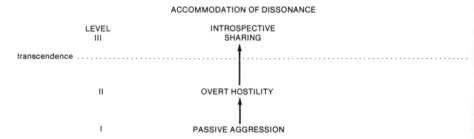

THE MYTH OF INDEPENDENCE

The concept of transcendence is generalizable to other human interaction models. One thrust of human relations training is toward making individuals more independent of others. The dependent person does not take risks for fear of upsetting the dependent relationships he nurtures. Without risk-taking, an individual cannot really grow because he is not free to experiment with behaviors which might provide the means through which he can grow. If the individual is able to move from dependence to independence, then he moves from a state of necessarily high trust to a state of extremely low trust. If he is independent of others, he is self-sustaining and need not trust others for comfort, security, love, or other needs. Independence precludes involvement with others, which might necessitate trust. It is "his own thing," and he alone is responsible for it. Moving from a state of child-like, must-trust-for-survival dependence upon others (the point at which many people enter a human relations group) to a state of independence is a very positive step. It allows the person to risk the rejection or displeasure of others because he is not dependent upon them. This risk-taking often takes the form of freedom to express feelings both verbally and nonverbally. In the joy of his new-found freedom, the newly independent person feels sure that he has come to terms with the world in the most effective way possible, often with disastrous results when he reenters his "real" world after the experience of a human relations training group.

In a sense, once the individual has taken the risk to become independent, his behavior no longer can be considered risk-taking since he has "nothing" (his dependent relationships) to lose by his free expression of himself. His behavior, which may seem to dependent people to be risky, is, in fact, "riskless."

As in the model of transcendence as it relates to dissonance (Figure 1), the dependent state may be labeled Level I, in parallel with the passive-aggressive state, and the independent state, Level II, in parallel with the overtly-hostile state. Level III, then, is the state of interdependence, in which the person is sometimes dependent and sometimes depended-upon. (See Figure 2.)

Figure 2

DEPENDENCY STATES

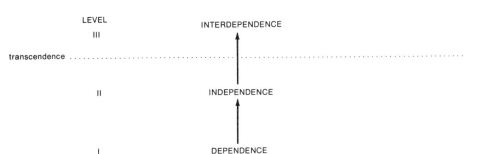

Interdependence is central to Gibb's TORI Theory and is the essential state to which individuals must transcend in order to function most productively in terms of their own needs and the needs of others. As with the parallel state, introspective sharing, the individual cannot go immediately from a state of dependence to a state of interdependence. A dependent person who has never experienced independence is not aware that he has the strength that will allow him to sustain another who needs to be dependent for a time.

Level II has limitations which are very pronounced in terms of sustaining interpersonal relationships with others because the Level II person functions without others. It is only when he transcends to Level III that his caring for others can become caring involvement. Therefore, on Level I, the dependent person lets others care for him but often does not risk expressing his own caring for fear of rejection. When he proceeds to Level II, he can risk expressing his caring; however, he does not trust others enough to allow himself to become vulnerable (in the way he was in his dependent state) by acknowledging his need for being cared for. When he becomes sure of himself in his independent state, he may transcend to interdependence, in which he can become involved in relationships with others in which each depends upon the other for caring and each feels secure in expressing caring. As in the three levels of accommodation of dissonance, the interdependent individual has transcended his need for independence and has moved to a more productive level. Again, it is often the goal in human relations training groups to facilitate independence, and this is a desirable goal; however, it cannot be the end of growth, but merely an important step in the process toward self-actualization.

TRANSCENDENCE IN TRANSACTIONAL ANALYSIS

In a third human interaction model, transactional analysis, Level I can be thought of as the state in which the individual usually has either his *Child* or his *Parent* in control. (His *Adult* exists and is functioning, but it is not well-developed.) The existential position is "I'm not-OK, You're OK." Since the "not-OK" *Child* is the primary factor in determining the individual's behavior, he will probably respond to dissonance in a passive-aggressive way. He cannot risk open hostility with his *Parent* or the *Parent* in others. His archaic *Parent* "tapes" produced by Judeo-Christian ethical demands caution him: "It's not nice to fight!" "Don't argue, just do as you're told!" "I know what's best!" These directives reconfirm his being "not-OK" and leave him frustrated and angry, but silent.

If the *Adult* in the individual has been allowed to develop and is processing reality in an efficient manner, he may transcend to Level II. On this level his *Adult* discovers that there are times for open expression of hostility and that, realistically, the individual cannot be productive if he is continually in the dependent, "not-OK" mode. Therefore, the now-stronger *Adult* will be in control on those occasions when the data of the situation indicate that the dissonance should be acted upon. The *Adult* makes it possible for the *Child* to risk the parental disapproval of both the *Parent* within himself and *Parent* within those with whom he is in conflict. At this second level, the existential positions remains "I'm not-OK, You're OK," though the *Parent* may manifest "I'm OK, You're not-OK" in the games the individual plays to help take the pressure off the "not-OK" *Child*.

If the *Adult* is processing reality in such a way that the individual is able to redefine his existential position as "I'm OK, You're OK," he may transcend to Level III — the emancipated *Adult* (Figure 3.) It is at this level that the individual can experience true intimacy and interdependence, which foster introspective sharing.

See Harris, Thomas, *I'm OK, You're OK*, Harper, New York City, 1969.

Figure 3

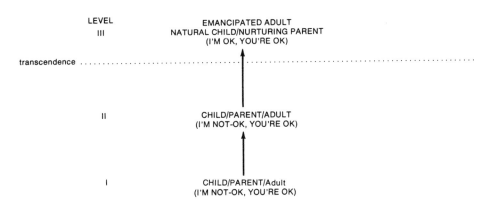

TRANSACTIONAL ANALYSIS

LEVEL   EMANCIPATED ADULT
III   NATURAL CHILD/NURTURING PARENT
(I'M OK, YOU'RE OK)

transcendence

II   CHILD/PARENT/ADULT
(I'M NOT-OK, YOU'RE OK)

I   CHILD/PARENT/Adult
(I'M NOT-OK, YOU'RE OK)

Level III allows the natural *Child* (pre-"not-OK") to emerge once more and encourages the nurturing *Parent*. Both the natural *Child* and the nurturing *Parent* are healthy elements in an intimate, interdependent relationship with "self" and with others who have transcended to Level III. As in the previous illustrations, the individual must achieve Level II before transcendence to Level III is possible. For the individual to become the emancipated *Adult*, he must first have developed a well-functioning *Adult* at the second level. There is no possibility for the "not-OK" *Child* to become the natural, "OK" *Child* again without the reality testing of a strong *Adult*.

RELATING ON LEVELS I, II, AND III

Within the conceptual framework of transcendence, true communication or genuine relating can happen only in transactions between individuals at the same level or between those at contiguous levels of functioning. In other words, an individual engaged in introspective sharing on an interdependent, emancipated-*Adult* level cannot truly communicate with a passive-aggressive, dependent individual whose irrational *Child* or prejudiced, perhaps punitive *Parent* is in control: there is no common ground for understanding to occur. A Level II individual is able to communicate with a Level I individual because the "not-OK" *Child* is a part of both of them: this is their common ground. Likewise, a dependent individual cannot relate in an interdependent way since he is not yet aware of his ability or has not yet developed his ability to function independently. Communication will break down when it is essential for him to perform an independent function within the interchange. He must first share the capability of independence in common with the other individual. Finally, since according to the present theory, the passive-aggressive individual denies his hostile feelings, he cannot communicate with an individual who needs to share feelings of hostility in order to achieve an introspective level of conflict resolution. Figure 4 illustrates parallel nature of the three models of transcendence.

Figure 4

TRANSCENDENCE MODELS

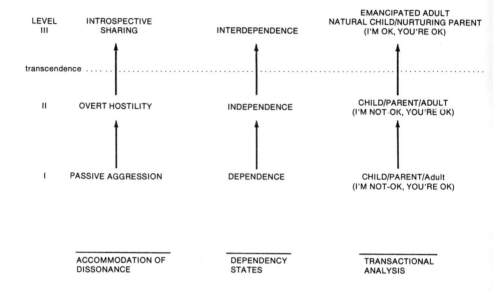

LEVEL III	INTROSPECTIVE SHARING	INTERDEPENDENCE	EMANCIPATED ADULT NATURAL CHILD/NURTURING PARENT (I'M OK, YOU'RE OK)

transcendence . . . . .

II	OVERT HOSTILITY	INDEPENDENCE	CHILD/PARENT/ADULT (I'M NOT OK, YOU'RE OK)

I	PASSIVE AGGRESSION	DEPENDENCE	CHILD/PARENT/Adult (I'M NOT-OK, YOU'RE OK)

ACCOMMODATION OF DISSONANCE	DEPENDENCY STATES	TRANSACTIONAL ANALYSIS

CONCLUSION

Transcendence may be viewed in light of an adolescent's rites of passage. He asserts his independence and becomes overtly hostile when conflicted. He is, however, still essentially a child who is slowly developing a discerning, responsible, decision-making capability that will finally result in his becoming mature. He is actively testing and sorting through all the ethics, mores, and disciplines that he has been asked to take for granted from birth. From time to time he may appear to be rejecting the valuable with the worthless, the proven judgements with the prejudices. He "trusts no one over thirty" and trusts peers only as projections of himself. Yet, without this turmoil, which is in effect a complex computer program which must somehow be made to "run," there is no way for his emergence to be complete. If the process is thwarted, the individual may never reach Level II, the keystone to maturity, much less Level III, where personal fulfillment lies.

The human relations training group facilitator must continue to focus on the development of Level II capabilities in participants since this is an essential step in the self-actualizing process. However, he needs also to introduce the concept of Level III responses and work toward this goal with those participants who are ready to make the transcendence.

CONTRACTS IN ENCOUNTER GROUPS

Gerard Egan

The notion of contract is offered here as one possible way of clearing up some of the confusion associated with both the conceptualization and the practice of encounter groups. Some critical, ethical and procedural issues can be clarified and handled, I believe, in a contractual framework. Since this is a handbook, this article will be relatively short and practical. I deal more extensively with contracts in sensitivity training elsewhere (Egan, 1970, 1971).

The notion of contract, though not widespread, is not a new one in the psychology of human encounter. Pratt and Tooley (1964, 1966) and Shapiro (1968) suggest contractual models to conceptualize both interpersonal transactions and the relationships a person has with himself. For Pratt and Tooley all of life is a patterning of contractual arrangements which men make with themselves and with others. Contracts, then, become the instrumentalities for both the creation and exchange of values among men. They go so far as to say that "men are their contracts" (1966, p. 882). Shapiro (1968) suggests that an important source of difficulty in close interpersonal relationships is the lack of explicit interpersonal agreements: "It is often difficult to get people to say openly and explicitly what they want and need from one another" (p. 172). It is difficult for participants to do this in an encounter group, even when this is one of the explicit goals of the group. In short, it is suggested here that contractual clarity, in both intra- and interpersonal relationships, is a useful, if not necessary, foundation for effective interpersonal living.

CONTRACTS AND THERAPY

Contracts have been used, however sparingly, to give greater clarity and definition to the structures and processes involved in what Truax and Mitchell (1968) call "human encounters that change behavior," the encounters that constitute counseling and psychotherapy. Goldstein, Heller, and Sechrest (1966) have combed the research literature in various areas of psychology in search for hypotheses with respect to procedures that would increase the effectiveness of therapeutic encounters. One of their hypotheses states that "giving patients prior information about the nature of psychotherapy, the theories underlying it, and the techniques to be used will facilitate progress in psychotherapy" (p. 245). They go on to say that they find it "remarkable (I believe they mean "deplorable") that psychotherapists have apparently been unwilling to impart to their patients more than a little of the process of psychotherapy" (p. 245). Few therapists spell out the therapeutic contract, especially a contract that includes not only patient but also therapist and situation variables. In a word, the client looking for therapy of a traditional stamp must too often buy a pig-in-a-poke. Encounter groups, too, fall into the general category of "human encounters that change behavior." Its practitioners would be well advised to avoid mistakes similar to those of the counselor or therapist.

Contracts, whether they are called that or not, govern much of the behavior of those engaged in "peer self-help psychotherapy groups" (Hurvitz, 1970) such as Alcoholics Anonymous. For instance, the participants in groups such as these agree (contract) to submit themselves to a good deal of social pressure to change their behavior, but they do so in return for the fellowship of the group and the promise of a better life.

Behavioral modification programs use "behavior contracts" (Krumboltz and Thoresen, 1969) to structure the administration of reinforcements. For instance, all those concerned with a particular behavior problem (e.g., disruptive student, teacher, principal, and parents) meet with the counselor to commit themselves to a contract designed to change behavior (in this case, the behavior of the disruptive student). The student learns that he will be dismissed from class as soon as he disrupts it. The principal commits himself merely to checking the student out of school without further comment. The parents agree not to administer further verbal or behavioral punishment at home. The contract clarifies and controls the situation. Beneficial punishment (dismissal from class) works because the contract prevents it from being contaminated by irrelevant forms of punishment. The student learns to control his behavior because ultimately he does not want to leave the classroom.

OPERATIONALIZING THE GROUP GOALS

Peter Drucker in his *Age of Discontinuity* (1969) claims that many organizations (education, government, church) remain ineffective because they do not have clear criteria by which they can judge success or failure. There is a great deal of evidence in the psychological literature indicating that groups achieve a high degree of operationality only through clear goals and clear means to these goals. March and Simon (1958) distinguish between operational and nonoperational goals. A nonoperational goal is one that is quite general in itself and is not realized by a particular sequence of group activities. For instance, a common encounter-group goal, "to become sensitive to others," is not very concrete. To become effective it must receive some kind of operational definition and then the kinds of interpersonal transactions that lead to such "sensitivity" (however it is defined) must be spelled out. Contracts can define encounter-group experiences and delineate in concrete, operational terms the goals of such groups.

Raven and Rietsema (1957) found that members with a clear picture of the group goal and the paths to it had a deeper involvement with these goals, more sympathy with group emotions, and a greater readiness to accept influence from the group than those who were unclear about goals and means. Deeper involvement in the encounter-group process, greater sensitivity to the emotional dimensions of the group, and an openness to influence from others are certainly assets in encounter groups. Contracts can clarify in concrete, operational terms the kinds of interaction geared to achieving the goals of the encounter group.

Furthermore, there is a great deal of evidence that cooperation (*not* its look-alikes — conformity, dependency) rather than competition makes for smoother performance and increased productivity in a variety of group situations. There is also a great deal of evidence that cohesiveness in groups is enhanced if members work together for common rather than mutually exclusive and individual ends (Lott and Lott, 1965). Groups whose members are concerned primarily with self-oriented rather than group-oriented needs are relatively ineffective (Fouriezos, Hutt, and Guetzkow, 1950). However, if the members of a group commit themselves by contract to the same goals and processes, clearly defined, before they enter the group, then it is more likely that they will cooperate with one another. Since they are working for common goals, it is also more likely that they will become cohesive more quickly. And cohesive groups are generally more productive than noncohesive groups (Lott and Lott, 1965).

CONTRACTS IN ENCOUNTER GROUPS

A contract can help stimulate a high degree of operationality in the encounter group in various ways.

(1) *Definition of the group experience.* Good ethics suggests that the prospective member has a right to know what he is getting himself into. This is especially true in view of the bewildering variety of groups presently available. Even though two different group experiences are given the same name — let us say "encounter group" — there is no assurance that one experience will resemble the other, for differing sponsoring agencies and different group leaders have different conceptions of encounter-group process. If the sponsoring agency does not divulge the nature of the experience and thereby asks the prospective client to buy a pig-in-a-poke (even a succulent pig), then the buyer has every reason to beware.

Ethics aside, the logic of commitment demands that prospective members know what kind of group they are about to join. If they know what kind of experience to expect, they can commit themselves to it in a way that would otherwise be impossible. It is my hypothesis that such clarity would insure a higher degree of what Golembiewski (1962) calls psychological (participative) rather than merely formal (spectator, nonparticipative) membership in the group. It is an agonizing experience to try to integrate a couple of people into an encounter group who did not realize what they were getting themselves into. The energies the group uses to deal with the uncommitted could more profitably be used elsewhere.

(2) *High visibility rather than ambiguity as a group value.* A number of theoreticians see "planned goallessness" as essential to a variety of laboratory-training groups (e.g., Benne, 1964; Bennis, 1964). The group, it is hypothesized, must begin goalless since one of the principal goals of the group is to *create* its own goals. The interactions involved in this creative process contribute to the growth of the participants. Tuckman (1965) sees this struggle for viable goals as essential to the establishment of group cohesiveness: "All the relevant T-group development studies see the stage of conflict and polarization as being followed by a stage characterized by the reduction of conflict, resolution of the polarized issues, and establishment of group harmony in the place of disruption. It is a 'patching-up' phase in which group norms and values emerge" (p. 392).

In practice, however, I do not think that this is an accurate picture of present-day encounter-group experience. Most groups begin with a greater specificity of goals than is admitted. The sponsoring agency, the group leader, even the participants themselves — especially as participants become more and more sophisticated with respect to encounter-group theory and practice — all have certain goals and procedures in mind, even though they might be vague and undifferentiated. Goals, however hidden, abound! To assume, then, that such a group starts goalless is not realistic. What happens is that a great deal of effort goes into sharing and refining goals already possessed. I find one practical difficulty with such a procedure. The members often spend so much time elaborating goals and structures to provide a framework within which they can interact with one another that they often have no time left to engage in the contract so painfully elaborated. It is true that the formulation of a viable interactional contract often demands intense interpersonal interactions and is often quite growthful. But this process, I believe, belongs in a kind of laboratory experience that differs from the encounter-group laboratory. Slater (1966) in his *Microcosm* discusses an academic laboratory experience the goal of which is to learn about the nature of small-group formation and interaction through the actual process of becoming such a group. "To learn about groups by becoming a group," however, is not the goal of the encounter group as I see it. Ambiguity is essential to Slater's experiment but not to the encounter group. The primary goal of an encounter group is the development of relationships among the participants, not the elaboration of an interactional contract. The least that may be said is that goallessness is neither an accurate nor necessarily a desired state of affairs at the beginning of an encounter-group experience and that, whatever the advantages of a goallessness approach, it is not the only viable approach to laboratory experiences. I advocate high visibility in small groups as a way of preventing manipulation on the part of the sponsoring agency, the leader, or the participants themselves. A simple contract both defines the experience and allows the participants to get to the substantive work of the group more quickly.

One of the reasons why planned ambiguity is deemed essential to the encounter-group process is that ambiguity breeds anxiety and anxiety is a drive that keeps members at the work of the group. There is no doubt that a moderate degree of anxiety is helpful in groups. The group that is too comfortable gets little or nothing done. However, there is no reason why ambiguity should be the source of anxiety in the group. If the members enter the group by contract, if they see the kinds of behavior expected of them, then the source of anxiety is the contract itself. I think that contract anxiety is preferable to anxiety stemming from ambiguity because the former is more real. It serves as a drive toward goals that are clearly defined.

The contract can be dramatized in various ways. It need not be just a written document. One way of dramatizing the contract is to show prospective participants or participants videotapes or movies of good group interaction. However, care should be taken not to raise anxiety too much. For instance, showing a movie such as Rogers' *Journey into Self* may be too anxiety arousing for neophyte encounter-group participants. A series of short videotapes may be more useful. These tapes can show the various phases in the life of a group (samples of these phases, rather, for they should be short) and thus serve as a graded series of stimuli.

(3) *Linking concrete interactional processes to concrete goals.* In the encounter group the contract should outline the procedural goals and the kinds of interactions appropriate to the pursuit of these goals. One reason for poor research results in the investigation of encounter groups is a lack of goal clarity: the goals of the sponsoring agency or facilitator, the goals of individual participants, and the interaction and integration of the two. It is difficult to design an experiment when outcome is not defined operationally and when the means for achieving a particular set of goals are not clearly delineated.

Perhaps the best way to demonstrate what I mean by linking concrete interactional processes to concrete goals is to outline a sample contract. The following contract, then, is addressed to the prospective participant.

AN ENCOUNTER-GROUP CONTRACT

GOALS

The general goal. The general goal of this group is the establishment of an intimate community within which the members are free to investigate their interpersonal styles and experiment with interpersonal behaviors that are not normally a part of that style.

A general procedural goal. The procedural goal is simple to state but difficult to put into practice. It is this: Each member of this group is to try to establish and develop a relationship of some intimacy with each of the other members of the group. Each member should come to know each other member in more than a superficial way. This goal is difficult to put into practice

188

because it means that each person must take the initiative to go out of himself and contact each of the other members of the group. It is not assumed here that you will be successful in establishing a relationship in each case. However, you will learn a great deal from both your successes and your failures.

Diagnosis as a goal. As each member interacts with the others he both observes his own behavior and receives feedback with respect to the impact he is having on others. This feedback gives him the opportunity to get a clearer picture of and deeper feeling for his interactional style. In this process the participant can learn much about both his interpersonal strengths and his interpersonal weaknesses.

Experimentation with "new" behavior as a goal. As each member learns more about how effective or ineffective he is in contacting others, he can attempt to change those behaviors that prevent him from involving himself creatively with others. This, for him, would be "new" behavior. For instance, if a participant tends to control others and keep them from interacting with him by monopolizing the conversation, he can change by inviting others to dialogue. The person who tends to fall silent in groups experiments with "new" behavior by speaking up.

Personal goals. The goals outlined briefly are the contractual goals of the group. However, each member comes with certain personal goals. These goals and the ways they might conflict with the stated goals of the group should be shared openly with the other participants, for the group will tend to stagnate if individual members pursue their own "hidden agendas."

INTERACTIONS

Certain interactions are common to all encounter groups. One function of this contract is to point out these interactional "values." If all the participants commit themselves to these values, then the chance of establishing a cooperative community in which the above goals can be pursued is heightened considerably.

Self-disclosure. Self-disclosure in the encounter group is important, but not an end in itself. If the other is to get to know me, enter into a relationship with me, I must reveal myself to him in some way. The participant, therefore, should be open primarily about what is happening to himself as he goes about the business of contacting others and trying to establish relationships with them. "Secret dropping" may be sensational but it is not a value in the group. The participant is important, not his secrets. If a participant reveals his life outside the group, he should do so because it is relevant to what is happening here-and-now and because it helps him establish and develop relationships more effectively in the group. It is up to each participant to choose what he wants to disclose about himself in order to establish contact with others.

Expression of feeling. Second, the contracts call for expression of feeling. This does not mean that the participant is asked to manufacture feeling and emotion. Rather he is asked not to suppress the feelings that naturally arise in the give-and-take of the group, but to deal with them as openly and as honestly as possible. Suppressed emotions tend eventually either to explode or to dribble out in unproductive ways.

Support. Third, and perhaps most important, the encounter contract calls for support, whatever name it may be given — respect, nonpossessive warmth, acceptance, love, care, concern, "being for" the other, or a combination of all of these. Without a climate of support encounter groups can degenerate into the destructive caricatures often described in the popular press. On the other hand, if a person receives adequate support in the group, then he can usually tolerate a good deal of strong interaction. Without a climate of support there can be no climate of trust. Without trust there can be no intimate community. Support can be expressed in many different ways, both verbally and nonverbally, but it must be *expressed* if it is to have impact on the other. Support that stays locked up inside a participant is no support at all.

Confrontation. If there is an adequate climate of support, of "being for" one another, then the participants can benefit greatly by learning how to challenge one another effectively. Confrontation does not mean "telling the other off." This is merely punishment, and punishment is rarely growthful. The participant should confront only if he follows these two simple rules. (1) Confront only if you care about the other and your confrontation is a sign of that care. (2) And confront in order to get involved with the other, as a way of establishing a relationship with him. Remember, it is possible to confront another with his unused strengths as well as his demonstrated weaknesses. There is evidence that the former is a more growthful process. Remember also that your confrontation will be better received if you first build up a base of support for the other.

Response to confrontation. Most of us, when confronted, react either by defending ourselves or by attacking our confronter — or both. The encounter contract, however, calls for something more growthful than defense and attack — self-exploration in the context of the encounter community. "What you say disturbs me, but I think that I should explore it with you and the others here" is not an easy response, but it can be very growthful. Both the one who confronts and the one being confronted should learn to check out the substance of the confrontation with the other members of the group.

PROCEDURAL RULES

Certain procedural rules help make for a climate of greater contact and immediacy in the group. The following rules, then, govern the interaction:

(1) *The here-and-now.* Deal with the here-and-now. When you talk about things that are happening or have happened outside the group, do so only if what you are saying can be made relevant to your interaction with *these* people in *this* group. The there-and-then can prove quite boring, especially if it is not helping you establish and develop relationships in the group. This does not mean that you may never deal with your life outside the group, but you should deal with it in such a way as to pursue the goals of this group.

(2) *Initiative.* Do not wait to be contacted by others. Take the initiative, reach out, contact others. The importance of initiative cannot be overstressed.

(3) *Speak to individuals.* As a general rule, speak to individual members rather than to the entire group. After all, the goal is to establish and develop relationships with individual members. Speeches to the entire group do not often contribute to this end. Furthermore, they tend to become too long, abstract, and boring. The group cursed with consecutive monologues is in bad straits.

(4) *"Owning" the interactions of others.* Part of taking initiative is "owning" the interactions of others. In the group when two people speak to each other, it is not just a private interaction. Other participants may and even should "own" the interaction not just by listening but by contributing their own thoughts and feelings. Each member should try to own as many of the interactions as possible.

(5) *Speak for yourself in the group.* Avoid using the word "we." When you use "we," you are speaking for the group. Rather speak for yourself. The word "we" tends to polarize; it sets the person spoken to off from the group. Furthermore, when you are speaking of yourself use the pronoun "I" rather than its substitutes — "we," "you," "one," "people," etc. Strangely enough, the pronouns you use can make a difference in the group.

(6) *Say it in the group.* A wise person has said that there is one excellent criterion for determining the level of trust in the group: Do people say in the group what they tend to say outside the group (to wives, friends, participants from the group to whom they feel closer). As much as possible, then, say what you mean *in* the group.

190

LEADERSHIP

The facilitator is in the group because he is interested in interpersonal growth. While it is true that he brings certain special resources to the group because of his theoretical background and experience, his purpose is to put whatever resources he has at the service of the group. He subscribes to the same contract as the other members do. In the beginning the facilitator will be more active, for one of his functions is to model the kinds of behavior called for by the contract. Another way of putting this is that he will strive to be a good member from the beginning. Another one of his functions is to invite others to engage in contractual behavior. However, the ideal is that whatever leadership (in terms of contractual behavior) he manifests should become diffused in the group. Eventually in the group there should be no leader but a high degree of shared leadership. This will be the case if individual members take the initiative to contact one another according to the terms of this contract.

CONTRACTS AND RESEARCH

It is a truism that macro- as opposed to molecular research is very difficult in the behavioral sciences. This is certainly true with respect to research in the areas of laboratory training in general and the encounter group in particular. The most obvious problem is control. Laboratories use a wide variety of techniques — for example, lectures, exercises, both verbal and nonverbal, and different kinds of face-to-face conversation. Trainers use a variety of styles: some are quite passive, while others are very active. Laboratories take place in a variety of settings with different kinds of populations — e.g. volunteers who attend a two week residential laboratory, students in courses in interpersonal relations, nonvolunteers representing a cross-section of an organization, volunteers in weekly local groups conducted by different kinds of leaders. It is practically impossible to replicate studies, for descriptions of what takes place in the training situation are either non-existent or too sparse to be meaningful. The goals for different kinds of group experiences are often extremely vague — and this naturally affects outcome studies. The processes considered necessary to achieve even these vague goals are not given any kind of operational definition.

If research is to be done and if the possibility of replication is to become a reality, then the object of study must be some kind of unitary phenomenon. Contracts delineate goals, leadership styles, and the kinds of interaction in which members engage. In short, contracts offer the possibility of a unitary phenomenon. A wide variety of contracts would produce a wide variety of group experiences, but each kind could be replicated in some meaningful sense of that term.

Most outcome studies deal with group scores. The problem with group scores, however, is that individual differences are lost. If a dozen people attend a group experience and six of them participate fully while the other six remain spectators, it is unfair to lump all together in assessing the outcome of the experience. Mere exposure to the group experience, at least in my opinion, is not expected to do anything. A contract approach makes it possible to measure, again in some meaningful way, the degree of each member's participation, for there are well-defined criteria of participation. High-participators should differ in outcome from low-participators.

A contract approach to self-actualization through the small-group experience might not appeal to some, but at least it does standardize the experience to some degree. If such standardization is impossible, then so is research, and all that an interested party can do is listen to the testimony, both positive and negative, given by those who engage in small-group experiences.

GROUP FACILITATION WITH CONTRACTS AND A CHECKLIST

The sample contract is not a definitive outline of what encounter groups should be.

Obviously there can be a variety of contracts leading to a wide variety of group experiences. In some groups the contract can take the place of a formal leader. Leaderless groups that are filled with leadership are most exciting.

The contract is not meant to control members, to restrict their freedom unduly. Its purpose is rather to channel the energies of the group toward specific goals. For instance, in the contract outlined above, each participant still has a good deal of *lebensraum*. While the contract, for example, indicates that self-disclosure is a value, it does not dictate either the content or the level of self-disclosure. Each participant must determine for himself how and to what degree he is going to reveal himself in the group. Self-disclosure should be an organic process arising from the participant's desire to achieve the overall goal of the laboratory and from the give-and-take involved in the process of establishing and developing relationships.

One of the needs a participant has as he enters the group is to know whether he is successful or not. He has to have some way of knowing whether he is achieving or not. But without explicit group and/or personal goals, this is difficult, if not impossible. The contract provides each participant with some kind of criterion for determining success or failure.

The following is a checklist I have devised to help me understand what is taking place in groups as I supervise student facilitators. But the checklist has much wider use. I give a few copies of it to both facilitator and group members and have them use it to check out their own behavior several times during the life of the group. The list helps the participants identify areas of strength and areas of weakness. This is at the heart of the diagnostic process mentioned above and provides starting points for experimentation with "new" forms of behavior within the group. For instance, because of the contract and the checklist many people come to realize in a rather dramatic way just how passive they are in interpersonal situations. They realize that they hardly ever initiate interactions. Others must come to them; they are reactors rather than actors in life.

192

ENCOUNTER GROUP CHECKLIST

1. *Tone.* What is the tone of the group (spontaneous, dead, cautious, etc.)?

2. *Commitment to goals.* Answer the following questions in view of the general procedural goal: Each member is to attempt to establish and develop a relationship of some intimacy with each of the other members.
   a. Are members working at establishing relationships with one another?
   b. Have a number of significant relationships emerged?
   c. Are relationships becoming deeper or remaining superficial?
   d. Is there consensus that the group is moving forward?

3. *Initiative.*
   a. Do members actively reach out and contact one another or do they have to be pushed into it?
   b. Is there some risk-taking behavior in the group?

4. *A climate of immediacy.*
   a. Do members deal with the here-and-now rather than the there-and-then?
   b. Are there a large number of one-to-one conversations as opposed to speeches to the group?
   c. Is the content of interactions concrete and specific rather than general and abstract?
   d. Do members use "I" when they mean I instead of substitutes (one, you, etc)?
   e. Do members avoid speaking for the group, using the pronoun "we"?

5. *Cooperation.*
   a. *Cooperation.* Is there a climate of cooperation rather than one of antagonism, passivity or competition?
   b. *Polarizations.* Are there polarizations in the group that affect the quality of interactions (e.g. leaders vs members, active members vs passive members, etc.)?
   c. *Owning interactions.* Do members tend to "own" the dyadic interactions that take place in the group? When two members are having difficulty talking to each other, do other group members help them? Do those having difficulty seek the help of others?
   d. *Check it out.* Do the members, when they confront one another check out their feelings and evaluations with other members?
   e. *Hostility.* Is there any degree of hostility in the group? Does the group or do individual members wallow in it or do they seek to resolve it? Is there covert hostility? If so, what is done to bring it out into the open?

6. *The principal modes of interaction.*
   a. *Self-disclosure.*
   Was it appropriate, that is, geared to establishing here-and-now relationships of some intimacy?
   Was then-and-there disclosure related to the here-and-now, that is, specifically to this

group or one's relationship to this group?

Was it related to the process of encountering (establishing relationships) rather than counseling (dealing with there-and-then problems)?

Was it meaningful disclosure or superficial?

b. *Expression of feeling.*

Did people deal with feelings and emotions?

Did expression of feeling help establish and develop relationships?

Were feelings authentic or forced?

Are participants able to express themselves spontaneously?

c. *Support.*

Was there an adequate climate of respect, acceptance, support?

Were members active in giving support or is the climate of support principally a permissive, passive thing?

Did the group prevent any member from clawing at anyone?

d. *Confrontation.*

Were people willing to challenge one another?

Did members confront one another because they cared about one another and wanted to get involved?

Was there any degree of merely punitive confrontation?

Is conflict allowed in the group? Is it dealt with creatively or merely allowed to degenerate into hostility?

Is confrontation really an invitation to another to move into the group in a more fruitful way? Do the members take the initiative to invite one another into the group in various ways?

e. *Response to confrontation.*

Did members reply to responsible confrontation by self-exploration rather than defensiveness or counterattack?

If the person confronted found it difficult to accept what he heard, did he check it out with other members of the group? Did the other members take the initiative to confirm confrontation without "ganging up" on the one being confronted?

7. *Trust.*

a. Is the level of trust deepening in the group?

b. Do members say in the group what they say outside?

c. If there are problems with trust, do the members deal with them openly?

8. *Nonverbal communication.* What do members say nonverbally that they do not say verbally (e.g. concerning their anxiety, boredom, withdrawal, etc.)?

9. *Leadership.*

a. Does the facilitator model contractual behavior?

b. Was the facilitator acting too much like a leader, that is, trying to get others to do things rather than doing things with others?

c. Is leadership becoming diffused in the group? Or are the members sitting back and leaving most of the initiating to the facilitator? Who are those who are exercising leadership?

d. If necessary, did the facilitator see to it that no one became the object of destructive behavior on the part of others?

10. *Exercises* (if any).

   a. If used were they appropriate? Did they fit into what was happening?

   b. Were they well introduced? Were the instructions clear?

   c. Were they forced upon an unwilling group?

   d. Is there too much dependence on exercises?

   e. Does the group always flee exercises even though they might be helpful?

   f. Did the exercises used accomplish their goals?

11. *Anxiety*.

   a. What is the anxiety level of the group? Too high? Too low?

   b. Is there always some motivating tension or is the group too comfortable?

12. *Modes of flight and problematic interactions*.

   a. What are the principal ways in which the group as a whole took flight?

   b. In what ways are individuals resisting the process of the group?

   c. Do members continue to claim that "they do not know what to do"?

   d. *Analysis.* Do members spend a great deal of time analyzing past interactions (an ounce of interaction followed by a pound of analysis)?

   e. *Interpretation.* Do members tend to interpret and hypothesize about one anothers' behavior instead of meeting one another directly?

   f. *Quiet members.* Did quieter members move into the group on their own initiative? If not, how was the problem handled? Do individuals or the group rationalize nonparticipation?

   g. *Control.* Are there members who control the group by specific behaviors (e.g. by always having the focus of attention on themselves, by cynicism, by hostility, by silence, etc.)?

   h. *Pairing.* Were coalitions formed that impeded the progress of the group?

   i. *Tacit decisions.* Has the group made any tacit decisions which affect the quality of the interaction (e.g., not to discuss certain subjects, not to allow conflict, not to get too close, etc.)?

   j. *Dealing-with-one*.
   Does the group tend to deal with one person at a time?
   If so, is that person usually consulted about being the center of attention for an extended period of time?
   Does dealing-with-one mean that others may not contact one another until the person in the focus of attention is "finished"?
   Do some people withdraw from the interaction when one person is dealt with for an extended period of time?
   If this is a problem for the group, is it dealt with openly?

13. What is needed to improve the quality of the group?

Obviously other kinds of checklists could be drawn up for different kinds of groups. The checklist should be related to the goals — overriding, procedural, and interactional — of the group.

REFERENCES

Benne, K. D. From polarization to paradox. In L. P. Bradford, J. R. Gibb, and K. D. Benne (Eds.), *T-group theory and laboratory method*. New York: Wiley, 1964. pp. 216-247.

Bennis, W. G. Patterns and vicissitudes in T-Group development. In L. P. Bradford, J. R. Gibb, and K. D. Benne (Eds.), *T-group theory and laboratory method*. New York: Wiley, 1964. pp. 80-135.

Drucker, P. F. *The age of discontinuity*. New York: Harper and Row, 1969.

Egan, G. *Encounter: Group processes for interpersonal growth*. Monterey, Calif.: Brooks/Cole, 1970.

Egan, G. Contractual approaches to the modification of behavior in encounter groups. In W. Hunt (Ed.), *Human behavior and its control*. Cambridge, Mass.: Schenkman, 1971.

Fouriezos, N. T., Hutt, M. L., & Guetzkow, H. Measurement of self-oriented needs in discussion groups. *Journal of Abnormal and Social Psychology*, 1950, *45*, 682-690.

Goldstein, A. P., Heller, K., & Sechrest, L. B. *Psychotherapy and the psychology of behavior change*. New York: Wiley, 1966.

Golembiewski, R. T. *The small group: An analysis of research concepts and operations*. Chicago: University of Chicago Press, 1962.

Hurvitz, N. Peer self-help psychotherapy groups and their implications for psychotherapy. *Psychotherapy: Theory, Research and Practice*, 1970, *7*, 41-49.

Krumboltz, J. D., & Thoresen, C. E. *Behavioral counseling*. New York: Holt, Rinehart & Winston, 1969.

Lott, A. J., & Lott, B. E. Group cohesiveness as interpersonal attraction: A review of relationships with antecedent and consequent variables. *Psychological Bulletin*, 1965, *64*, 259-309.

March, J. G., & Simon, H. A. *Organizations*. New York: Wiley, 1958.

Pratt, S., & Tooley, J. Contract psychology and the actualizing transactional field. *International Journal of Social Psychiatry*, 1964. (Special Ed. No. 1; Congress Issue: Theoretical Aspects and Research).

Pratt, S., & Tooley, J. Human actualization teams: the perspective of contract psychology. *American Journal of Orthopsychiatry*, 1966, *36*, 881-895.

Raven, B. H., & Rietsema, J. The effects of varied clarity of goal and group path upon the individual and his relation to the group. *Human Relations*, 1957, *10*, 29-44.

Shapiro, S. B. Some aspects of a theory of interpersonal contracts. *Psychological Reports*, 1968, *22*, 171-183.

Slater, P. E. *Microcosm: Structural, psychological, and religious evolution in groups*. New York: Wiley, 1966.

Truax, C. B., & Mitchell, K. M. The psychotherapeutic and the psychonoxious: Human encounters that change behavior. *Buffalo Studies*, 1968, *4*, 55-92.

Tuckman, B. W. Developmental sequence in small groups. *Psychological Bulletin*, 1965, *63*, 384-399.

196

OPENNESS, COLLUSION AND FEEDBACK

J. William Pfeiffer and John E. Jones

"Tell it like it is" is a saying that is popular today. It is based on the assumption that complete honesty is a preferred human condition, but it might better be said, "Don't tell it like it isn't." Leveling, or responding with absolute openness, is sometimes inappropriate and harmful. What is to be avoided is deceiving other persons. This paper focuses on problems of openness as they are experienced in human communication. The intent is to suggest a way for genuine communication to take place while preventing systems from being blown apart by insensitivity.

THE OPEN-CLOSED CONTINUUM

OPENNESS. Each of us is a part of a number of interpersonal systems. There are interlocking networks of people in our families, our work staffs, our social circles, etc., and these systems are maintained in part by commonly held expectations about appropriate behavior. Each of the systems within which we interact with other persons can be tensed or even "blown" by too much openness. Unrestricted, untethered "truth" can create high levels of anxiety and can cause persons in a system to become less able to accomplish their goals. Stream-of-consciousness is a valid literary technique, but it can be highly dysfunctional in interpersonal relationships.

An example of *inappropriate openness* is depicted in the movie, *Bob & Carol & Ted & Alice.* Bob and Carol have just "turned on" to themselves in a weekend growth center experience, and they are having dinner at a restaurant with the other couple. Carol pours out her feelings in such a way as to embarrass Ted and Alice. She confronts the waiter with feeling data and then follows him to the kitchen, where she apologizes to him in front of his co-workers — increasing his embarrassment. She is displaying insensitive sensitivity; that is, she is aware of herself but oblivious of the impact she is having on others. This phenomenon of being more expressive of oneself than the situation will tolerate we have labeled "Carolesque" openness. A person who displays Carolesque behavior is "in touch" with his own feelings to the exclusion of any awareness of the impact of his behavior on others.

Destructive openness can result from an inordinate value being placed upon "telling it like it is," from insensitivity to the recipients of the communication, or from a desire to be punitive. If the effect of open self-disclosure is to make another person defensive or highly anxious, there is a high potential for destructiveness. If the open communication is markedly judgmental of others, the chance that it will be harmful is increased. For example, a husband and wife may be out for the evening, and during the course of the conversation, she asks how he likes the new dress she is wearing. His honest reaction may be highly negative; however, if he is frank, it will be a "brutal frankness." Not only will she be hurt over his rejection of her choice of attire, but she will experience great frustration in that the situation is not modifiable since it is too late for her to change to another outfit. Total openness could only ruin the evening for both of them. The husband need not be "dishonest" if he uses some non-feeling words such as "striking" or "different" in response to her question and chooses to deal with his negative reaction to the dress at a more appropriate time. He hasn't told it "like it is," but neither has he told it "like it isn't" — true inauthenticity.

A number of motives may be served by sharing one's feelings and ideas with others. One's intent may be to help, to impress, to seduce, to punish, to exploit, or to cathart. The reasons behind the sharing, as well as its effects on the listener(s), determine the ethicality of self-disclosure. Openness *qua* openness is not justifiable except in a human context in which readiness and willingness for honest interchange have been assessed. Choosing what to share in interaction with another person or system is purposive behavior. Therefore, openness can be helpful or harmful, effective or ineffective, appropriate or inappropriate, depending on one's motives, on one's ability to be sensitive to the probable effects of the sharing, and on the readiness of the recipient(s) of the data. It may be hypothesized that a person's capacity for openness with himself regarding his motives for open communication defines a limit on his ability to be sensitive to the needs of the situation. If a person deceives himself about his aim, he can probably also distort the cues he gets from other people in the system. On the other hand, when a person is conscious of having a hidden agenda, his communication is not likely to be genuine in that he may "sit on" a large part of his reaction.

The concept of ethical authenticity, which promotes growth in a system, we have termed *strategic openness*. Strategic openness means determining how much open data flow the system can stand and then giving it about a ten percent boost — enough to stretch it but not to shatter it. This risk-taking is an attempt to open up the system by mild pushing and is far more effective than attempting to "drag it kicking and screaming" into whatever recognition of conditions or sets of values the initiator of the openness had in mind. Strategically-open behavior underlies attempts at seduction, but the intent can be either benevolent or malevolent. Being strategically open implies a responsibility to check out the system carefully, being alert to cues that say to go on and to cues that say to stop.

COLLUSION. Collusion is characterized by an unwillingness to take risks and an unwillingness to check out assumptions about the expectations of others. It is confounded by being a contract of tacit and implicit terms. It drastically underestimates the ability of the system (and the members of the system) to deal with openness. It is closedness reinforced by default.

In the experience of organization development consultants, a fairly common assessment in the sensing (or diagnosing) period is that the key issue is the ineffectiveness of a manager.

In one such sensing phase, the common, independently issued complaint of six subordinates was "the problem with this organization is that old J. B. is a lousy manager. He is reactive, slow to make decisions, and frequently preoccupied with something other than the business at hand." In the interview with J. B., he revealed that he was "giving a great deal of thought to stepping down." He continued, "With the kids grown, through college, and both living out on the Coast there isn't a hell-of-a-lot to keep me interested in my work. My wife and I have enough money so that I really don't need to work anymore; some days I just feel more like golfing or just sitting around than I do going to the office." At the next staff meeting J. B. decided to send up a trial balloon about retiring. It went something like this.

— J. B.: I've been thinking it over and what I think this division needs is a new chief, someone with more energy than I have . . .

— Subordinates (in chorus): Oh no, J. B.! We couldn't get along without you.

What has taken place in this annecdote is an example of collusion — the opposite of being too open. When collusion is identified, *e.g.*, in the J. B. annecdote, the unified response of the colluders is to deny the data or to attack the person who has exposed the collusion.

FUNCTIONALITY IN COMMUNICATION

It may be useful to consider openness as a non-linear phenomenon. Too much and too little openness can both be dysfunctional in human systems.

A non-linear conceptualization of the open-closed continuum in interpersonal relations.

The diagram above depicts the functional-dysfunctional aspects of openness. Closed communications (collusion) can be equally as dysfunctional as completely open expression (Carolesque). Strategic openness functions to ameliorate the system rather than to "blow" it or to hide its reality. Persons in a system which has an openness problem may vacillate between too much and too little sharing. A system that can tolerate high levels of honest interchange of feelings and ideas is characterized by trust and interpersonal sensitivity. Persons are free to give, receive, and solicit feedback on the effects of their own and others' behavior as they interact.

FEEDBACK. Feedback is a method of sharing feelings directed toward another and is generally considered a phenomenon of encounter or T-groups; however, we are constantly engaged in feedback activity in our minds, whether or not the data is ever shared. Feedback sharing may be incorporated into our daily experience as a means of *constructive openness*, based on an intent to help. When openness is applied to feedback, some definite criteria can be established. Feedback is more constructive when it has the following characteristics[1]:

It is descriptive rather than evaluative.

It is specific rather than general.

It takes the needs of the system (two-person, multi-persons) into account.

It focuses on modifiable behavior.

It is solicited rather than imposed.

It is well-timed.

It is validated with the receiver.

It is validated with others.

Evaluative feedback induces defensive reactions and makes listening difficult. To be told that one is not OK often requires that one defend himself. On the other hand, having the effects of one's behavior described leaves the listener the option of making his own evaluation. Giving evaluative feedback is promoting one's own "should" system rather than increasing the freedom of the other to decide for himself.

General feedback is most often not useful because the recipient is left to guess about what he may wish to attempt to change in his behavior. A message such as, "You are a pushy person," is less effective in promoting learning than are messages that focus on definite, observable behaviors. "When you cut off Joe while he was talking, I felt irritated with you," is highly specific feedback that leaves the listener free to choose what he wants to do with it.

---

[1] Adapted from theory session material contained in the NTL-IABS *1968 Summer Reading Book.*

The third feedback criterion, taking needs into account, relates directly to the concept of strategic openness. Whose needs are being met at whose expense? The person who is contemplating being open about his reactions to another person needs to "locate" himself, *i.e.*, he needs to consider why it seems important to share his reactions. In order for the feedback to be constructive, he needs to take into account not only where he is but also where the other person is. He needs to assess the readiness and willingness of the other person to receive the reaction, and he needs not to deceive himself about his own motives.

Focusing on modifiable behavior increases the freedom of the recipient of feedback. To call attention to behaviors over which a person has little or no control, such as tics or other nervous mannerisms, simply leads to frustration.

Solicited feedback is more easily heard than is imposed feedback. The person who asks to be told what his impact is on others is probably more ready and willing to engage in high-level openness than is the person who feels "dumped on," or attacked. Imposed feedback often elicits defensiveness and denial. When the recipient of the feedback has himself named the behavior on which he wants a reading, he is far more likely to listen.

The timing of feedback is critical. "Gunnysacking," or withholding one's reaction until later, is a common interpersonal phenomenon, and sharing reactions about events in the past is less constructive than giving immediate feedback. To be told, "Last week you upset me when you didn't call," is less useful than to be confronted with that reaction relatively soon after the behavior has occurred.

The choice of whether and when to express the feelings which one experiences is not a single one. It is best made from data about the interpersonal situation in which emotion is generated and from the style the person has in responding to his "inner life." In a committee meeting, for example, one of the members becomes irritated at the parliamentary maneuverings of the chairman. He may not permit himself to be conscious of the negative affect, and this would be what analysts call repression. He may engage in suppression, or a conscious choice to focus his awareness on something else besides his feelings. A third type of response would be to choose not to confront the chairman but to maintain consciousness of the irritation. Finally, he may confront the other person. Choosing not to confront can be a low-profile, copping-out style as well as a conscious attempt to be sensitive to others. Feedback can be considered timely, then, if it is given as soon as it is appropriate.

Validating feedback makes sense for two reasons. First, what is heard is very often not what is intended, and, second, a given person's reaction may not be shared by others. Feedback should be at least a two-way process. The recipient of the feedback needs to determine the range of reactions that he causes in others by his behavior.

To be open in giving feedback to another person or to a group, then, is neither effective nor ineffective except as the communication is based on sensitivity to self and to others. It is not inauthentic to be careful in giving feedback, but "softsoaping" one's reaction can carry the message, "You can't take it." If the intent is to enlarge the freedom of the recipient of the feedback, the message should increase options rather than "nail" the other person.

Ideally, openness should be both strategic and constructive. It should enlarge the range of options of the recipients without shutting them down emotionally. It requires demanding self-appraisal of motives by the person who chooses to be open because he must assume responsibility for the open behavior (just as he must for any of his behaviors), with the added dimension that he is imposing the results of his behavior on others. A person's openness must be dealt with, in some fashion, by those with whom he has chosen to share feelings and ideas or give feedback. Therefore, openness should never exceed the system expectations to the extent of reinforcing closed behavior in others; rather, it should become a growth experience for both the "open" person and the system with which he is interacting.

IMPLICATIONS

The group facilitator needs to be aware of both the problems and possibilities relative to openness, collusion, and feedback. A number of these implications are suggested by the points of view expressed in this paper. Feedback criteria can be taught rather easily in small group meetings either experientially or didactically. Building and maintaining the norms implied in these "standards" can result in constructive openness and trust.

The facilitator should be careful in surfacing evidence of collusion in a human system. He needs to find a non-threatening way of helping the colluders to "own" and to deal with their complicity. It is equally dangerous to generate or focus on more data than the system can process. One example of too much data would be calling attention to feelings of members in task group that have not voluntarily committed themselves to studying their interpersonal process. Another example is a facilitator who "models" openness in the initial session of a growth group but expresses so much feeling that participants become unduly anxious. Hypotheses about a system's readiness for increased openness need to be tested. The facilitator should be wary of a tendency to project his own position onto others or to be party to the collusion that may exist in the system. He needs to check out the assumptions that he is making about the client system and to flush out what assumptions persons in the system are making about him.

Openness and trust grow in a nurturing environment; they cannot be expected to be engendered instantaneously. The level of openness in growth group meetings usually cannot automatically be reproduced in "back-home" settings. The facilitator needs to negotiate (and re-negotiate) the level of openness that is to be expected in his relations with others and with groups with which he works.

THE CONCEPT OF STRUCTURE IN EXPERIENTIAL LEARNING

Ruth R. Middleman
and
Gale Goldberg

The importance of the here-and-now, of action and reaction in the living moment, as a potent dynamic in the learning process is widely accepted. There is general agreement that *knowing* which derives from direct experience is significantly different from *knowing about*, which the more vicarious, didactic methods yield.

Despite the common acknowledgement of the importance of the living moment, however, interaction is typically analyzed in terms of the individual's internal, subjective perceptions and/or the developmental process itself. Little emphasis has been placed upon analysis of the complex system of interrelated elements that *is* the here and now situation.

This discussion deals with structure in two ways: (1) as an approach to understanding human interaction in social situations, and (2) as a deliberately employed vehicle for creating, in microcosm, particular social situations for learning purposes.

Structure, in the first instance, is a noun. It refers to the total system of interrelated elements viewed from the perspective of wholeness. It is concerned with the gestalt, the total configuration, the ordered interplay of the various constituent parts. It is concerned with the totality that exists and can be identified beyond its parts, even in the absence of some of its constituent elements. It is concerned with the conditions under which individuals engage each other. The structure of a social situation is the anatomy of that social situation.

Structure, in its second sense, is a verb. It refers to constructing particular conditions to amplify certain elements for purposes of study. When one structures a learning situation, one imposes a certain frame of reference on it. This frame of reference emphasizes some aspects of the situation and screens out others. Thus, the social situation is delimited and a particular focus emerges. The notion of "structured group experience" in human relations training is based upon structure in this latter sense.

STRUCTURAL APPROACH TO ANALYSIS OF THE HERE-AND-NOW

Underlying a structural approach to analysis of the here-and-now is an assumption that the elements which comprise every instance of human interaction are systematically interrelated, and that the meaning of any single element resides in the system of interrelationships and not in the element itself. For example, the amount and type of communication among individuals, the manifest barometer of interaction, cannot be understood except as it relates to such other elements as member roles, the norms governing role relationships, and the type of task facing the group. And all of these elements vary according to size of group, available resources, locus of power, time of day, physical environment, ad infinitum.

A key concept is that of *pattern*. Pattern implies that there is an order to the elements of a situation and that these elements occur with some regularity. While variations on basic patterns due to individual and subcultural differences occur, they can be understood beyond their differences only as they are seen as a general class of event. In this way the concept of pattern unites previously isolated phenomena. When the arrangement of elements is understood in one situation, this understanding can be generalized and applied to other situations.

Patterns of interaction behavior are learned in early childhood, and performed thereafter without conscious awareness. Much of human relations training has been concerned with bringing characteristic styles of interaction into conscious awareness, evaluating them with respect to their utility for different business and professional roles, and modifying those particular aspects of one's style which limit his effectiveness.

Irrespective of characteristic styles of interaction, certain patterns of elements in social situations evoke common behaviors. For example, limited resources in the face of a task to be accomplished tend to produce frustration. A person's choice of fight behavior or flight behavior to express this frustration is also more a function of the roles and norms of the situation than of his personality per se. A structural approach to understanding the here-and-now emphasizes the patterns of elements in given situations that provide opportunity for certain behavioral alternatives while limiting opportunity for other behavioral alternatives. Thus, the structure of social situations needs to be understood, evaluated, and modified where aspects of it limit human effectiveness.

EXPERIENTIAL LEARNING SITUATIONS

Human relations training relies heavily upon experiential learning. In fact this is its single most distinguishing characteristic. However, not all of experience-based learning makes use of structure. For example, the very *lack of structure* provides the central dynamic for the best known form of human relations training, the T-Group. Experiential learning can be conceptualized in the following way:

	STRUCTURED	NON-STRUCTURED
Interactional	1	3
Noninteractional	2	4

As the diagram illustrates, the two dimensions — structure and interaction — provide a four category frame of reference for classifying various forms of experience-based learning. Box 1 includes structured learning situations of an interactional nature. For example, *Towers: An Intergroup Competition Exercise*[1] belongs here. Similarly, *Win As Much As You Can*[2] and *Miniversity*[3] are of the same order. Box 2 refers to structured situations of a non-interactional nature. Specific examples include *In-Basket*[4] and *Guided Individual Fantasies*.[5] Non-structured

---

[1]This footnote as well as all of the following are drawn from Pfeiffer, J. W. and Jones, J. E. A *Handbook of Structured Experiences for Human Relations Training*. Iowa City, Iowa: University Associates Press, Vol. 1, 1969: Vol. II, 1970; Vol. III, 1971. For simplicity, only the volume and page will be cited. Vol. III, p. 22
[2]Vol. II, p. 66
[3]Vol. II, p. 6
[4]Vol. II, p. 44
[5]Vol. I, p. 79

situations of an interactional nature such as the T-Group belong in Box 3. Box 4 includes non-structured situations of a non-interactional nature such as feeling the contours of one's face or listening to one's own heart beat. Major concern in this discussion is with boxes 1 and 2, with structured learning situations of both an interactional and a non-interactional nature.

A structured learning situation is a closed system deliberately constructed and set in motion by the trainer or facilitator. It has a boundary which separates it from the talk about the situation as well. For example, within a given period of time several different structured learning situations may be introduced by the trainer and experienced by the participants. Interaction proceeds within and outcomes and consequences are delimited by the boundary of the particular situation.

Within this boundary a set of conditions is established which affects the roles and/or the rules, and/or the processes of interaction. Finally, the trainer or facilitator introduces a task to be pursued under the structured conditions. This task constitutes the moving dynamic of the learning situation. Participants must function within those particular conditions and experience both the opportunities and constraints on pursuit of the task and human behavior in general that are generated by these conditions.

The task which the trainer introduces may be one of two types. On the one hand, it may be a *structured task* with a defined goal to be achieved (a payoff). On the other hand, it may be a *non-structured task* without a defined goal to be achieved.

In the case of the structured task the primary attention of participants within the boundary of the constructed learning situation is focused upon issues of productivity, goal achievement, task accomplishment, efficiency, etc. Likewise, the talk attending work on the task is about the task itself. For example, in the *NASA Exercise*[6], the goal is to rank order fifteen items with respect to their utility in space. The talk among participants is about the relative importance of each item. The *NASA Exercise*, then, is a structured task. Discussion of the decision making process, inter-personal behavior, and the personal price paid for task achievement is reserved for the processing time, after the task has been completed, i.e. outside the boundary.

In the case of the non-structured task, there is both manifest and latent content. The manifest content is not relevant to the central focus, but is used as a medium through which the latent content may operate. For example, in the *Listening Triads*[7], manifest content may be a topic such as the pros and cons of Black power or of premarital sex or abortion, and the like. While the participants discuss the manifest content, however, their focus is upon hearing the other side of the argument, accurately enough to summarize it, and at the same time effectively presenting the side of the argument assigned to them. Tasks such as these are considered non-structured (although the conditions under which they are operative *are* structured) because they are intrinsically endless. Since they have no particular resolution, goal, or payoff beyond increased awareness or improved performance in the moment, they must be arbitrarily ended by the trainer or facilitator calling time. As in the case of the structured task, processing in the case of the non-structured task takes place outside the boundary of the constructed learning situation, after the constructed learning situation has been ended.

Underlying the deliberate use of structure for learning purposes are certain basic principles that provide clues for constructing learning situations. The use of structure presupposes an holistic approach. Emphasis is upon encapsulating the all, the totality, the gestalt, the wholeness that is greater than and independent of the sum of its parts. In dealing with totalities, however, issues of figure and ground arise. Often, the ground can camouflage or completely obscure the figure. Further, since perception is selective, various figures may emerge for various perceivers. In short, individuals simply cannot attend equally and simultaneously to all aspects of a complex social situation.

---

[6]Vol. I, p. 52
[7]Vol. I, p. 31

For purposes of learning, therefore, it is necessary to delimit the arena and spotlight the particular figure or selected aspect of ground which is to be explored and examined. Hence, simplicity within structure is prerequisite. The facilitator must abstract, from among the complex, multivariate aspects that comprise "real life" social situation, those essential elements, those elements which capture the essence of the situation, eliminating the morass of potentially distracting variables (the "noise") from the constructed learning situation. For example, in each round of *Win As Much As You Can*[8], a structured task within a structured learning situation, participants choose either X or Y. These letters have no particular meaning. Emphasis is on the way in which decisions are made and how people bargain with each other. If, instead of X or Y, participants were to choose one or the other of two political candidates, the number of variables in the situation would increase tremendously (male/female; youth/age; Black/White; liberal/ conservative; etc.), obscuring the intended focus upon the dynamics of collective and representative decision-making itself.

The above example also illustrates another feature of the structured learning situation: the provision of focus. Through simplicity within structure, the energies of the participants are directed to a pin-point of attention, funneled into convergence on a central emphasis that gives direction and effectiveness to the enterprise.

Once the essential elements of a social situation to be explored have been identified and abstracted for use in the structured learning situation, they must be recast in a paradigm that magnifies and intensifies their operation and possible effects. For example, the dynamics of power can take the form of a parent/child situation, a labor/management situation, a political lobbying situation, etc. The power itself can be represented by numbers of chips, centrality of physical position in relation to other participants when information needs to be collected or disseminated, possession of a resource essential to completion of the task introduced by the facilitator, and the like.

Power is an elusive concept, while chips, for example, are concrete. Using chips to represent power, therefore, concretizes the concept of power and makes it available for study. Other elusive concepts can similarly be made available by concretizing them in a symbolic form. For example, a puzzle can represent a problem to be solved, while such functional roles as leader, supporter, and sympathizer can be represented by a baton, an Ace bandage, and a crying towel respectively.

ADVANTAGES OF THE STRUCTURED LEARNING SITUATION

For adult learners, the structured learning situation with either a structured or a non-structured task, has certain advantages which non-structured situations, e.g. the T-group, do not possess. First and foremost is the de-emphasis, in the structured situation, upon the personality of the trainer or facilitator. The learning challenge is lodged in the situation itself, with the facilitating person *less central within the boundaries* of the constructed learning situation. This is not to imply that the facilitator need be less skilled nor less sensitive. Rather, it is he who constructs the situation (much of his work is done prior to the session), sets it in motion, and conducts the important processing period after the constructed situation has ended.

In contrast, the trainer in the non-structured situation (T-group) is most central within that situation, permitting all kinds of projections and counter-projections to be generated, and takes no responsibility for processing with participants outside the boundaries of that situation. Each person is left to grope and sort out his own learnings, however long this may take, and to live with whatever order of experience he has had. Furthermore, the use of structure sets limits on the

---

[8]Vol. II, p. 66

power of the trainer, assuring the integrity of each individual's experience, against the potential vagaries of style, mood, current enthusiasm, and recent life experience of a single central person.

Another feature of the structured learning situation is the psychological safety factor provided by the boundary of each structured situation. Since each situation is a complete entity, the consequences of one's way of being in one situation can end with that situation. One can learn and be different in the next situation. He need not continue to suffer the repercussion of an early, disliked behavior for the duration.

Further, because there is a boundary which punctuates the structured learning situation and separates it from the processing period that follows, as well as from previous and subsequent constructed situations, opportunities for learning are maximized. Participants can engage whole-heartedly in tasks within the boundaries of the constructed situation as well as separate themselves from that situation when they step outside the boundary to view the situation in retrospect. And as they look back on the conditions and ensuing behaviors — their own and the others — they are less encumbered by the emotional impact of events within the boundary. From their position "outside", they can view each situation as one instance of broader, more general principles of human behavior and social conditions. Such a format suggests education rather than therapy.

EXAMPLES OF STRUCTURED LEARNING SITUATIONS

A. *STRUCTURED TASKS WITHIN STRUCTURED LEARNING SITUATIONS*

THE IMPACT OF STRUCTURE ON GROUPS AND COMMITTEES.

GOAL

To explore the consequences of too much and too little structure upon the execution of a group task.

GROUP SIZE

Minimum of 20. This is multi-group activity. Each group should be composed of 4-8 persons, arranged in five different groups.

TIME REQUIRED

2½ to 3 hours plus processing time.

MATERIALS USED

5 envelopes containing instructions for each of the 5 groups.

PROCESS

This activity is designed for a conference held in a city and the group tasks presented reflect this. It should take place the first evening of the conference and will be like a recreational/social part of the conference in addition to a learning experience. It has also been used for a particular organization and a different task which does not take participants out of the meeting room can be substituted.

I. The facilitator distributes to each of the five groups one envelope of instructions and explains that they will now have an opportunity to get to know the city. They have 2½ hours to follow the directions they receive. He explains that they will reconvene at a stipulated time to discuss their reactions.

II. When the groups return the facilitator leads a general discussion of this activity, eliciting comments on what happened in their groups, what feelings were generated, how much of the directions were followed, what effect did the directions have on the group, and general implications for working with adult committees. There is usually ample opportunity for recognition of the prevalence of over-planning agendas and overdirecting group movement.

DIRECTIONS GIVEN TO THE GROUPS

Group 1

Have a good time.

Group 2

Group gets a printed guidebook, "This Week In _____," and have a good time.

Group 3

Stay together for dinner. Have dinner at either Neptune's Seafood House, 513 Main St. or The Steak and Chop House, 2217 Market St. After dinner, you need not stay together as a group if you don't want to but everyone should go to at least one of the following places: Bijou movie theater (corner Main and Market); open air concert, Roosevelt Park; WXYZ, late night radio show (717 E. Broad St.); Flamingo Bar, 559 Flamingo Ave.; Teddy's Topless, 816 Broadway; Sound and Light, Convention Hall; St. Mary's Cathedra, 14 Magnolia Sq.; the campus of Watsamata U. Have a good time.

Group 4

Stay together all evening. Have dinner at either the Rathskeller, 692 W. Main St. or Pasquale's, 893 Broad St. After dinner go to either the Lennox Cinema, Corner Main and Lennox, or the Centre, 991 E. Broad St. After the movies have a drink at either Danny's Den, 1662 7th Ave. or the Showboat, Wharf at 19th St. Have a good time.

Group 5

Stay together all evening. Have dinner at the Homestead, 1492 Primrose Path. After dinner visit the Commercial Auditorium's porcelain and china display. Then go to the Latin Quarter, 777 West Bank St. Have a good time.

(Note: In the indoor version [which can be accomplished in 1 hour] a task such as "Plan an all day session for x-group's retreat" can be used with 5 different degrees of structured directions added).

THE IMPACT OF NONVERBAL BEHAVIOR

GOALS

I. To demonstrate the effects of nonverbal behavior upon individuals

II. To illustrate how unconscious individuals are of the dynamics of nonverbal cues.

GROUP SIZE

Any number. Best arrangement is small groups of 5 or 6 with two persons interacting and the rest observing this interaction.

TIME REQUIRED

Ten minutes for each activity, followed by reporting period for each group plus processing time for total group.

MATERIALS USED

I. Construction paper, scissors, tape.

II. Written instructions. A set for each partner in each dyad.

III. Nonverbal observation guides may be given to observers (optional).

PHYSICAL SETTING

Room with ample space for small groups to meet and not over-hear each other. Each dyad positioned at a small work table.

PROCESS

I. The facilitator is careful not to mention that this activity is concerned with nonverbal behaviors. He asks the group to break into five smaller groups in any way they wish, stating that he will be distributing instructions to two in each group who will engage in a task with each other while the others observe the interaction. (If observation forms are used, these are now distributed to the observers who position themselves for observation purposes.)

II. Each dyad works on its task while the observers watch.

III. When the tasks are completed, the facilitator, moving from group to group, asks for reports on what happened, what feelings were generated, etc., in the following order: (1) from the partner in the dyad who received no nonverbal directions, (2) from the partner who received the non-verbal directions. After each pair in each small group reports, the facilitator calls on the observers in each group to present their observations.

IV. The total group then discusses the variables noted, the impact of the nonverbal behaviors, the implications of this in this situation and in general, etc.

Task: Decide upon and construct a three-dimensional symbol of your dyad. You have 10 minutes to accomplish this.

INSTRUCTIONS:

Partner A: With your partner decide upon and construct a three-dimensional symbol of your dyad. You have 10 minutes. (Same for each dyad.)

Partner B:

Dyad 1: With your partner decide upon and construct a three-dimensional symbol of your dyad. You have 10 minutes. While you're talking and working, gradually move to stand or sit too close to your partner. Continue to stay too close.

Dyad 2: (Same first instructions). While you are talking and working, gradually spread out the materials so that you take over both the materials and the work space.

Dyad 3: (Same first instructions). While you are talking and working, stare directly into your partner's eyes and keep staring.

Dyad 4: (Same first instructions). While you are talking and working, gradually move closer to your partner and begin to touch him as you are talking. Gradually touch him more and more as you work.

Dyad 5: (Same first instructions). While you are talking and working, gradually increase the volume of your voice and move around so as to face your partner directly as often as possible.

TAKING IN THE WHOLE GROUP

GOAL

I. To understand the importance of eye contact with every member of the group during discussions.

II. To acquire skill in using eye contact to draw silent members into the discussion or modify the overparticipation of a dominant member.

GROUP SIZE

Unlimited number of small groups of 5-10 participants each.

TIME REQUIRED

45 minutes

PROCESS

I. The facilitator may make some introductory remarks about the importance of developing skills in working with small groups and that this will be a chance to practice such skills.

II. The small groups are set up through voluntary choice. One or two in each group are asked to observe the process of the discussion.

III. The facilitator asks each group to select one person to act as discussion leader. The activity will be repeated twice, the first is the naive phase where each discussion leader tries to do his best in his own way. The second phase is introduced after the facilitator calls time on the first discussion, calls for reports from the observers as to how well they thought the leader took in the whole group and what things did they notice he did to accomplish this.

IV. After the first round of discussions and reports (about 15 minutes) the facilitator calls to one side a volunteer from each group who will lead the second discussion. The same observers perform their roles.

V. The facilitator verbally gives the following instructions to the new discussion leaders. "Pay careful attention to how you use your eyes. Make sure that you scan the whole group during the whole discussion and make eye contact with every person. If you notice someone has not contributed anything verbally, try staring at him and see if he will come in. If someone is too long winded, look away from him to the others. Do not simply look at the person who is talking."

VI. Second discussion is held. Following this, the observers report what they noticed. What, if any differences, were there in this discussion from the previous one.

VII. Facilitator engages the total group in discussion of the possibilities in using eye contact more deliberately. Note: Any discussion topic will do for this activity. The facilitator should select one that he knows is of interest to his group.

NOTES
ON
FREEDOM

Stanley M. Herman

For some time the main thrust of organization development efforts has been directed at changing organization environments in ways that will make them more supportive and facilitative to people. I believe that emphasis has been useful but not complete. I want to suggest a different approach, one that is largely derived from the theory and practice of Gestalt therapy. My objective here is not to provide instruction on making the organization world safer, pleasanter or easier for the individual but rather to help the individual to recognize, develop and experience his own potency and ability to cope with his organization world, whatever its present condition. Further, I would like to encourage him to discover for himself his own unique wants of that environment and his capacity to influence and shape it in ways that get him more of what he wants.

The worst barrier to the individual and his free expression of himself in the organization setting is probably fear — fear of others and even more importantly, fear of one's self. In the following paper I will comment on some of the ways in which we tie ourselves up and keep ourselves from experiencing our freedom.

THE MYTH OF OMNIPOTENCE

For many years an important focus for theories of management has been the area of power and control. Even before Douglas MacGregor's theory X and theory Y management, literature advocated caution in the manager's use of power and control. The cases for participative or permissive or otherwise tempered styles of supervision were made in many theories. By now it has become clear to almost every manager or supervisor who sees himself as "beyond the dark ages" that bosses are not supposed to be domineering and authoritarian (or at least if they are they are not supposed to seem that way to their subordinates).

It is clearly true that a dictatorial or oppressive style of management is no longer generally acceptable in the United States, but I believe that the real basis for this truth is not found in philosophical images of theoretical democracy; rather, it stems from the high probability that most people who work in present day organizations are unwilling to tolerate oppression. They will find a way of rising up against it either overtly or covertly, through sabotage.

For many managers the image of "democratic leadership" has not served as a useful model. Their attempts to regulate their own behavior to make it "fit the image" have been strained and unnatural and frequently received with discomfort or suspicion by their subordinates. A man is a man; if his behavior is authentic, it must reflect his own internal personal realities at any given point in time, not a prescribed external ideal. *Genuine growth requires that a person first recognize and acknowledge his own present qualities before he can proceed in his own natural development.*

In the practice of psychotherapy, therapists repeatedly encounter the guilt and anxiety ridden patient who tortures himself with fantasies of how he has abused or injured others. So does he bring himself to a state of such self-mistrust or self-hate that he becomes unable to encounter people around him and can only turn inward. His vitality and excitement are lost as he spends his energy in restraining and punishing himself.

In an organization culture where the exercise of direct power is ostensibly disapproved by the established norms of the organization many people in positions of authority may experience a comparable (though, of course, less extreme) pattern. They may become vaguely uncomfortable or even terribly concerned about the "awesome force" they have over other people. I call this "syndrome" the myth of omnipotence.

The myth of omnipotence is a specter that can paralyze potency. The manager who believes too much in his own power to harm begins to hold himself back to avoid hurting others. I believe this withheld thrust has adverse affects *both* on the withholder and on those from whom he withholds. In the course of my organization consulting I have encountered many cases in which the manager of an organization struggles painfully within himself to try to force his behavior to conform to an image of managership in which he is constantly benign, non-authoritative, encouraging and facilitative toward his subordinates, but at the same time within himself he feels and holds back his own wants, opinions, and desires to move things ahead. He also experiences "negative" emotions toward his subordinates, such as irritation, criticism, and impatience, and yet withholds these because (like a "good parent") a "good manager" does not express such things to (his children) those who are below him.

In some ways the myth of omnipotence could have its compensations. If I believe the myth I can, at least internally, feel myself (in comparison to my subordinates) stronger and more capable. However, the manager seldom enjoys that clarity. Instead he struggles with intermittent ambivalence and lack of fulfillment. Perhaps more important, his subordinates also suffer from the ambiguity of the signals he sends out. On the one hand the manager's words are encouraging, patient, and deferential, while on the other hand the expressions on his face, his tone, his body signs (e.g., fidgeting, tension etc.) indicate conflicting responses and these too are perceived by his subordinates, though seldom if ever dealt with.

I believe it would be far healthier for the manager to fully express his feelings, negative as well as positive, and to allow himself fuller expression of his directive impulses as well. With their full expression his subordinates could more completely experience the totality of the manager's reality. Then they could accept it or contest it as they saw fit. I believe that from this interchange of *full expression* and *full reaction* both the manager and his subordinates could grow in a most meaningful way. Their growth would be along at least two dimensions. First, in the interpersonal and intrapersonal sense, they would come to really know each other more richly and authentically, and through a heightened awareness of their own feelings, they would come to know themselves better as well. Secondly, with repeated practice and greater familiarity between each other, the substance of their ideas could also be more adequately tested and new, more effective ways of working together developed.

The consultant can concentrate on helping managers and subordinates to fully express "where they are" both on issues and in relationships to each other. He can highlight their interpersonal process and help them to discover their own vitality and the satisfaction and excitement of full expression. He can help them to become aware of their own predictive fantasies, i.e., for the manager, "If I really let myself go I would oppress, overpower, do terrible damage to my subordinates;" or for the subordinate, "I must be very careful because this is a very dangerous environment." When these murky, catastrophic expectations have been surfaced, the consultant can help the manager and his subordinates to explore and test them against reality. Finally, he can assist them in working out individual arrangements between people that will allow for greater self expression and fulfillment.

I need to emphasize here that while some of the processes may seem quite similar, the approach I am advocating is not the same as the more typical practice by many O.D. consultants in which they facilitate "confrontation," then help the parties to "see how they adversely affect each other" (particularly how the manager adversely affects the subordinate), and finally encourage the establishment of a detente in which the "dominant" boss takes on the assignment of being more considerate and encouraging to his "weaker" subordinates.

WHEN "THEORY" IMPEDES PRODUCTIVE PROCESS

O.D. theory has, for most of its brief history, stressed the support of the subordinate, the reticent team member, etc. and the solution of disagreement through rational processes. In the context of our national culture and traditions this is not surprising, nor do I object to the general underlying philosophy. Unfortunately, however, some of our approaches have attempted to "help" the "weaker member" by providing an easier world for him through advocating the restraint (usually by "self control" and under the moral pressure of "human relations rightness") of the "powerful" manager or team member. I believe this approach is counter productive. Not only does it foster the inhibiting omnipotence myth and guilt feelings of the manager discussed earlier, but it can also be experienced as a confirmation of his own inferiority or "invalidism" by the individual who is granted the so called "benefits" of other people holding themselves back for his sake. Better by far to help this individual to discover, use and rejoice in his strength and ability to move forward for himself than to have others take turns pushing his wheel chair for him.

Robert W. Resnick, a Gestalt-oriented psychotherapist, makes the point this way: "Many therapists see themselves as members of the "helping professions" engaged in the "helping relationship." Beware! Such people are dangerous. If successful, they kill the humanness in their patients by preventing their growth. This insidious process is somehow worse realizing such therapists typically want the reverse. They want their patients to grow, to live, and to be, and they guarantee the antithesis with their "help." The distinction between true support and "help" is clear; to do for the others what he is capable of doing for himself insures his not becoming aware that he can stand on his own two feet . . ."

In one organization I worked with the high level manager of a large staff had developed a strong, indeed passionate, commitment to "O.D. values." Included in these values, as he saw it, was the requirement for a manager to be fair, rational and helpful to those who reported to him. Most of the time he conformed to these requirements quite easily and naturally. He was, however, an individual of great personal force, with strong emotions and subject to occasional moodiness. Those who reported to him recognized these qualities and had gradually grown accustomed to them, though as might be expected their comfort with his style differed.

Over a considerable period of time this strong, able manager grew increasingly discontent and unhappy with his relationships to several members of his staff, and the staff members, in turn, were also troubled. The "problem" can best be illustrated by the patterns of interaction in the manager's staff meetings. These were generally conducted in a fairly free-flowing and participative style with the floor pretty much available to anyone who wanted it. Sometimes the meetings were quite business like and at other times they consisted mostly of a series of rambling discourses punctuated occasionally by concise irrelevancies. For the most part the manager and his staff were fairly well satisfied by the patterns, both the focused discussions and the "non-productive" ones. From time to time, however, and for no very apparent reason except his mood at the moment, the manager would suddenly jump into the discussion with all the force of a safe dropped from a ten story window, usually landing on one of about three or four members of his staff. Frequently his "attack" was logically sound, though sometimes it was not; in any event, it was not so much the substance as the vehemence and unexpectedness that seemed to most affect those who were the recipients.

The responses of those who were "attacked" by the boss varied but few were silent or completely unresponsive. (This was clearly not an oppressive environment.) Some replied by defending their position with counter logic. One used humor, including self-depreciating comments to "reduce the tension." Still another acted and sometimes verbally expressed his feelings of being "punished" by the boss. Whichever the response, what most frequently seemed to happen was that after a round or two or three of exchange the boss would cease to respond, frequently settling into a glum, silent posture. When that happened the entire group would experience a long awkward pause, with no explicit resolution of the issue, if indeed an issue was even identifiable from the brief exchange.

As I worked with the group over some period of time it became clear to me that the manager was quite aware of the effects of his attacks on his staff members — perhaps too aware. These effects had been pointed out to him before a number of times. Why then did he, an enlightened, devoted, "theory Y" manager, continue this behavior?

The answer is because the feelings behind the behavior were part of him — parts of the whole of his humanness, power and emotionality: those same qualities for which his staff and many others respected and trusted him. What then could be done? To preach abstinence or even temperance to this manager hardly seemed worthwhile. Even if he resolved to stop his verbal interruptions his feelings would still be sensed by others and would float like a pervasive phantom among them all. No, the answer was not for this manager to back away from his impulsive behavior but rather *to go further into it*. Not to cut himself off, after an exchange or two, with his guilt feelings about abusing his subordinates, and then to settle into melancholy self blame, but rather to stay engaged with them in the battle until it reached its natural conclusion.

After some discussions with the manager and a period of his own reflection he began gradually to allow himself to follow through further in his so called attacks. At the same time the people attacked were also encouraged to continue to respond, even counter-attack if they felt like it. Further, other members of the staff also joined the fray (usually on the side of their colleague).

As the group re-examined its processes some time later, members recognized that this turbulent meeting had produced for the entire group a greater sense of vitality, excitement and relatedness than they had felt for many months, and that this feeling had carried over into subsequent staff meetings as well (including the calm business-like ones). The manager reported in addition that in their "fight" he had gained a new sense of respect for the staff member who stood up to him. In subsequent similar encounters other staff members also began to stand their ground more firmly.

It is, of course possible that some managers, if encouraged to fully express themselves, would turn out to be intolerable tyrants. I believe there are few such people. In the context of Gestalt theory the "intolerable tyrant" is likely to be an individual suffering the myth of his own personal total helplessness. Thus he defends himself by trying to control completely all those around him. In the therapy for such individuals, as they are able to confront their feelings of helplessness and come to recognize for themselves that they are not as totally helpless as they felt then the tyrannical behavior begins to disappear. At any rate I suspect that a straightforward undisguised tyrant is easier and better to deal with than a disguised one.

I WILL DO YOU NO FAVOR

If I withhold my voice of anger from you
    for your sake
You, in listening too hard to me,
Will hear more anger than ever any
    real voice of mine would have held

If I curb my raucous ribald pleasure voice
    for anticipation of your sensibilities
You will know I have curbed and pleasure will be dimmed
    and overlaid with grimy speculation as to why.
(What else than pleasure was there that
    he did not say?)

If I damp my robust affection for you and keep my arms
    that want to hug you bound at my sides
(As would seem more appropriate
    for men of our station and trade)
Your arms, or perhaps only fingers, will twitch too,
    stifled and pinched off meanly
And perhaps in spite against their mind-formed shackles
    will tense to fists

All that I withhold diminishes me
    and cheats you
All that you withhold diminishes you
    and cheats me
When we hold back ourselves
    for each others sake
That is no service to us either one
We only collude in the weakening
    of us both.

ATTACK AND DEFENSE

Another concept of training that I believe has been distorted and at times carried to dysfunctional generalization has to do with defensiveness. The practice in organization development of asking people to withhold temporarily their rebuttals in order to more fully understand a case being made by the opposition can be a sensible and useful one at times. However, by some trainers and consultants, this has been translated into the caveat "don't be defensive." This phrase is used many times as a way to club the resistor into the posture of listening. I say posture advisedly and mean just that, for very frequently the instruction not to be defensive merely results in the subject closing his mouth and at the same time closing his ears, mind and heart as well. We need to recognize that defensiveness (as well as attackingness) are natural behaviors for people and only after an individual has the opportunity to complete either his attack or defense can he *really listen* to the other within the full meaning of that word.

I believe that in working with people in organizations the consultant would do well to keep this hypothesis in mind. He would do well to encourage the full expression of attack and defense behaviors *prior* to the time he encourages reasonable and objective listening. He may find much to his surprise that if the two parties are encouraged to fully express their conflicting positions the resolution of their apparent differences may occur in a different way than might have been initially anticipated.

In one organization I served as consultant in dealing with the long standing feud between an administrative officer and a young woman who was the head of the clerical work force of the organization. The young woman's complaints were that the administrator usually ignored the girls in the office, had excessively high standards for their performance and was unwilling to listen to the girls' complaints sympathetically. Thus she was required she felt to act as an intermediary between the office staff and the professional part of the organization.

After some period of discussion the administrative officer generally agreed to being guilty as charged and was about to resolve to try to do better. An initial inclination I had at that point was to help the two parties systematize their agreement into some list of "action items" that would regularize the connection between the administrative officer and the clerical group. However, I resisted that temptation and instead began to work with the administrative officer by encouraging him to get in touch with what he really wanted for *himself*, rather than in response to the complaints being made about him. After some work using the Gestalt approach of first heightening the polarities of the conflicting urges within the administrative officer, (rather than trying to resolve them) it became clear that he was at this point in his life unable or unwilling to establish and sustain really personal contact with other people. It was also apparent that if he were to agree to the requests being made of him by the clerical supervisor he would do so in a ritualistic and strained way, and it was doubtful that such contacts would have the desired effect.

In working further with the clerical supervisor as well, it gradually became clear that her underlying and more real complaint had not so much to do with the administrative officer's lack of attention to the girls in the office (actually she was quite competent, able, and even found it satisfying to deal with the girls' problems herself) but rather her desire was for more personal interaction with the administrative officer herself. As she came to recognize her own wants and his difficulty with that kind of interaction she became very empathetic, as did others in the group, and the nature of her demands changed. The change was not out of compromise, or pity, or a willingness to decrease her expectations, but rather a natural emerging feeling that she and others *wanted to* accept the administrative officer as he was right now.

Paradoxically, with the administrative officer's new awareness and *willingness* to accept himself as a person who was not easily able or inclined to be personal with others on a sustained basis, he began to grow and change in the direction of being more comfortable in personal relationships. I understand from subsequent contacts with the organization that the relationships between these key people and among the office force in general have improved greatly since our work together.

BEHAVIOR CHANGE

Too often people come out of T-groups, team building sessions and other group experiences having learned a set of new rules for how to behave appropriately. Trying to change your behavior according to some one else's rules about participation, openness, confrontation, or whatever, in order to conform to the latest fashions of "human relations" is no good. It is more important to recognize who you are, what you do, and how you do it, *now*. Natural growth and change derive from fully experiencing and appreciating yourself as you are now. Planned or "exhibitionistic" behavior change is usually strained and difficult to maintain. It will probably deteriorate over time and under stress, and will not be comfortable for you or perceived as genuine by others. It takes a great deal of energy to keep the new style under control, energy that could better be used for other more self fulfilling purposes.

One of the more discouraging phenomena for O.D. consultants is the continual repetition of certain problems. The consultant works with two conflicting parties or organizations, he helps them to bring out their differences, to examine and discuss, and finally to come together on an apparent solution. But a day, a week, or a month later they are in conflict again over the same or a similar issue. The consultant may be called back in to repeat the problem solving process, but once more the truce breaks down. By this time both clients and consultant have likely grown discouraged, cynical, or both about the process.

My guess is that most frequently the root of such "failures" is in the fact that the solutions developed by the parties involved were too symptomatic rather than core problems, and called for forced behavior changes that were not consonant with the present natures of the parties involved. The effort required for maintaining such changes could not be sustained.

SPONTANEITY

Most of us spend a great deal of our time predicting the effect of our behavior on someone else, and then of course, we predict the reaction of that other person to us. For some the predictive "disease" carries them into round after round of future speculation: if I do this, he will do that, then I'll do this, then he'll do that etc., etc. Predicting kills spontaneity and so obstructs energy and the potential for excitement and pleasure.

Probably one of the most radical proposals anyone dealing with organization theory could make in these times would be to advocate increasing spontaneity in the organization. Our emphasis for a number of decades has been on increased planning, control, and other forms of regulative activity that can produce predictable results. Of course, in the complexity of present day organizational requirements the need for planned action is undeniable. However, what has occurred as a result of this largely successful approach to addressing the organizations' technical needs has been the extension of the philosophy of deliberation and planning to a point where addressing all aspects of existence within the organization, including human interaction, seems to demand governed and predictable behavior.

One cost of constantly adhering to this norm of self control has been that we have deprived ourselves of much of our capacity to enjoy ourselves and each other. Some of us have even forgotten what it used to be like to be ourselves without care or caution. We are able to appreciate the experience only vicariously. We may, for example, enjoy the antics of a film character like Zorba, or the innocent spontaneity of a child. At most, perhaps on occasion at a party, well lubricated by alcohol, we may allow some of our own boisterous or sentimental feelings to come through without suppression for awhile. But in the latter case there is frequently the next mornings' worry and regret: what did I do, what did I say, did I seem silly to others, antagonistic? And so last nights' enjoyment turns sourly to this days' embarrassment and the resolve of "never again."

I believe there is more room for spontaneity, earthiness, and joy within organizations than is commonly suspected. I have seen work groups of professionals as well as non-professionals in which there was a climate of easiness that allowed and encouraged boisterousness, playfulness, and other "unconventional" and "undignified" behavior. These groups were strong and effective. I am not sure whether their strength and effectiveness grew out of the easiness of the climate or vice versa. I suspect both may have encouraged each other. I believe that the organization consultant who personally prizes freedom can work with his client group in ways that will help and encourage them to be able to find ways of dealing with each other more spontaneously and freely, and with more enjoyment.

The main thrust of this paper has been toward encouraging authenticity in individuals, and the freer expression of the entire range of feelings — both "positive" and "negative" — that make us human. The consultant can help individuals in working groups to experiment. In small and relatively low risk ways at first he can encourage them to deal with each other more authentically, not merely around problem solving or work related issues but in the normal intercourse of their day to day relations. There are a number of exercises or structured experiments to help facilitate this development, but most important again is the model of the consultant's own behavior as he relates. How much of himself is he willing to put up front? I am not speaking now of the self-revealing-confessor-of-old-sins model, but rather who and how I am now. How willing am I to say plainly what I want *for myself* (rather than to concentrate exclusively on "helping" others)? How willing am I to express my own hostility, frustration, affection, sadness, and silliness as these feelings rise within me, and equally important, to say *explicitly*, "no, I will not reveal myself" when that is where I am? How willing am I to "speak before I think" from time-to-time? In essence, how willing am I to trust myself to let go, a little at a time, of my protective shield of behavioral science (BS) word sophistication in favor of my own innocence?

For those who find some part of themselves intrigued by these ideas, I offer the suggestion: start your personal experiment in spontaneity with someone that you feel fairly comfortable with. Begin with your own venture rather than placing any requirement on him. Sit together and tell him or her what you want *now*, your awareness *now* of what you are experiencing, emotionally, physically within yourself, outside yourself. Allow your awareness to go its own way without pain or purpose. Avoid explanations and "reasons why." When you find yourself censoring your feelings or thoughts, be aware of that and make it explicit, but do not force yourself beyond your present limits of expression. Your limits will expand later, naturally and without forcing. If the experience seems strange and uncomfortable, acknowledge that it is. Leave off, when you are inclined to and return again when you are ready.

For those who have had no prior experience in Gestalt therapy this experiment will probably seem quite awkward and purposeless at first. But there is a kind of magic in the spontaneous sharing of awareness that may at some moment come through for you and the other. If it does you may discover a quality of relationship that you never before enjoyed.

BOAST

Say you are good
Say you are good at — say both.
Loudly, smilingly, but not
with embarrassment

There is much shit that has
been burdened upon us
But not much worse than the downing,
gripey voice that says in mincy tones:
Do not a boaster be

What rot!
What smothering, stunting rot
Be free!
Love yourself greatly and with gusto
Love those qualities about you that you love

Give to you pleasure
You deserve it
It is wise that you appreciate yourself best
You know you best

Your finger to the tch'ing, clucking
wrinkled prunes who say
Do not a boaster be
Listen to them closely and you will hear
their boasts too
Not clean and happy full
But small and undistinguished
pings — flecks of crap
A name dropped here, a simpering
disclaimer there, a modest
hint of fluttering eyelash desperation

So on and on they go
Unfinished self-choking, unconvincing
and worse yet unconvinced.
Others stare briefly, or glance away
Or conspiringly act impressed
and, taking their petty due,
drop their own flecks too

A boaster be
A lover of yourself, what you are
and what you do
That is good, my friend.
I will love you more for it, not less

THE TYRANNY OF THE UNDERDOG

An important part of Gestalt therapy is the concept of polarities, the extremes within each of us (i.e. weakness-strength, activism-passivity, etc.) that together comprise our full natures. One of the manifestations of polarity is the "topdog" vs. "underdog." The topdog is that part of us that mostly serves the function of director and disciplinarian, that part of our personality that tells us what we *should do*. The underdog is the resistive part of us, that part that balks at the bossiness of the topdog and attempts to subvert or derail his directives.

The underdog may work at his mission by pleading that we are unable to do what the topdog demands, or he may delay and promise to do it tomorrow, or he may divert the topdog's directions, and so on. Fritz Perls in his development of Gestalt therapy theory believed that the underdog in each individual almost always triumphed in the long run over the topdog.

Relationships between some individuals within organizations have many of the same characteristics as this topdog-underdog conflict. The apparently powerful directive person makes demands on the ostensibly weaker underdog, but somehow, the demands are never quite met. While the topdog's pressure may be great, the underdog's ability to divert, deflect, or delay is often greater. So-called weak parties in a variety of relationships may have very great, though not immediately apparent, advantages in their ability to resist without attacking and to use, like a judo expert, the strong person's own strength against him. I have worked with a number of teams in which one or two members, undoubtedly without conscious intent, skillfully manipulated the apparently stronger members of the group, including the boss into "helping" them. This helping takes many forms. It can be protecting the quiet member, taking his side in a competitive situation, being more sympathetic to his problems and inabilities to meet his commitments than would be the case for other members of the team, etc. One of the most harmful accommodations to the "weak party" involves others holding back their forcefulness and vitality in order to keep from offending or upsetting the weak one.

As a consultant or counselor to the relationship between "dominant" and "submissive" people, it is important not to encourage the strong individual to withhold his strength for the sake of the weak one. It is most important to help the weak one to discover the form of his present real strength (which may very well be his ability to manipulate others into doing his work for him) and to bring this strength into his awareness. Once this has been accomplished he will then be able to move toward choosing whether he wishes to continue to use his present style or a more direct means of satisfying his needs.

OGRE BUILDING

Almost all of us in organizations have great capacity to build ogres fearsome enough to scare ourselves half to death. The ogre may be a supervisor, especially one at a higher level than those we are accustomed to dealing with, another organization, or, perhaps most insidious of all, "the system." Ogres can be very useful sometimes in helping us to avoid doing what we don't really want to do anyway. I have no special objection to the use of the ogre for that purpose if indeed we are conscious of what we are doing and that we *want* to do it. More frequently, however, we are not aware of what we are doing and our ogres are not so clearly useful or desirable. They are compounded of some degree of organizational reality plus our own projections and predictions of dire consequences. Organization development methodology is frequently useful in dealing with ogres, especially the mutual ogres dreamed up by internally competitive organizations for each other. I believe more can be done, especially in working with individuals, in helping them to discover their own courage and potential capacity to confront and deal with their own ogres.

In the case of "complaining people" (that is those who see others and/or their environment as oppressive and preventing them from doing what they would want to do "if only things were different"), it is a good idea for the consultant or counselor to begin working with his client in a way that concentrates on identifying the client's own sense of power. That may not be easy; the complainer's power is not readily apparent. On the contrary, he usually spends much of his time denying he has any power at all. All power belongs to "the others": his boss, his more influential (or articulate, or aggressive) co-workers or, most oppressive of all, to "the company."

As a consultant I am suspicious of these complaints. This is not to say that I think the complainer is intentionally deceptive, nor do I doubt that wide spread inequalities of opportunity for certain classes of organization citizens do exist; rather I have found that most people do possess some form of power even if that power is passive, resistive, or a withholding kind that they use to manipulate others in their world (often by triggering feelings of guilt among the more active and assertive people with whom they deal).

In a large government agency, I was involved with a team-building session between the top management group (including the chief and his central staff) and a group of field supervisors, each of whom headed a local service office. The pattern of complaints, and there were many from each "side," was clear and repeated. For the central staff it was that those in the field seldom seemed to be able to respond to the requests for new information that they were asked to provide, nor did they try out proposed innovations developed by the central staff for use in the field (except occasionally in a most cursory way that practically assured the failure of the new approach.) Finally, after repeated efforts, the central staff people had subtly abandoned their efforts to direct the field supervisors and adopted what they felt to be the more modern management approach of asking the field people to submit their own ideas for innovation and improvement. This approach fared no better.

What was very noticeable to me as I heard the presentation of this information from the central staff people was their almost complete lack of emotion. This pattern of relationships which I imagined had been going on for about a year, must have produced frustration for the agency chief and his staff, yet in listening to the presenters I heard only careful neutrality, infinite patience, and dispassionate though devoted interest in objective "problem-solving."

It took considerably longer for the case of the field supervisors to really emerge. Their first responses to the complaints of the central staff were rather desultory and almost apologetic. They had very heavy work loads, many new people to train, spent a great deal of time on public relations, and so on, all of which limited their ability to concentrate on new things. Besides, they felt it was quite unlikely that they could develop any new methods that would really be well regarded by the central staff, since the central staff people were obviously so much better informed about the latest trends in their specialized field than they were. Similarly, the information emerged that in the past year a few of the field supervisors felt they had attempted to institute some of the recommended new approaches of the central staff but had not done well at it. While they had not been overtly criticized by the staff they had "felt" disapproved of.

As a consultant here I experienced myself at a choice point, I could "help" the field supervisors by encouraging the central staff to examine its olympian posture with respect to the field people: how their cool paternalism put down the supervisors, and ways they might change this pattern into a more encouraging one. Secondly, I could pursue the problem solving approach by helping the total group to recognize specific areas of weakness in the supervisors' skills and then to develop training programs for building those skills. Thirdly, I could encourage the field supervisors to go even further into their complaints. I chose the third.

What emerged in response to my request for the supervisors (in a fishbowl arrangement) to elaborate further on their grievances against the staff was a veritable river of complaints, many of which went back for years. In essence, though, the field supervisors felt like second class citizens, without influence or power in their dealings with the staff. They didn't know what the staff meant by "innovation" and what's more they didn't much care. (They did have some good ideas from time-to-time which they put into effect without fanfare, and seldom told the staff anything about them.)

When the venting had subsided some, I asked the field supervisors to talk about how they characteristically dealt with the staff. After a slow start the supervisors rolled out a substantial list of "passive-resistance" and "playing stupid" techniques. In a little while they were enjoying their catalogue immensely (and so were the staff people, who prior to this time had perceived themselves as in the superior position, and so very much responsible for the opposed feelings of the supervisors).

Some time later, after the supervisors had become aware of the way in which they exerted their own resistive power in their dealings with the staff, we were able to turn successfully to the possibilities of developing different modes of interaction between the groups. Now, however, they were able to do so, not as impotent sufferers, but as men.

SELF ACCEPTANCE FOR INDIVIDUALS AND ORGANIZATIONS

I believe that a necessary pre-requisite for real change in a person (as opposed to forced or exhibitionistic change) is his acceptance of where he is now. If I can allow myself to fully experience and to be what I am now — my character, style, etc. — then my growth will follow naturally as it does with other live and changing organisms in nature. I believe this same principle can apply to individuals within organizations in the right circumstances and perhaps to organizations themselves.

Many of us have seen people and total organizations in which there is so much self doubt or even self contempt that they are practically immobilized and so incapable of performing well, even though good potential capacity exists. In such cases "objective analysis" of problems and causes, and advice on alternative behavior seldom helps. The dearth of internal vitality and drive is just too great a barrier, so that even when better possibilities are pointed out no one is able to muster the courage or enthusiasm to try them out. This frequently accounts, incidentally, for the lack of follow-up after team building sessions and other organization development interventions in many organizations.

I believe it is important as a first step in working with an organization, particularly one that is in such serious trouble, to help its members to recognize according to their own sense of reality where and what the organization is now. This includes not merely the trouble and problems that the organization experiences but also the strengths and functional purposes of its current operating style. Sometimes it may well be that these two sides of the coin are not entirely separable, that is, the same quality or characteristic that is a serious problem for the organization also serves as its way of coping with the environment. This way of coping may be outdated, inadequate, and even self defeating in the long run, but it does *serve some purpose*.

The preceding case example of the staff and field personnel in the government agency can illustrate this point.

While the functions of development and innovation were not being optimally performed between the central staff and field groups some purposes were being served. The field supervisors coped well with the central staff by "playing uneducated and inadequate" thus precluding the staff from having high expectations of them. The central staff protected itself well from the possible unpleasantness of a real confrontation with the supervisors by "playing objective and understanding". There are many classic illustrations of exquisite protectionism in bureaucracies where the bureaucratic processes are so beautifully designed they absorb and render inert any effort to change the system. (A number of U.S. Presidents and Secretaries of State have paid this tribute of frustration to the Department of State.)

In working with an organization's leaders and members, various approaches can be used to help them to get firmly in touch with what functions are being served, what needs are being

222

met, and what protections are being built by their current behavior. Paradoxically then, in his beginning efforts the consultant may be most useful in helping the organization to understand the usefulness, however limited, of what it is *now* doing. When that has been done and these patterns have been fully identified, experienced and appreciated, then the organization may be able to go on to a process of change and to a more effective way of addressing its environment. The resulting changes, rather than being forced or exhibitionistic, will be more real, better integrated, and more likely to succeed on a longer term basis.

The consultant may begin this approach by working with the organization team in helping them to actually list what is "good" about the current way in which the organization operates, and what is "bad" about the current way. He can have them briefly review and explore the good elements until they are fully appreciated, then have them address the bad elements, beginning by identifying what purpose each of these operating modes serves. The bad elements should be as fully explored and appreciated as the good elements. After the appreciation step has been fulfilled then the consultant may help the group explore whether there is a desire to change some of the items from both the good and bad lists and what will be required in order to do so. Finally, after these have been fully explored, he can help the group to go on to actual planning for change that would include both structural and non-structural aspects.

Another approach (taken from the Gestalt Therapy model) would be for the consultant to have individuals in the organization identify the major positive forces and negative forces at work in the organization. Subsequently he would help the group to compare the positives and negatives in ways that clearly polarize them into sets of forces, and finally have the positive and negative forces in each set "dialogue with each other" until an "integration" emerged.

CONCLUSION

In the model of the consultant's role I have been advocating the primary step is not to help people embark on self-improvement programs, rather it is to encourage them to recognize and appreciate where they are now. Then the consultant may help them to find their own unique paths forward to change and growth. It is important to recognize that this change and growth, at best, will occur naturally rather than being self-forced. Paradoxically, natural change in an individual does not preclude his boss or others from exerting power or expressing their wants strongly and explicitly. *What is explicit and up-front is usually not harmful, though it may be difficult to deal with.* Covert, withheld or truncated expression is frequently harmful. In most circumstances the consultant will do best to encourage in both individuals and organizations the full recognition and completion of their negative feelings rather than a premature "objectivity" or problem solving approach.

We have in our field of behavioral science placed great emphasis on the negative consequences of authoritarian management for both organizations and individuals. In voices sometimes gentle and sometimes determined we have addressed the power figures in organizations and called upon them to depart from old patterns, to risk a new approach, and to allow greater and more meaningful participation in the organization affairs by those below them in the hierarchy. Many of us have made substantial contributions to helping managers to recognize and exercise their responsibilities toward their subordinates. This has in the main been good and worthwhile. The time has come though, I believe, for us to begin to address subordinates as well. To help both manager and subordinates become aware of the alienating and vitality-sapping consequences of "playing helpless" or "playing helpful." To question ourselves and to encourage others to question unthinking acceptance of and adaptation to someone else's rules of good human relations, without regard to how those rules feel inside.

I believe it is worthwhile to urge ourselves and others to take new risks, risks of greater self assertion, more spontaneity and more willingness to experiment with aggression as well as love. If we in O.D. do indeed believe in a wider distribution of power, it would be well for us to stop trying to deny power's existence, muffle it, wish it away, or disguise it under velvet wrappings. Rather we can encourage as many people as possible, at *all* levels of the organization from highest manager to lowest subordinate to discover his own and use it.

OBJECTIVITY

I am not cool anymore
Dispassionate calm no longer moves
   me to admiring nods
I do not smile appreciatively
   at the neatly disciplined point
Nor at neatly checked restraint
Nor neatly channeled moderation

I am more messy now
And I like it better

The smoothly quiet logic that purrs
Like a Detroit built engine from
   the smoothly quiet throats of
   practiced men impresses me not
I suspect the emissions of those throats
   as much
   as I suspect the emissions of those engines

Pure reason is not pure
It is the product of an isolated head
And no head can be isolated
   yet still alive

A man is a total of all of himself
   plus probably more
And his reason issues from him —
   all of him
What is isolated is distorted or dead

It is no real message and not
   worth my hearing

Objectivity is a concept
And if I take it to mean my best attempt
To hold my prejudice in check
   for just a moment as I hear
It seems a decent thing to try
But if I make of it a more
   pretentious thing than that
I will only frown
And grow enmeshed in guards, and counter
   guards, and counter, counter guards
In senseless toiling to balance
   off the balances
To assure the fairness for all
   possible and potential points of view
Until, like some over sterilized
   laboratory culture
I am no fitting host for any
   viable position to take hold.

Fairness is a virtue I still find
But it is only one of many
And I would choose to find my fairness
In the clashes of expressions that allow
Life space for passions as well as reasons
Rather than in the noiseless mausoleums
   of disconnected minds.

COUNSELING AND CLINICAL TRAINING APPLICATIONS OF HUMAN RELATIONS THEORY AND PRACTICE

Richard Levin

The following are the personal observations of a trained clinical psychologist in his mid-fifties who has come on the human relations training scene in the last five years and who has been struck by the potency of human relations training for his wing of the helping professions. These comments are a highly personal view of the actuality of as well as the potential (and the gap between) in the application of human relations theory and techniques in formal programs training psychologists.

Early in the history of clinical psychology training several graduate programs across the country required, in the halcyon days of psychoanalysis, that all graduate students in psychology programs have a "didactic analysis" as part of the experiential requirements for achieving a doctoral degree. Over the years disillusionment with the exclusiveness of the analytic model as the method for dealing with human misery, as well as other theory content requirements in growing programs, forced the abandonment of this didactic analysis requirement. While there were coercive aspects of this particular requirement, the notion of learning something more about yourself in interaction with another person strikes me as being reasonable and needed. Perhaps the original attraction for me in human relations training activities, in the National Training Laboratories (NTL) model that I know best, has been the "therapy for normals" aspect of sensitivity training. The student in a helping profession, especially, needs a systematic arena in which he can interact with another and share his views of another's behaviors as well as have the other's impressions of his behavior fed back to him. Then the useful, self-learning-in-an-emotional-situation aspect of didactic therapy can be preserved. I see no other situation in which self-learning could be gained as fruitfully and as effectively as in a small-group human relations experience.

In addition to the therapy-for-normals aspect of sensitivity training, a body of theory and practice coming from many sources, including education, the performing arts, and applied psychology, is provided by activities in training. It is the positive quality of this theory of human behavior that has struck me particularly. Perhaps its impact on me was a function of where I had been within clinical psychology, and perhaps it provided for me some view of the nature of man-in-interaction that has struck me as important and needed. I had learned to focus on psychopathologic aspects of man. Viewing much of interpersonal behavior as ego-protective, shielding, and guarding, I had seen it crucial to cleverly diagnose and richly describe the myriad blemishes in the emotional wrappings of man. To what end? How much more fruitful to view man as an increasingly striving, coping, competence-asserting animal.

These ultra concerns with the fragility or destructiveness of man that I had had were modified a good deal by my participant and trainer experiences in human relations laboratories. In my first co-training experience with NTL, an initial T-group meeting on the first night of an eight-day lab, a woman participant spent what was (to me) an unusual amount of energy being verbally destructive to many others in the group. My initial reaction, carefully learned from earlier group therapy experiences with verbally assaultive folk like this, was to take this woman out of the group. I so recommended to my co-trainer, pointing out that her destructiveness seemed to predict an early end to her learning effectiveness, if not the group's. After some discussion we decided not to take her out, and I think this experience was a critical one for me. In the following eight days during which she began to talk and feel out some of her initial concerns with herself and with her being in the laboratory with several of the other participants, she revealed much more of a wholeness and purpose than my initial "castrating female" subcategory would have allowed. Had we removed her from the group, we could not have seen the warmth and compassion she later evidenced.

Activities which promote norms of personal responsibility, growth, and consciousness are to me the core of human interaction training activities for the budding mental health worker. Instead of looking for examples of defensive behavior to fit neat categories of locked-in habitual patterns for alleviating anxiety, initial efforts at coping should be seen as positive features of the person, qualities that are modifiable when the individual is provided appropriate feedback. In short, the basic theory or philosophy, as I see it in human relations training, is that of looking for strengths and effectiveness in human behavior.

Where does the developing counselor and clinical psychologist within his graduate program *experientially* receive this other view of human behavior? Surely he can read much of humanistic psychology — Maslow, Rogers, Shutz, etc. But how does a philosophy of effective human relations get experienced? One method for providing an opportunity for a student to gain these experiences is one with which I have personally experimented in a doctoral clinical program and am now trying out in a master's-level clinical program. It consists of the following steps for the student to go through to increase interpersonal competence as to acquire effective trainer or facilitator skills.

Step 1. Under the benevolent, facilitating auspices of senior faculty, the student interested in developing group skills and discovering something of his own potential in group situations meet as participants in a sensitivity or T-group. It is recommended that the experience extend through a minimum of one academic quarter or semester. Often to be most effective the group continues its life throughout the academic year. The issues of individual inclusion, appropriate group topics, the emotional life of students in a competitive program, and the many other problems that students, as humans, have would be dealt with in a group setting.

Step 2 consists of the student's serving as a junior co-trainer with a senior staff co-trainer working in a sensitivity group situation; typically undergraduate students volunteer to participate in this kind of experience. Here the clinical student can learn further of his reactions in a facilitating role, wrestle with the duel allegiances of participant and trainer, and rap with his instructor about the mysteries of the whole process. He should begin to read fairly extensively in the literature of group process, if he hasn't already done so.

Step 3 would be that of acting as a senior co-trainer with a less-advanced student as junior co-trainer. This would be done without the physical presence of the staff member but with the option of the staff member's checking the procedure on video or audio tapes.

This is the specific design in which this particular way of looking at human behavior has been implemented by me. The advantages of this procedure consist of the student's being a real living, breathing, interacting member of a growing group. The student is able to predict in broad outline the group issues by reading theory and by experiencing personally how these issues get played out. A student-trainer should not be permitted to retreat into highly intellectualized accounts of what seems to be going on out there, although his initial tendency to do so is strong. He has to be "up front" with respect to where his emotions are and what he is experiencing in order for him to be truly effective and functional and to be seen as such by the other participants in the group. He has to learn what was, at least for me, a difficult lesson, to trust the group process and the group itself to handle problems that he has previously believed should be handled appropriately only by an "expert." These include removing "disturbed" members from the group and feeling it necessary to categorize and implicitly "put down" the classes of behavior that are uncomfortable for him to experience in others. All of these "lessons" can, I think, only be learned in an experiential framework, in which the present feeling content of the situation is dealt with, rather than in a retreat into the past or a glimpse of the future.

Here and there around the country sensitivity training in the classroom is offered sometimes through social psychology activities and sometimes directly through counseling but more often through structures outside of the formal graduate programs. To my knowledge there is little real systematic presentation of a body of theory and practice relating to human relations, as described here, in the bulk of clinical training and counseling programs. I think the time is ripe for such a beginning.

Appended to this article is an account from the point of view of a faculty facilitator, Dr. Don Clark, of a sensitivity group that he and his wife conducted for first quarter graduate students in the Clinical Training Program at Appalachian State University.

FROM THE INSIDE

Sue and I had our stereotype of graduate students. They would wear us down with words. So we started right off the first session not talking — just doing body-tapping, a non-threatening, massage-type thing. We wanted to get through our feelings about psychology graduate students, and we wanted them aware of another way of relating.

We got close fast and left with a glow.

The second session two students invited friends. Sue let her aggravation be known because she had put a lot of herself into that first session and the people in that room were already special to her. Someone said they hadn't realized anyone had meant anything to anybody. The implication was they had just faked the warm feelings that first night and Sue felt betrayed. When she finished raising hell, one visitor excused himself fast. The rest of the session involved encouraging the other visitor to stay.

Next session was heavy. Some people almost didn't come. People were sitting off in corners taking little verbal pot-shots at Sue for last time's episode. When it finally hit me that they really thought we might have staged what happened and didn't realize Sue was honestly hurt, I got mad. All I could think of was that I was sitting in a room full of would-be psychologists soon to be helping others and they were acting more like patients in a therapy session. They seemed absolutely incapable of recognizing genuine feelings and totally incapable of dealing with their own.

I got so mad I just grabbed the most verbal member and arm-wrestled the hell out of both of us. It was great.

But at the next session, when he returned with, "You just jumped me to defend your wife," I knew I didn't like that guy and I told him so. What's more, I said I didn't think I would ever like him, and you know what he said? He said he finally believed we were for real, and he felt better.

After that the anger just seemed to get behind us. We had some great sessions. They began to learn to be quiet when their words were only words and to touch when it seemed sincere. We laughed and cried together and worried about our own phoninesses and each other's.

We gave them the best we had. Mostly we wanted them to experience us as authentic persons, and maybe they would gain courage to be more authentic. We wanted them to experience genuine involvement with other people. We wanted them to be more sensitive (I was glad when they finally recognized that graduate professors need lots of love, too.). And we wanted them to discover how they came across to others.

Anyway, we feel better about their working with other people because some of them did some mighty good things for us.

INTRODUCTION TO
THE RESOURCES SECTION

In the past few years there has been an explosion in the products field in human relations training. Interest in the area of simulated societies and simulation techniques has fostered an immense amount of product development and at the same time quite a bit of data. Information about human potential and its development has appeared in the form of printed and non-printed media — films, filmstrips, kits, books, handbooks, etc. — and it is the purpose of this section to help the group facilitator to gain some perspective on what materials and resources are available to him as he works with small groups.

There are four parts to the resources section. In the first part Frank Johnson extracts and summarizes the essential information available about the various associations in the human potential movement which the practitioner may wish to join. Brent Ruben, who is a specialist on communications and simulations, reviews representative materials in these areas and gives some guidelines for the selection and experimentation with commercially prepared materials available for use in groups. Norm Felsenthal has researched the area of films and other media resources and gives information about their availability and content for the practitioner.

The book review section focuses on six important publications, recently printed, that are well worth exploring by the person who works in groups. The basic criterion for selection of these books for review by experienced group facilitators is that each book should have some potential utility for the practitioner in the human relations training field. William Schutz's book, *Here Comes Everybody*, is reviewed by Jack Sherwood of Purdue. Schutz is most famous for his book, *Joy*. In, *Here Comes Everybody*, he explains what he calls the "encounter culture" and offers it as an alternative to the culture that we have been developing. Carl Rogers needs no introduction. Will Poland of the University of Cincinnati reviews Rogers' latest contribution, one of a long series in a brilliant career fostering human growth. Gerald Egan's book, *Encounter*, which explicates most clearly the concept of contract groups, is reviewed by Dick Heslin, also of Purdue. Robert Golembiewski and Blumberg's *Sensitivity Training* is a book of readings that contains some selections which are unavailable in any other place except in mimeograph or hard-to-get form, and Bob Le Lieuvre of Indiana University at Indianapolis spells out the merits of that collection. Tom Holman reviews *The Changing College Classroom*, by Runkle, one book which we believe needs to be read by people who are concerned with the application of human relations training technology and theory to the classroom. The Addison-Wesley OD series, is a set of books that is a must for every person who is interested in working with people inside organizations, and Tom Lyons of the University of Michigan evaluates those books from the point of view of their resourcefulness to the consultant in organization development.

We intend in future editions of the *Annual* to continue cataloging and critiquing the significant media presentations that are available to group facilitators, and we would appreciate hearing about their issuance. The development of the technology of human relations training has received great impetus from the advent of video-tape replay, inexpensive reproduction of materials, and so on. It is the objective of this section of the *Annual* to help the user to determine what is worth purchasing and how one goes about evaluating materials on his own.

ALPHABET SOUP

Frank Johnson

In most fields, the air eventually gets cluttered with a multitude of initials. The field of human relations is no exception. Following is an overview of organizations involved to varying degrees in Human Relations Training and related concerns.

NTL

NTL is the pioneer organization in applied behavioral science. It hearkens back almost directly to Kurt Lewin, who was the grandfather of us all. There are a number of tales about the inception, the one I like best goes like this:

Once upon a time, in a country called Connecticut, a short course was held for teachers. A few grad students had been asked to sit in and observe by the three men who were leading the session, and afterwards, they would gather in one of the local pubs and discuss what had gone on during the day. As often happens, some of the participants in the course edged their way into the "social hour." They decided, and told others in the class, that the observations as to what was happening, and why, were much more interesting than the content. To some professors that would come as a shock, but these men (Leland Bradford, Ronald Lippert, and Kenneth Benne) reacted creatively by helping to develop a conference the following summer at Gould Academy in Bethel, Maine to involve educators, psychologists, and sociologists in a discussion of the methods of education. Thus, in 1947, the National Training Laboratories was born.

The primary theme of the first year was process observation and group dynamics. However, it quickly became apparent that there were many personal payoffs in this methodology. As more attention was paid to these, the phrase "sensitivity training" was used to denote becoming more aware of one's self and others.

NTL began as a non-profit branch of the National Education Association (NEA), but in 1967 became a corporation — the NTL Institute for Applied Behavioral Science.

As the organization developed, there grew up a body of people who were able to provide leadership in laboratory learning situations. The NTL Network provided those in the field with some feelings of kinship and certification, although NTL never saw itself as a professional accreditation body. Recently, NTL was advised that the organization might be legally liable for anyone who worked anywhere as an NTL Trainer. This has resulted in a freezing of the present membership levels and the formation of a study group to look into the process of professional certification (see IAASS).

NTL is located at 1201 Sixteenth Street, N.W., in Washington, D. C., 20036. For further information, inquire of Vladamir Dupre who is the president.

O D NETWORK

One of the interests of behavioral science is the improvement and humanization of organizational life. Particular approaches of the experiential process have proved highly useful in work situations.

The Organizational Development Network was founded in 1964 to provide an affiliation and linkage among people who have similar concerns. Later it became a part of NTL.

Membership in the O D Network is both on an organization and an individual basis. There are two meetings a year and a newsletter. There are also helpful mailings about job openings, research, and other items of interest. For further information write Virginia Stacy at the NTL address (see above).

ARABS

The Association of Religion and Applied Behavioral Science was started in 1968 by a group of sixteen men who had a mutual concern for applying the tools of social psychology to the life of religious institutions.

The present membership of over 500 consists of those who share such interests, and who have had a basic HR lab experience (at least).

A further concern was of maintaining the high standards of those who were using such tools. A system was developed which provides denominations and other organizations with a directory of men qualified to lead small groups and conduct organizational change. The qualification system is a five-step process which utilizes evaluation and peer feedback. Anyone who trains would be interested in copies of the rating instruments which are based upon two levels: Laboratory Trainer and Professional.

For further information, write William Yon, Executive Director, at 521 North 20th Street, Birmingham, Alabama, 35203.

ASTD

The American Society for Training and Development is a must for those who are interested in organizational development. The cost includes a fine journal and your name in *Who's Who in Training and Development*. Membership also means involvement in a local chapter and there are certain division options as well, such as organizational development and community development. It is a society to develop the expansion of skills and standards for all professionals who are responsible for training and development. To find out more, write P.O. Box 5307, Madison, Wisconsin, 53705, or contact the chapter in your area.

IAASS

The International Association of Applied Social Scientists is a professional association, incorporated in June, 1971. The bylaws of the association recognize two principal foci of effort within this emerging profession:

a) Persons who work with small groups to facilitate re-education and learning of members through the use of collaborative and scientific methods; and,

b) Persons who intervene in larger social systems to facilitate system changes through the use of collaborative and scientific methods.

(See article on IAASS by Kenneth Benne and Steven Ruma).

This organization will attempt to be an accrediting agency for persons who work in small groups and organization development, while maintaining a cross-discipline membership.

For further information, contact Dr. Steven J. Ruma, 1755 Massachusetts Ave., N.W., Suite 300, Washington, D. C., 20039.

APA

The American Psychological Association was founded in 1892 and exists to advance psychology as a science, as a profession, and as a means of human welfare. The membership is limited to psychology educators and psychologists. They do have registration for non-members at their annual meetings — the one for next year is in Hawaii! For further information write the APA at 1200 Seventeenth Street, N.W., Washington, D. C. 20036.

AHP

The Association for Humanistic Psychology was begun as a step-child and also an alternative to the APA. The membership was deliberately designed to be inclusive of all those who feel motivated toward the helping professions and is based upon the value system that we all be more human. At the annual meeting (which usually precedes the APA Convention), the AHP tries to be experimental in subject matter and in style. There are a number of local chapters which provide the opportunity for more frequent meetings. For further information write AHP, 416 Hoffman Street, San Francisco, California 94114.

APA

Another APA with even more stringent membership requirements — the American Psychiatric Association. This is the professional society consisting solely of psychiatrists. Their address is 1700 Eighteenth Street, N.W., Washington, D. C. 20099.

AGPA

The American Group Psychotherapy Association includes psychiatrists, psychologists, social workers, and others in the mental health field who are interested in the practice and theory of group psychotherapy. Their offices are at 1790 Broadway, Room 702, New York City, New York 10019.

APGA

Not to be confused with the above is the American Personnel and Guidance Association. The purposes and the membership are broad. It includes guidance and personnel workers in elementary and secondary schools, in higher education, and in community agencies, organizations, government, industry, and business. Did I leave anyone out? There are many divisions, including the American College Personnel Association in which a study group is developing guidelines to rate group leaders. Write to 1605 New Hampshire Ave. N.W., Washington, D. C. 20009.

ASA

The American Sociological Association often has active local chapters. It is wide open as a professional society of sociologists, social scientists, and others interested in research, teaching, and the application of sociology. There is a division for those who are mainly interested in Social Psychology. Offices are at 1001 Connecticut Avenue, N.W., Washington, D. C. 20036.

AMA

The American Management Association includes professional management executives in industry, commerce, government, service and non-commercial organizations, and teachers of management. Its purpose is simple — to help managers do a better job. They provide a good many educational services to further this goal. The offices are at 135 W. 50th, New York City, New York 10020.

Two other organizations which may be of interest to some of you are:

AAPC American Association of Pastoral Counselors,
201 E 19th Street, New York, New York, 10003.

AAMC American Association of Marriage Counselors,
27 Woodcliff Drive, Madison, New Jersey, 07940.

The list is not exhaustive, but it should be a good start for those interested in sharing resources in the related fields of applied behavioral science.

GAMES
AND SIMULATIONS:
MATERIALS
SOURCES, AND LEARNING CONCEPTS

Brent D. Ruben

Experience-based learning is rapidly becoming a familiar concept to nearly everyone involved in the realm of social education, from preschool to postgraduate work. A few years ago terms like "games," "simulations," and "structured exercises," had little meaning beyond the gymnasium or the industrial research laboratory. Today they are an important part of a vocabulary used by the applied behavioral scientist, the educator, and the group facilitator alike.

The accelerating growth of experiential learning is a mixed blessing. The market is flooded with games, simulation kits, and so called "how-to-do-it" manuals, but there is an alarming absence of persons with more than a passing knowledge of the basic concepts of experience-based learning design and application. Reflecting this fact, this paper consists of two separate but related sections: one providing a listing and brief discussion of some of the sources of packaged game and simulation kits; the second presenting a cursory treatment of some basic experiential learning concepts together with a selected list of correlative readings and resources.

GAMES AND SIMULATIONS

Games and simulations are available in various sizes and shapes, covering a variety of topics and content areas, at prices ranging from less than $1.00 to well over $100.00. Some are designed for use with as few as one or two participants; others are constructed for 200-300 participants.

Though there are many differences between the various social games and simulations, all represent abstractions on certain elements of human, individual and social behavior. These abstractions are reconstructed in miniaturized fashion to create a dynamic and involving laboratory learning environment. Thus such factors as competition, play, and peer group pressure — all forms of social interaction which play an important part in our daily lives — are brought into the classroom, becoming a relevant source of, or at least motivation toward, learning.

Many of the packaged instruction games and simulations have little or no apparent applicability to the typical goals of the small group. If these are to be useful, significant adaptation is required. Some, on the other hand, are obviously pertinent. In studying the listings of publisher and distributor brochures, a number of titles and descriptions suggests themselves as relevant and consistent with the foci of small group and laboratory work. Among those are GHETTO, GENERATION GAP, PLANS, CRISIS, EDPLAN, CULTURE CONTACT, TRACTS, IMPACT, BODY TALK, BLACKS AND WHITES, AND SQUIRMS.

GHETTO, distributed by Western Publishing Company, is constructed to provide participants with a sense of the conditions under which the urban poor strive to improve their situation in the face of continual frustrations. It is designed for use with seven to ten junior high- through adult-level players, takes two to four hours to play, and is priced at $20.00

GENERATION GAP, also distributed by Western, is a simulation of the interaction between a parent and an adolescent son or daughter around particular issues where conflicts of attitudes are likely to arise. The interactions and conflicts are regulated by a set of rules and a power structure representative of that of the family setting. The kit is designed for use with four to ten junior high through high school players, requires less than one hour to play, and costs $10.00.

PLANS, available through Simile II, is a game in which participants are involved as members of an interest group which seeks to influence the directions of American society. Six interest groups are used in all: military, civil rights, nationalists, internationalists, business, and labor. The game is appropriate for use with twenty-five to thirty-five junior high through adult level participants, requires three to eight hours to play, and sells for between $20.00 and $50.00, depending upon the number of players involved.

CRISIS, also available through Simile II, is a simulation of international conflict, in which players serve on teams representing one of six fictional nations. The nations vary in strength and military capacity and collectively must resolve situations essential to their mutual well-being. The game is designed for use with twenty-five to thirty-five junior high school through adult participants, requires two to four hours to play, and sells for between $35.00 and $50.00, depending upon the number of player kits desired.

EDPLAN, available from Abt Associates, is an education system planning game constructed to illustrate the major issues involved in planning educational strategies and to suggest various alternatives to dealing with those issues. The simulation game is designed for use with twenty-nine to thirty-six high schoolers, teachers, administrators, or PTA and costs $25.00.

CULTURE CONTACT, also distributed by Abt, is a role-play game designed to focus upon the sorts of misunderstanding and potential conflict which can arise when a trading expedition docks at an island inhabited by a pre-industrial society. It is designed for use with twenty to thirty upper elementary through high school level players and costs $25.00.

TRACTS, available from Instructional Simulations, is a simulation designed to focus upon the social and political issues involved in controversy inherent in core city land use. The game is constructed for use with twelve to forty junior high through adult-level participants, requires two to four hours to play, and costs $39.00.

IMPACT, also available from Instructional Simulations, is a group problem-solving simulation which focuses upon decision-making in community action. It seeks to illustrate the results of individual and collective actions upon an imaginary community, its institutions, associations and residents.

BODY TALK, a Psychology Today game, focuses upon the realm of nonverbal communication and is designed to heighten participant awareness of their own nonverbal behavior. The game is designed for use by adult players and costs $5.95.

BLACKS AND WHITES, another Psychology Today game, is designed to provide participants with an awareness of what is involved in being black and poor and to suggest the nature of ghetto conditions. The game is designed for use by adult players and costs $6.95.

SQUIRMS, available through Contemporary Drama Service, are sets of role-play simulations organized around particular levels, topics, and contexts. A kit of general role-play interaction situations is available for use with elementary, junior high, high school, college and adult participants. Specialized kits, which focus on problems associated with the generation gap and sex education, are also available. Each package costs $5.00.

These are some of the instructional games and simulations of potential use in the context of the small group laboratory. A comprehensive list of sources and details regarding those mentioned here are available from publishers and distributors, who each have available catalogues and brochures of their offerings.

In addition to simulations and games described above, I have included at the end of this paper listings of related articles and resource books under the following subheadings: Experience-Based Learning, Instructional Simulations and Games, and Instructional Role-Playing and

236

Structured Group Exercises. Also included is a list of the mailing addresses of the major commercial sources of games and simulations.

Interestingly, the primary problem for the individual who wants to make use of these or other simulations and games is deciding how to think about what he and the people who design the games are up to. Only with this matter resolved can he hope to make reasonable applications of the techniques to his own spheres of activity. One way to focus upon the central issue is to consider the structure and functioning of experience-based activities in general. (Ruben, 1971.) Five elements are common to all: 1) participants in *roles*, 2) *interactions* between participants/roles, 3) *rules* governing interactions, 4) *goals* with respect to which the interactions occur, and 5) *criteria* for determining the attainment of the goals and the end of activity.

While each of these elements is present in all experience-based activities, their importance, composition, and origin differs greatly from one design to another. Sometimes the roles, interactions, rules, goals, and criteria are clearly specified by the design of the activity or by the trainer, and participants have little latitude in their determination. These I term *external parameter* activities. In other instances, most of the decisions as to participant roles, interactions, goals, and so on are made by participants, as a part of the activity. These are *internal parameters*.

The terms and the distinctions that they indicate can be important, since each type of activity is appropriate for a particular kind of teaching/learning objective. In the simplest sense the distinction has to do with whether it is desirable for participants to learn *particular and specific known* knowledges, behaviors, skills, or facts, or on the other hand, acquire general competency, question, inquire, make decisions, *create* knowledge. Where that which is to be learned can be specified and enumerated and where the objective is teaching known knowledge, a tightly structured, and controlled (external parameter) activity is necessary and desirable. One example of the appropriate use of external parameters is the case where the trainer or designer intersperses a number of "theory sessions" between T-Group meetings within a laboratory context. A structured situation is posited whereby participants exchange feedback with one another and evaluate what they have done against a set of criteria previously developed in their sessions. Through participation in this activity, all participants are exposed to and gain at least a passing familiarity with a particular set of known knowledges.

In contrast is the internal parameter activity, in which the goal is the creating of individual knowledge, the inventing of personal coping strategies, and increasing of self-awareness. It is neither necessary nor probably desirable for all participants to be exposed to the same experiences or to learn the same things. Such experiences can be characterized more by the *striving for* than the *attainment of*.

The classic example of the internal parameter experience — at least in theory — is the T-group or encounter group, where participant roles, patterns of interactions, rules, goals, and criteria evolve almost entirely from the activity of the participants, rather than being imposed by the designer or trainer.

A logical consequence of the use of external parameter activities is the encouragement of homogeneity among participants in the way they understand and experience the activities to which they are exposed, as well as the applications they come to make of their learning in other "back home" situations. Since internal parameter experiences are less likely to be similarly experienced by all participants, they can foster heterogeneity among participants and can permit the reaching of diverse and non-overlapping goals by those involved. Paradoxically, the most effective internal parameter activity may be dramatically ineffective viewed in terms of the goals associated with the external parameter experience. Where the learning goal is having each participant come to his own understanding and judgment of the relevance of "touching" or "honesty" for his own life pursuits, external parameter activities, which foster *similarity* in the way people are exposed, are clearly dysfunctional.

The parameters of experiential techniques are not usually at the extreme positions of being completely internal or completely external. Usually the extent to which they fall into one or the other category is a function of how the designer or utilizer thinks about what he's doing. The point to be underscored is that the design or selection of instructional games and simulations must necessarily be preceded by the design or selection of a framework within which the games and simulations will operate toward the growth goals of the particular group.

BASIC SOURCES

Experience-Based Learning

Archambault, Reginald, ed., *Lectures in the Philosophy of Education: 1899 by John Dewey*. New York: Random House, 1966.

Bennis, Warren G., Edgar H. Schein, Fred I. Steele, and David E. Berlew, *Interpersonal Dynamics*. Homewood, Ill.: The Dorsey Press, 1964.

Bruner, J. S., ed., *Learning About Learning: A Conference Report*. Washington: U.S. Government Printing Office, 1966.

Bruner, J. S., *The Process of Education*. Cambridge, Mass.: Harvard Press, 1961.

Bruner, J. S., *The Relevance of Education*. New York: Norton, 1971.

Bruner, J. S., *Toward a Theory of Instruction*. New York: Norton, 1966.

Budd, Richard W., "Communication, Education and Simulation: Some Thought on the Learning Process," Institute for Communication Studies, University of Iowa, Iowa City, Iowa, December, 1970.

Churchman, C. West, "Education in a Technological Age," Center for the Study of Democratic Institutions, Philosophy Colloquium, April, 1968.

Danish, Paul, *Champaign Report: A Conference on Educational Reform — A Student View*, Champaign, Illinois, September, 1966.

Dewey, John, *Experience and Education*. New York: Macmillan Company, 1938.

Forces in Learning, National Training Laboratories National Education Association, 1961.

Gardner, John W., *Self-Renewal: The Individual and the Innovative Society*. New York: Harper & Row, 1965.

Harvey, O. J., ed., *Experience, Structure and Adaptability*. New York: Springer Publishing Co., Inc., 1966.

Holt, John, *How Children Learn*. New York: Pitman Publishing Co., 1967.

MacLean, Malcolm S., Jr., "A Process Concept of Communication Education: A Position Statement for the Educational Policies Committee," School of Journalism, University of Iowa, 1966. (Mimeo.)

Montessori, Maria, *The Montessori Method*. New York: Schocken Books, 1964.

Montessori, Maria, *Spontaneous Activity in Education*. New York: Schocken Books, 1965.

Neil, A. S., *Summerhill: A Radical Approach to Child Rearing*. New York: Hart Publishing Co., 1960.

Postman, Neil and Charles Weingartner, *Teaching as a Subversive Activity*. New York: Delacorte Press, 1969.

Riesman, David, *Constraint and Variety of American Education*. Lincoln, Neb.: University of Nebraska Press, 1968.

Rogers, Carl R., *Freedom to Learn*. Columbus, Ohio: Charles E. Merrill Publishing Co., 1969.

Ruben, Brent D., "The General Problem-Solving Simulation," in *Experience Learning*, Robert S. Lee, ed. New York: Basic Books. (in press).

Schroder, Harold M., Michael J. Driver and Siegfried Streufert, *Human Information Processing*. New York: Holt, Rinehart & Winston, Inc. 1967.

Thayer, Lee, "Systems, Games and Learning," in *Experience Learning*, Robert S. Lee, ed. New York: Basic Books, (in press).

Thayer, Lee, "Human Communication: Tool, Game, Ecology," *Perspectives on Communication*, Carl E. Larson, Frank E. X. Dance, eds., Speech Communication Center, University of Wisconsin, Milwaukee, Wisconsin.

Thayer, Lee, "On Communication and Change: Some Provocations," *Systematics*, Vol. 6, No. 3, December, 1968.

Instructional Simulations and Games

Abt, Clark C., *Serious Games*. New York: The Viking Press, 1970.

Boocock, Sarane S. and E. O. Schild, ed., *Simulation Games in Learning*. Beverly Hills, Calif.: Sage Publications, Inc., 1968.

Cherryholmes, Cleo H., "Some Current Research on Effectiveness of Educational Simulations: Implications for Alternative Strategies." *American Behavioral Scientist*, Vol. X, No. 2, October, 1966.

Coleman, James S., "Games as Vehicles for Social Theory," *American Behavioral Scientist*, Vol. 12, July-August, 1969.

Coleman, James S., "Introduction: In Defense of Games," *American Behavioral Scientist*, Vol. 10, October, 1966.

Crawford, Meredith P., "Dimensions of Simulation," *American Psychologist*, Vol. 21, No. 8, August, 1966.

Dill, William R. and Neil Doppelt, "The Acquisition of Experience in Complex Management Game," *Management Science*, Vol. 10, No. 1, October, 1963.

MacLean, Malcolm S., Jr., "Theory, Method and Games in Communication," in *Mass Media and International Understanding*, France Vreg, ed., Ljubljana, Yugoslavia: School of Sociology, Political Science and Journalism, Part I, 1969.

McKenney, James and William R. Dill, "Influences on Learning in Simulation Games," *American Behavioral Scientist*, Vol. 10, October, 1966.

Raser, John R., *Simulation and Society: An Exploration of Scientific Gaming*. Boston: Allyn and Bacon, Inc., 1969.

Tansey, P. J. and Derick Unwin, *Simulation and Gaming in Education*. London: Methuen Education, Ltd., 1969.

Twelker, Paul A., ed., *Instructional Simulation Systems*. Corvallis, Oregon: Continuing Education Publications, Oregon State University, Department of Printing, 1969.

Werner, Roland and Joan T. Werner, *Bibliography of Simulations: Social Systems and Education.* LaJolla, Calif.: Western Behavioral Sciences Institute, 1969.
Wilson, J. P. and D. E. Adams, "A Selected Bibliography of Simulation and Related Subjects, 1960-1969," Pittsburgh, Kansas: Political Science, Kansas State College, April 6, 1970.
Youngers, John C. and John F. Aceti, *Simulation Games and Activities for Social Studies.* Dansville, N.Y.: The Instructor Publications, Inc. 1969.

Instructional Role-Playing and
Structured Group Exercises

Bavelas, Alex, "Role Playing and Management Training," *Sociatry*, Vol. I, No. 2, June, 1947.
Blansfield, Michael G., "Role-Playing as a Method in Executive Development," *Personnel Journal*, Vol. 34, 1953.
Chesler, Mark and Robert Fox, *Role-Playing Methods in the Classroom.* Chicago: Science Research Associates, Inc., 1966.
Corsini, Raymond J., Malcolm E. Shaw and Robert R. Blake, *Roleplaying in Business and Industry.* New York: Free Press of Glencoe, 1961.
Klein, Alan F., *How to Use Role Playing Effectively.* New York: Association Press, 1959.
Knowles, Malcolm and Hilda, *How to Develop Better Leaders.* New York: Association Press, 1955.
Lippitt, Ronald, "The Psychodrama in Leadership Training," *Sociometry*, Vol. VI, No. 3, August, 1943.
Maier, Norman, R. F. and A. R. Solem, "Audience Role Playing: A New Method in Human Relations Training," *Human Relations*, Vol. IV, No. 3, 1951.
Mial, Dorothy J. and Stanley Jacobson, "10 Interaction Exercises for the Classroom," National Training Laboratories.
Moreno, J. L. and Edgar F. Borgatta, "An Experiment with Sociodrama and Sociometry in Industry," *Sociometry*, Vol. XIV, No. 1, February, 1951.
Moreno, J. L., *Psychodrama*, Vol. I, New York: Beacon House, 1946.
Nylen, Donald J., Robert Mitchell and Anthony Stout, *Handbook of Staff Development and Human Relations Training: Materials Developed for Use in Africa.* Washington, D.C.: National Training Laboratories Institute for Applied Behavioral Science, 1967.
Parnes, Sidney J., *Creative Behavior Guidebook.* New York: Charles Scribner's Sons, 1967.
Parnes, Sidney J., *Creative Behavior Workbook.* New York: Charles Scribner's Sons, 1967.
Pfeiffer, J. William and John E. Jones, *A Handbook of Structured Experiences for Human Relations Training, Volumes I, II, III.* Iowa City, Iowa: University Associates Press, 1969, 1970, 1971.
Shaftel, Fannie R., *Role-Playing for Social Values: Decision-Making in the Social Studies.* Englewood Cliffs, N.J.: Prentice-Hall, 1967.

MAILING ADDRESSES OF
PUBLISHERS AND DISTRIBUTORS
OF GAMES AND SIMULATIONS

1. *Abt Associates, Inc.,* 55 Wheeler Street, Cambridge, Mass. 02138
2. *Academic Games Associates,* 430 East 33rd Street, Baltimore, Maryland, 21218
3. *Avalon-Hill,* 4517 Hartford Road, Baltimore, Maryland 21214
4. *Center for Simulation Studies,* 634 North Grand Avenue, St. Louis, Missouri 63103
5. *Contemporary Drama Service,* Arthur Meriweth, Inc.
6. *Didactic Systems, Inc.,* Box 500, Westbury, New York 11590
7. *Dynasty International,* 815 Park Avenue, New York, New York 10022
8. *Games Research, Inc.,* 48 Wareham Street, Boston, Mass. 02118
9. *Herder & Herder,* 232 Madison Avenue, New York, New York 10016
10. *Interact,* P.O. Box 262, Lakeside, Calif. 92040
11. *International Learning Corporation,* 3233 S. W. 2nd Avenue, Fort Lauderdale, Florida 33315
12. *Instructional Simulations, Inc.,* 2147 University Avenue, St. Paul, Minn. 55114
13. *MacMillan,* 866 Third Avenue, New York, New York 10022
14. *Psychology Today Games,* P.O. Box 60279, Terminal Annex, Los Angeles, Calif. 90080
15. *Scott, Foresman & Co.,* Glenview, Illinois 60025
16. *Science Research Associates,* 259 East Erie Street, Chicago, Illinois 60611
17. *Simile II,* P.O. Box 1023, 1150 Silverado, La Jolla, Calif. 92057
18. *Simulation Systems Program,* Teaching Research, A Division of the Oregon State System of Higher Education, Monmouth, Oregon 97361
19. *University Associates Press,* P.O. Box 615, Iowa City, Iowa 52240
20. *Urban Systems, Inc.,* 1033 Massachusetts Avenue, Cambridge, Mass. 02138
21. *Western Publishing Co.,* 850 Third Avenue, New York, New York 10022

MEDIA RESOURCES FOR HUMAN RELATIONS TRAINING

Norman Felsenthal

Communicators seeking to bridge the gap between theory and practice will find an ally in the motion picture. Instructional films can be invaluable as an aid for clarifying abstract concepts, illustrating specific points, and stimulating discussion.

This annotated film listing is intended to acquaint potential users with some of the motion pictures that are appropriate for communication-oriented activities. Most of these films are readily available from university extension film libraries.

Copyright dates and approximate rental fees for most films are included in the annotations. The fee listed is generally a five-day loan by Indiana University, the largest of the extension film libraries. Naturally, rentals vary but the fees set by universities are generally lower than those charged by commercial film distributors.

Motion pictures available for loan from the Indiana Audio-Visual Center library are noted by the "IU" designation within the annotation. Films available from the Psychological Cinema Register of Pennsylvania State University are marked "PCR." Many of the motion pictures designated "IU" and/or "PCR" are also available from other libraries.

Listed below are the addresses of selected university audio-visual centers with sizeable extension film libraries. Most of these libraries will send a catalog upon request.

NATION-WIDE

Audio-Visual Center
Extension Division
Indiana University
Bloomington, IN 47401

Psychological Cinema Register
Pennsylvania State University
6 Willard Building
University Park, PA 16802

EAST

Memorial Film Library
Boston University
765 Commonwealth Ave.
Boston, MA 02215

Audiovisual Center
University of Maine
Education Building
Orono, ME 04473

Film Library
New York University
26 Washington Place
New York, NY 10003

Film Library
Syracuse University
1455 E. Colvin Street
Syracuse, NY 13210

SOUTH

Media Center
Florida State University
Tallahassee, FL 32306

Film Library
Center for Continuing Education
University of Georgia
Athens, GA 30601

Educational Film Library
School of Education

University of Mississippi
University, MS 38677

Audio-Visual Aids Bureau
University of South Carolina
Carolina Coliseum
Columbia, SC 29208

MIDWEST

Visual Aids Service
University of Illinois
704 South 6 Street
Champaign, IL 61820

Bureau of Visual Instruction
University of Kansas
Bailey Hall, Room 6
Lawrence, KS 66044

Audio-Visual Education Center
University of Michigan
416 Fourth Street
Ann Arbor, MI 48103

Audio-Visual Center
University of Iowa
East Hall
Iowa City, Iowa 52240

Audiovisual Services
Kent State University
Kent, Ohio 44240

Bureau of Audiovisual Instruction
University of Wisconsin
1327 University Avenue
P.O. Box 2093
Madison, WI 53701

SOUTHWEST

Central Arizona Film Co-op
Arizona State University

Tempe, Arizona 85281

Film Library
Eastern New Mexico University
Portales, NM 88130

Audio-Visual Center
Oklahoma State University
Stillwater, OK 74074

Visual Instruction Bureau
Division of Extension
University of Texas
Austin, TX 78712

WEST

Educational Media Center
University of Colorado

Room 320, Stadium Bldg.
Boulder, CO 80302

Audiovisual Instruction
Oregon State System of Higher Educ.
133 Gill Coliseum
Corvallis, OR 97331

Extension Media Center
University of California
2223 Fulton Street
Berkeley, CA 94720

Division of Cinema
Univ. of Southern California
Los Angeles, CA 90007

When possible, films should be previewed prior to selection; they should always be previewed prior to utilization. Frequently, films can be previewed without charge if the potential user is able to visit the film library and do his viewing on the premises. Users who request that films be mailed are generally charged full rental fees regardless of how or if the films are used.

A wide variety of other audio-visual media are available but are not listed in this edition of the *Annual*. These media include overhead transparencies, video tapes, tape-slide packages, and audio tape cassettes. This latter resource is particularly popular with some human relations trainers. Two sources for audio tape cassettes specifically related to human relations activities are:

The Human Development Institute
A Division of Bell & Howell
20 Executive Park West, N.E.
Atlanta, GA 30329

Development Digest
P.O. Box 49483
Los Angeles, Calif. 90049

All films and film series annotated on the following pages are listed alphabetically under one of four subject headings — *General Communication and Communication Theory, Group Dynamics, Human Relations Training,* and *Managerial Training and Organizational Development.* Films in a designated series are listed under the series title; films within each series are listed sequentially when a particular viewing order is recommended, alphabetically when this is not the case. The NET designation is used to identify films originally produced for broadcast by National Educational Television.

GENERAL COMMUNICATION AND COMMUNICATION THEORY

BATTLE OF CHICAGO: THE DYNAMICS OF CONFRONTATION

A "multi-media package" which includes film, audio tapes, and text. Tapes include observations by historian, sociologist, psychologist, and political scientist. 45 min. The Film Group, 430 West Grant Place, Chicago, Illinois.

CASE HISTORY OF A RUMOR (CBS News)

Traces the development of a rumor as it changes from gossip to rumor to hysteria, ballooning a simple military exercise into a planned United Nations invasion of the United States. 1963, 54 min., $11.75, IU.

COMMUNICATION PRIMER

Animation and other techniques are used to illustrate communication models. Excellent overview of the Shannon-Weaver model, the concept of "noise," and the utilization of redundancy in language. Good basic film for those unfamiliar with conceptual theories of communication. 23 min., color, IU and others. $7.00.

ESP: THE HUMAN "X" FACTOR (NET)

Film visits the Parapsychology Laboratory at Duke University where J. B. Rhine explains why he is investigating extrasensory perception. Defines and demonstrates clairvoyance, psychokinesis, and precognition. 30 min., $6.75, PCR, IU, others.

EYE OF THE BEHOLDER, THE

The "classic" film on perception. Extremely well-produced. Dramatizes a twelve-hour period in the life of an artist. This dramatization is based on the incorrect perceptions of five persons who observed his actions. The second half of the film reviews the same twelve-hour period with emphasis on "what really happened." Three of the five incorrect perceptions are caused by psychological projection; the other two by faulty generalization. Some users like to stop the film half-way through to elicit viewer response before proceeding with the second half. (Note: This film is widely used. The instructor or trainer may wish to identify those in his audience who have previously seen the film and encourage them to help the presentation by not giving the film away.) 1954, 25 min., IU, PCR, others. Around $6.00.

FOLLOW THE LEADER

A film about children who play at war with make-believe guns; a disturbing study of mob psychology. 1965, 23 min., Carousel Films, Inc., 1501 Broadway, New York City, 10036.

HIPPIE TEMPTATION, THE (CBS)

Describes the Hippie culture and its impact on youth in contemporary American society. Harry Reasoner narrates this documentary and takes viewers into a Hippie colony in San Francisco's Haight-Ashbury district. He provides commentary on the reasons behind young people becoming Hippies and the great dependence of the Hippie culture on drugs, particularly LSD. The film summarizes the positive and negative aspects of young people trying to adjust to the often confusing middle-class world. 1968, 51 min., color, Contemporary/McGraw-Hill Films, 330 West 42nd Street, New York City, 10036.

LANGUAGE BY GESTURE

Unrehearsed meeting between two persons unable to speak one another's language. Learning a language without the aid of a translator is demonstrated. 28 min., $6.10, PCR.

MASLOW AND SELF-ACTUALIZATION — Two Parts

Abraham Maslow discusses the dimensions of self-actualization and elaborates on recent research and theory related to honesty, awareness, freedom and trust. 1968, each part 30 min., color. Psychological Films, 205 West 20th Street, Santa Ana, Calif. 92706.

MESSAGE TO NO ONE, THE (Champion Paper Series)

Highly stylized and "campish" dramatization of the problem of listening as it affects the members of a family. Very basic. Good for paraprofessional and lower-management. Also for older audiences. Lacks sophistication for educated and/or young adults. 1954, 26 min., color, various film libraries.

PERCEPTION AND COMMUNICATION

Introduces two theories of perception — cognitive and transitional — and illustrates these theories in a number of sequences. 32 min., color, IU, $6.00.

PROCESS OF COMMUNICATION

Extends models, theories, and practical examples of various aspects of communications as a process and shows diagrammatic communications models which encompass the concept of noise. 45 min., color, IU, $7.70.

PRODUCTION 5118 (Champion Paper Series)

A non-conventional view of human communication and the problem of understanding others. Dramatized incidents illustrate how and why person-to-person communications are frequently misperceived. 1954, 29 min., color, various film libraries.

PSYCHOLOGY OF HUMOR, A

University of Houston psychologist Richard Evans discusses the psychology of humor with comedians Buddy Hackett and Johnny Carson. 1964, 20 min., Association Films, Inc., 600 Madison Avenue, New York City, 10022.

TIME PIECE

Strange mixture of zany comedy and serious comment. Surrealistic. A filmic stream of consciousness. 1965, 10 min., color, $15.00, Contemporary/McGraw Hill Films, 330 West 42nd Street, New York City, 10036.

WHY MAN CREATES (Saul Bass for Kaiser Aluminum)

Highly unusual and provocative film. Academy Award-Winner as best short subject. Employs both live-action and animation. Eight separate and distinct episodes, each of which explores some facet of man's desire to be creative. 1968, 25 min., color, Free from Modern Talking Picture Service, 1212 Avenue of the Americas, New York City, 10036.

GROUP DYNAMICS

ALL I NEED IS A CONFERENCE

Older film but still relevant. Some do's and don'ts on how to lead a meeting. Reluctant conferees bring with them an unseen assortment of personal and business problems. Emphasizes that in order to deal successfully with whatever problem is on the table, you must first know how to deal with the people around it. 1954, 28 min., color.

DYNAMICS OF LEADERSHIP SERIES (NET)

Designed as a community training program for more effective group action, each of five films features group drama, interspersed with the commentary of Malcolm Knowles of Boston University. Each film, 30 min., $6.75, IU, others. Films in the series include:

Anatomy of a Group: Explores structure of a group, characteristic patterns and differences in individual participation, and the quality of communication among members.

Individual Motivation and Behavior: Attempts to illustrate the wide range of individual behavior within the group.

Diagnosing Group Operations: Examines conflicts within the group. Points out signs of conflict, withdrawal, factionalism, and group indecision.

Sharing the Leadership: Defines leadership and examines how it develops within the group. Explores self-serving functions, task functions, and group-serving functions.

Roadblocks to Communication: Illustrates faulty listening. Distinguishes between genuine disagreements and those due to misunderstanding. Explores the concept of "feedback" and explains the use of watchdog and reaction panels.

EXPERIMENTAL STUDIES IN SOCIAL CLIMATES OF GROUPS
(K. Lewin, R. Lippitt, and R. White)

Hidden camera views unrehearsed activities of a series of boys' clubs organized experimentally with either democratic, autocratic, or laissez faire atmospheres. Narrator explains each situation and discusses graphs which illustrate research results. From the original films of Kurt Lewin. 1953, 33 min., $6.50, PCR and others.

SOCIAL ANIMAL, THE (NET)

Excellent film for understanding certain "classic" research in social psychology. Film opens with overview of the Asch research on social conformity (line length), then presents, in sequence, Stanley Schachter, Leon Festinger, and Morton Deutsch. Each psychologist utilizes subjects in experimental settings to illustrate his research findings including group exclusion of deviates (Schachter), cognitive dissonance (Festinger) and interpersonal bargaining (Deutsch). 29 min., 1963, PCR, IU and others. $7.00.

HUMAN RELATIONS TRAINING

CHARLIE, YOU MADE THE NIGHT TOO LONG

Affluent whites are driving through a ghetto when their car breaks down. They seek refuge in a bar. Their attempts to get a cab and to seek help from an auto club are both unsuccessful. With a riot about to break out in the ghetto, the whites are confronted by militants. Angry exchanges occur but, in the process, real dialogue begins. Each side gets to know the other better. The head militant drives the whites home. 27 min., Association Films, Inc., 600 Madison Avenue, New York City, 10022.

COME OUT, COME OUT, WHOEVER YOU ARE (NET)

Many mental patients become so dependent upon the hospital that they do not want to be released. Film illustrates "confrontation therapy" with nine long-term patients. Patients are forced to examine their abnormal behavior. Within six months one man spoke his first word in 23 years and seven of the nine found jobs in the outside world. 1971, 59 min., IU, $13.50.

CONFLICT RESOLUTION RESEARCH

Psychological conflict problems examined. Dr. Morris Shamos talks with Dr. Morton Deutsch of Columbia University and Dr. Larry Solomon of the Western Behavioral Institute. Research in inter-personal conflict as experimented with in a laboratory, illustrated by film excerpts and demonstrations. 1966, 30 min., PCR, $2.00.

DEHUMANIZATION AND THE TOTAL INSTITUTION

Animated film calls attention to those practices in institutions which may adversely affect human dignity and suggests possible methods of eliminating the practices that lead to "dehumanization." Discussion guide accompanies film. *Not intended for the general public.* 1966, 15 min., Contemporary/McGraw-Hill Films, 330 West 42nd Street, New York City, 10036.

FEELING OF HOSTILITY, THE (Nat. Film Board of Canada)

Older well-produced film dramatizes the factors producing resentment and hostility in personal relationships. In the story of Clare we see how the death of her father and the later remarriage of her mother discouraged her in seeking affectional relationships with others. Though successful in college and business, she feels the lack of fellowship and understanding. The factors behind this emotional inadequacy are reviewed by a psychiatrist. 1951, 31 min., IU, PCR, others, $7.00.

FEELING OF REJECTION, THE (Nat. Film Board of Canada)

Older well-produced case history. A 23-year-old girl has physical disorders but no physical cause. A psychiatrist shows her the root of her troubles — childhood over-protection and discouragement of her efforts to express herself, resulting in a crippling fear of failure and a complete inability to assert herself. 1948, 21 min., IU, PCR, others. $5.50.

FEELINGS OF DEPRESSION (Nat. Film Board of Canada)

Older well-produced case history of a businessman whose feelings of depression have carried over from childhood to overshadow his adult life. Film illustrates how persisting reactions to early emotional problems render the subject incapable of enjoying a happy, normal life. 1948, 30 min., IU, PCR, others. $7.00.

FIDELITY OF REPORT

A silent audience-participation device designed to demonstrate degree of accuracy of observation and report. A dramatic action sequence shows women robbed while waiting for a bus. This action takes 60 seconds after which the projector is to be stopped. A standard set of questions (accompanying the film) is given to the audience to answer. The dramatic action is repeated by continuing the projection, and each observer is asked to check the accuracy of his own report of the event. 1946, 6 min., IU, PCR, others, $3.00.

GAMES PEOPLE PLAY: THE THEORY (NET)

Interviews with Eric Berne, during which he explains the assumption upon which his theory of transactional analysis is based. Berne also discusses the relationship of his method of transactional analysis to the more traditional methods of psychoanalysis and describes such games as "Rapo" and "PTA". 1967, 30 min., IU, PCR, others, $6.75.

GAMES PEOPLE PLAY: THE PRACTICE (NET)

Continutation of interviews with Eric Berne, during which he explains his use of the terms "game," "script," "ego state," and others. Explanation of the term "transaction" rather than "interaction." Relates the problems of one of his patients to a fairy tale which he says can be used to explain the "script" which the patient is unconsciously following. 1967, 30 min., IU, PCR, others, $6.75.

I WISH I KNEW HOW IT WOULD FEEL TO BE FREE

Candid interviews with Blacks living in a New Haven, Conn., ghetto. Intimate scenes in a pool-hall, barbershop, and on the street. Opinions of black power advocates and black law enforcement agents. Accompanied by music of Nina Simone. 1968, 20 min., PCR, $4.60.

JOURNEY INTO SELF (Carl Rogers)

Record of intensive basic encounter group session led by Carl Rogers and Richard Farson. Focuses on four of the eight individuals in the group and contains highlights of some of the most emotional moments of their interaction. 1968, 47 min., PCR, $50.00.

LOGOTHERAPY (Viktor Frankl)

An interview between Bordon Deckett and Viktor Frankl on the general subject of logotherapy. 1965, 27 min., Behavioral Sciences Media Laboratory, University of Oklahoma Medical Center, 800 N.E. 13th Street, Oklahoma City, 73104.

NOTABLE CONTRIBUTORS TO THE PSYCHOLOGY OF PERSONALITY
(A 22-film series produced under an NSF grant)

Excellent series. University of Houston psychologist Richard I. Evans conducts informal but penetrating discussions with eleven prominent psychologists and with playwright Arthur Miller. Each of the 22 films may be used independently. These films are not for neophytes. Viewers should have a prior knowledge of the works and philosophies of each film's subject before viewing the film. The series was produced between 1967 and 1970. Films in the series include:

Gordon Allport — Part One: Relationship with Freud, Allport's reactions to Freudian theory, Allport's own contributions including trait theory and the functional autonomy of motives. 50 min., $17.50.

Gordon Allport — Part Two: Allport's views on the development of self, his evaluation of personality testing and his thoughts concerning personality development, socialization and existentialism. 50 min., $17.50.

Raymond Cattell — Part One: Cattell's opinions on intelligence and personality measurement, heredity versus environment, motivation attitudes, dynamic calculus and the specification equation. 50 min., $17.50.

Raymond Cattell — Part Two: Discussion of OT techniques, psychological testing and psychotherapy. 50 min., $17.50.

Erik Erikson — Part One: Erikson's involvement with psychoanalysis followed by his theory on the eight stages of psycho-social development. 50 min., $17.50.

Erik Erikson — Part Two: The libido theory, ego identity and identity crisis; positive and negative identity; existentialism and cross cultural research are discussed by Erikson. 50 min., $17.50.

Hans Eysenck: The subject discusses his criticisms of Freudian theory and psychoanalysis, explains behavior theory, and refers to his focus on intraversion-extroversion. 30 min., color, $20.00.

Erich Fromm — Part One: Fromm discusses productive and non-productive character orientation and expounds on mechanisms of escape and individuation. 50 min., $17.50.

Erich Fromm — Part Two: Fromm's approach to psychotherapy: his theories and techniques, including the use of drugs and group therapy. 50 min., $17.50.

Ernest Hilgard — Part One: Brief history of Hilgard's work on learning theory, a discussion of the present status of psychoanalysis, and Hilgard's views of contemporary learning theory. 27 min., $10.00.

Ernest Hilgard — Part Two: Hilgard discusses his involvement with hypnosis as a research tool, his views on the uses of hypnosis, and his ideas on the field of psychology for today's college student. 30 min., $10.00.

Carl G. Jung: The subject discusses his differences with Freudian theory, his views of the unconscious, his introversion-extroversion theories, his concept of archetypes, and his reactions to some of the contemporary challenges to psychology. 32 min., $10.00.

Arthur Miller — Part One: The playwright discusses various conceptions of motivation, his own reactions to the psychoanalysis of an author through his work, and reveals his attitudes toward psychological theories and methods. 50 min., $17.50.

Arthur Miller — Part Two: Miller's own reactions to personality theories, the nature of the "message," his own reflections on contemporary problems. 55 min., $17.50.

Gardner Murphy — Part One: Murphy's views on motivation, learning, perception, ego autonomy and self-determination. 50 min., $17.50.

Gardner Murphy — Part Two: The measurement of uniqueness in personality, subliminal and extrasensory perception and hallucinogenic drugs. 50 min., $17.50.

Henry Murray — Part One: Murray shares his impressions of Freud and Jung. He also discusses the Thematic Apperception and Rorschach tests. 50 min., $17.50.

Henry Murray — Part Two: Murray's analysis of *Moby Dick* and its author, Herman Melville. Also a discussion of personality, the training of psychology students and molar versus molecular personality. 50 min., $17.50.

Nevitt Sanford — Part One: A history of the research project on the theory of authoritarian personality. Also Sanford's views on psychoanalysis and a discussion of the principal characteristics of the authoritarian personality. 31 min., $10.00.

Nevitt Sanford — Part Two: Sanford discusses the results of his research on American college students, sexual behavior on the campus, and his own reactions to criticisms of his authoritative personality theory. 25 min., $10.00.

B. F. Skinner — Part One: Skinner's views on motivation, operant conditioning, schedules of reinforcement/punishment, and teaching machines. 50 min., $17.50.

B. F. Skinner — Part Two: A discussion of *Walden Two* and the problems of creating a society based on positive rather than negative control. Also Skinner's evaluation of the American educational system and suggested applications of operant conditioning to society-at-large. 50 min., $17.50.

Rentals prices are those set by the distributor CCM Films, 866 Third Avenue, New York City, 10022. Many of these films are also available from university audio-visual centers; usually at a lower rental fee. PCR, I U, others.

NOTHING BUT A MAN

Semi-commercial and extremely well-dramatized film. Personal struggle of a Southern Black and his wife in a hostile society. Emotional adjustment to the problems of earning a livelihood and supporting a family, of living in peace and dignity, becomes poignantly difficult because the place is Alabama today and the man will not play the expected Negro role. 1965, 92 min., Brandon Films, Inc., 221 West 57th St., New York City, 10019.

NUDE MARATHON, A (Canadian Broadcasting Co.)

Documentary on the role of nudity in group therapy. Paul Bindrim, the originator of the method, works with normal adults as they move from physical isolation to physical intimacy established by nude body contact in a heated pool. Experiment initially suggested by Abraham Maslow. 1968, 25 min., PCR, $12.00.

OH DEM WATERMELONS

Symbolic and surrealistic satire. Lampoons the most derisive Negro stereotype in the book — the watermelon. Great discussion-getter for Black-White encounter groups. 1962, 12 min., color, Film-Makers' Cooperative, 175 Lexington Avenue, New York City, 10016, $15.00.

OVER-DEPENDENCY (Nat. Film Board of Canada)

Older well-produced case history. Young man's life is crippled by behavior patterns carried over from a too-dependent childhood. He finds it difficult to face and deal with ordinary problems of life. Professional counseling helps patient to re-trace childhood experiences and understand the emotional causes of his illness and fear. 1948, 31 min., IU, $7.00.

SOME PERSONAL LEARNINGS ABOUT INTERPERSONAL RELATIONSHIPS

Carl Rogers informally lectures about his experiences and philosophy of human interaction. Details need of people to be "heard" and to escape their self-imposed prisons. Stresses the need to be genuine and the willingness to be vulnerable in order to achieve interpersonal rapport with others. 1967, 33 min., IU, others, $7.75.

THEMES FROM ACTUALIZATION THERAPY (E. Shostrom and N. W. Ferry)

A series of seven films which carry one group through seven sessions of therapy. 1966, 45-50 min., each, Psychological Films, 205 West 20th Street, Santa Ana, California, 92706.

THIRTY-FOURTH HOUR, THE

Participants in a marathon basic encounter group try to be honest with each other, taking a good look at their own hang-ups. Participants include a priest, a nymphomaniac, an unfaithful wife, an unloving man, and others. 27 min., Association Films, Inc., 600 Madison Ave., New York City, 10022.

TITICUT FOLLIES

Prize-winning documentary made at the Institute for Criminally Insane at Bridgewater, Massachusetts. Highly controversial. Release of the film touched off a bitter political and legal battle in Massachusetts. 80 min., Grove Press Film Library, 80 University Place, New York City, 10003.

VERY NICE, VERY NICE (Nat. Film Board of Canada)

Award-winning film takes a cutting look behind the business-as-usual face we put on life and shows anxieties we want to forget. Made of dozens of pictures which seem familiar, with fragments of speech heard in passing and between times, a voice saying, "Very nice, very nice." 1969, 7 min., Contemporary/McGraw-Hill Films, 330 West 42nd Street, New York City, 10036.

MANAGERIAL TRAINING AND ORGANIZATIONAL DEVELOPMENT

EFFECTIVE COMMUNICATION SERIES (David Berlo)

Well-produced series but geared to the para-professional or lower-management level. David Berlo proposes ways to overcome a variety of communication obstacles. Dramatizations are utilized in each film to illustrate relevant points. The five films include: Avoiding Communication Breakdown, Meanings Are in People, Communication Feedback, Changing Attitudes Through Communication, and Communicating Management's Point of View. 1969, each film 24 min., color. $45.00.

Rental price is for one-week loan from the distributor: BNA Films, Bureau of National Affairs, 5615 Fishers Lane, Rockville, Maryland, 20852. Special rates for two-day "previews" are available from BNA. Many university film libraries have some or all of the films in this series and generally charge lower rental rates. BNA has established five free preview centers in Atlanta, Chicago, Los Angeles, New York, and Rockville, Maryland. Any of the BNA films may be previewed at no charge but prior reservations are requested. Write to the Rockville, Maryland address for additional information.

EFFECTIVE EXECUTIVE SERIES (Peter Drucker)

Peter Drucker plays his accustomed role as management consultant to the mythical Hudson-Lansing Corporation. The five films in the series include: Managing Time, What Can I Contribute?, Focus on Tomorrow, Effective Decisions, and Staffing for Strength. Each film, 25 min., color, $50.00.

Rental price quoted here is for one week rental from the distributor: BNA Films. Other rates and film sources available. Free viewing at five BNA preview centers.

INNER MAN STEPS OUT, THE

Illustrates problems in industrial supervision. Animation explains that two "inner men" exist inside of everyone — representing each person's need for security and importance. 1951, 35 min.

MAN THE MANAGER

Animated film traces the development of management responsibilities and capabilities from prehistory down to modern times, focusing on the manager's growing ability to determine "out of present facts, a picture of future possibilities." 1965, 14 min., color, $5.00, IU, others.

MAN THE MANAGER: CASE HISTORIES

Three 2 to 3-minute dramatizations of situations where important concepts have been ignored. Each case may be viewed and discussed separately. May be used independently or as a follow-up to the film, MAN THE MANAGER. 1965, 16 min., around $5.00, IU and others.

MORE THAN WORDS

Outlines basic principles and methods for effective person-to-person communication. Dramatizes examples of communication breakdown in supervision and management. Combines animation with live sequences. 1961, 14 min., color, IU, others.

MOTIVATION AND PRODUCTIVITY SERIES (Saul Gellerman and others)

An extraordinary film series. Well-known management consultants present their theories on motivation. Dramatic enactments are inserted to pose a problem, illustrate an alternative, and/or stimulate viewer discussion. The films may be used either as a series or individually. Individual films are listed in their recommended sequence.

Strategy for Productive Behavior: Designed as the introductory film for those planning to use

250

the entire series. Saul Gellerman discusses the broad implications of behavioral science for management. 1970, 20 min., color, $30.00.

Motivation Through Job Enrichment: Frederick Herzberg describes his "Motivation Hygiene Theory," emphasizing that motivation is found only in the job itself, in the opportunity to satisfy the human need for accomplishment. 1969, 28 min., color, $50.00.

The Self-Motivated Achiever: David McClelland discusses the problems of identifying and dealing with individuals who possess a high need for achievement. 1969, 28 min., color, $50.00.

Understanding Motivation: Saul Gellerman explains the individual needs of workers and how their motivation is a product of the kind of world they *think* they live in. 1969, 28 min., color, $50.00.

Theory X and Theory Y — Part One: Three former colleagues of the late Douglas McGregor discuss McGregor's best known contribution — the distinction between two contrasting sets of assumptions about human nature. 1970, 25 min., color, $50.00.

Theory X and Theory Y — Part Two: Stresses the application of the theory. Illustrates why a "Theory Y" manager will be likely to elicit greater productivity from his employees. 1970, 25 min., color, $50.00.

Human Nature and Organizational Realities: Chris Argyris discusses his experience in motivating employees at lower levels of an organization and improving interpersonal relations at all levels of management. 1969, 28 min., color, $50.00.

The Management of Human Assets: Rensis Likert comments on the training and direction a company must take to obtain high-producing work-groups. 1969, 28 min., color, $50.00.

Motivation in Perspective: The concluding film in the series. Saul Gellerman summarizes, compares, and contrasts the research and application of behavioral science to management. 1970, 20 min., color, $30.00.

Rental prices quoted here are for one-week rentals from the distributor: BNA Films. Other rates and film sources available.

Discussion guides and supportive audio cassettes for this series are also available from BNA. Free viewing at five BNA preview centers.

MOTIVATION TO WORK SERIES (Frederick Herzberg)

Using his "motivation-hygiene" theory as a base, Frederick Herzberg probes the problem of increasing efficiency in business and industry. The five films in the series include: The Modern Meaning of Efficiency; KITA, or, What Have You Done for Me Lately?; Job Enrichment in Action; Building a Climate for Individual Growth; and The ABC Man: The Manager in Mid-Career. 1969, each film 25 min., color, $50.00.

Above price is one-week rental from BNA. Free viewing at five BNA preview centers.

MANAGEMENT BY OBJECTIVES SERIES (John Humble)

English management consultant John Humble appears as the principal spokesman in this four-film series. Film titles include Management by Objectives, Defining the Manager's Job, Performance and Potential Review, and Colt — A Case History. 1969, each film 25 min., color, $50.00. Supplementary overhead transparencies available.

Above price is for one-week rental from BNA. Free viewing at five BNA preview centers.

NEED TO ACHIEVE, THE (David McClelland — NET)

McClelland demonstrates the tests with which he seeks to verify his psychological theory — that the economic growth or decline of nations is dependent to a large extent upon the entrepreneurs of these nations. The need to achieve is one of a variety of phenomena studied in motivational research. 1963, 30 min., PCR, IU, others. Around $7.50.

ORGANIZATIONAL RENEWAL SERIES (Gordon Lippitt)

This five-film series defines and illustrates Gordon Lippitt's research in organization development. Film titles include: Growth Stages of Organizations; Confrontation, Search, and Coping; Individuality and Teamwork; Coping with Change; and How Organizational Renewal Works. 1969. Each film 25 min., color, $50.00.

Above price is one-week rental from BNA. Other rates and film sources available. Free viewing at five BNA preview centers.

A ROCKET WITHOUT
A GUIDANCE SYSTEM

Review of Schutz, W. C. *Here Comes Everybody.*
New York: Harper & Row, 1971. pp. xviii + 295. $6.95.

Reviewed by John J. Sherwood

"Understanding the body is central to the philosophy of open encounter." This is the lead sentence on page one of Schutz's new book. It represents what is new in his latest effort to provide laser-like guidance to the human potential movement. While the body played a part in his earlier book on encounter, *Joy*, it is much more central here. The subtitle is *Bodymind and Encounter Culture*, and on the front of the dust jacket everybody is hyphenated so that the title reads: *Here Comes Every-Body*.

The title is from Joyce's *Finnegan's Wake* and is Schutz's clever way of saying in the important ways all men are alike.

But more than that, Schutz has a word for everybody — every person and every body — parents and children, teachers and students, spouses and couples, bosses and subordinates, politicians and diplomats, and the church and the theatre. He has ideas about anatomy that are just as sweeping, from the head and neck to the heart and lungs to the thighs, calves, and feet — and, of course, the penis and vagina.

Unfortunately since Bradford, Gibb & Benne's *T-Group Theory and Laboratory Method* in 1964, the human potential movement — encounter culture, sensitivity training, human relations, T-groups, sensory awareness, et cetera — has not produced a body of theory which is necessary to move to the next step beyond the elaboration of where it presently stands. The work of Fritz Perls in Gestalt therapy comes closest to leading a breakthrough, but Gestalt concepts are essentially ways to help us generate more and more useful data about one another. Schutz sets out to provide for the theoretical integration of three aspects of living — the psychological or mind, the physical or body, and the interpersonal or life with other people. He also continues to mention the soul and the spirit, but these last ideas always seem to be left over.

Techniques without theory are like words without syntax or, in this case — because of the excitement of some of Schutz's ideas — like a rocket without a guidance system. His treatment of theory is disappointing on two counts. First, he treats the relationship between mind and body, an issue that has busied philosophers and researchers for centuries, in an annoyingly simplistic way — for example, "lack of personal warmth is often accompanied by a constricted heart" . . . "respiratory ailments are probably related to inclusion problems" . . . "upper arm tension is often relieved by embracing someone." The point is made that the body and its reactions are enormously important, and we should attend to bodily reactions, posture, and appearance more than we customarily do. Most of the guidance we receive from Schutz is, however, folklore on the one hand, such as the heart as valentine, and sexually-oriented interpretations on the other, such as threats to masculinity being often felt in the neck. It seems that since Schutz has crashed through the *Portnoy's Complaint*-barrier, he wants to help us all cross that barrier to a fuller realization of our sexuality — even though some never had such a barrier to cross, and others have crossed it long ago.

The body is not seen as something to be enjoyed or as a vehicle for doing things. It is conceived as a storehouse of energy and tensions and sexuality. The body is most often viewed as a problem. It is something which keeps us from being and doing, rather than a source of potential and pleasure.

The second disappointment is the way in which the ideas of the East are introduced. Attempts are made to give spiritual and mystical notions a Western basis by showing parallels to established Western ideas. Rather than exploring the utility of spiritualism by entering it and living with its concepts, Schutz tries to translate such ideas into his own scheme. In reading H.C.E., I got stuck on page 65, which is ten pages into the section on mysticism and spirituality. I didn't read beyond for several weeks, although I carried the book everywhere. I really wanted to learn about mysticism and spirituality, but had great difficulty with the way they are presented here. I didn't find the help I need in understanding the perspectives of the East.

Schutz knows Rolfing well and treats it enthusiastically. Rolfing is a ten-session, sequential, physical technique which is designed to bring the body more into awareness and to make it more available by liberating it of limiting and distorting tensions which may have become incorporated within the muscle organization. This section is intriguing. As I was reading, I wanted to be a Rolfee — i.e., someone to whom this is done.

His discussion of a typical open encounter workshop and the detailed account of a sample microlab are both very interesting. They lead to a statement of the 27 *Rules of Open Encounter*. These are a collection of reasoned and reasonable guides to increasing personal growth and self-insight and enhancing open, direct, responsible communication between people. Only two of the rules are likely to cause much discussion. The one dealing with nudity will be debated, simply because it concerns taking off clothes in a group. The rationale presented for nudity is, however, reasonable, and undressing is clearly a matter of individual choice. Schutz also provides for such choice by advertising his preferences, so that the public has a pretty good idea about what it's getting into.

A more controversial rule is probably, "Whatever you are most afraid of is the thing it is most valuable to do." This is likely to upset some clinicians. Frankly, it is a bit too quixotic for me to accept as anything other than melodramatic advice.

The section on rules ends with a statement that these rules describe the nature of behavior and interaction that Schutz desires in an open encounter group. He then says about the rules that, "They are based directly on the theoretical ideas presented earlier." I was startled by the assertion that these guides are tied directly to theory. The theory is neither sufficient nor clearly enough described to allow my acceptance of that assertion. Schutz's 27 rules are a nice, useful collection of guidelines.

Most of what follows is a potpourri of encounter techniques, often with clever and entertaining vignettes from Schutz's experience with their use. The book lacks the crispness of *Joy*. Perhaps this is because there is much overlap with *Joy*, which I believe is better organized and represents a more substantial contribution. A lot of H.C.E. is flat. Often I had "the feeling of cold potatoes," because it seems that things are said and accounts are offered "without much energy." It is as if they are recounted tales. Energy is one of Schutz's favorite concepts. Rule Number 25 of the *Rules of Open Encounter* reads: "If you are saying something about yourself that you have said before, stop and say something else." I found the discussion to be flat particularly on those several occasions when he stated that he was giving fuel to critics by being as open as he was now going to be. The openness usually involved his perceptions of his own needs. These statements often read as if they had been said so many times before that they have become stereotyped — e.g., "I do like to look at beautiful, shapely women, and justified nudity gives me a good rationale; it even allows me to touch them . . ." He reports learning from his father during an interchange about a child-

254

hood hero, Lou Gehrig, not to overlook anything that might undermine his case. His self-revealing statements about his own needs seem to follow what he learned from his father. They do not give critics the ammunition he suggests, nearly so much as they cover his tracks, so that after the critics have had their say, Schutz has the last word — "I told you so!"

The fact that Schutz is ostensibly in touch with his own needs does not change the fact that he appears to use others to gratify his own needs. The essential question for me is: Is it at the expense of the client or the participant in encounter? The stories he tells present him as manipulative and coercive, and most important, as apparently not trusting *the process* of encounter itself. To the extent that there is a theoretical basis to encounter, it rests on the assumption that people can be trusted to become resourceful enough to learn from their own insights, their own timely interventions, and the power of the interaction of their own personalities. His discussion of responsibility repeats the Gestalt position that each person is ultimately responsible for his own behavior. As Perls puts it, "I am not in this world to live up to your expectations. And you are not in this world to live up to mine." When taken literally, this gives Schutz license "to allow virtually any behavior to occur, but to insist that it be discussed openly at all points." And also, "If the method is applied inappropriately it is usually simply ineffective" (i.e., neither inhibiting nor destructive). I find him vulnerable on both points, as I do on the following bit of advice, "Whenever the energy level starts to lag, a nonverbal activity can usually revitalize it." While this assertion is probably accurate, it is the transferability to daily life that raises serious questions about such a strategy. To be perfectly fair to Schutz, this latter statement was made in the section on sample microlabs. The book is, however, filled with snappy devices without concern for building problem-solving skills and concepts within encounter groups. He makes a strong case, which I accept, for replacing "interpretation" with experience. He does not address problems of building capacity to carry on growth and change, such that each of us becomes more able to continue to shape our lives in more joyous ways. My hunch is that Schutz produces much evangelic fervor, including a literal laying on of hands, which requires recharging periodically because it is not self-sustaining.

His travels through his "latest" encounter techniques are by turns informative (e.g., Rolfing), incomplete (e.g., yoga), and confusing (e.g., breathing). Interspersed throughout the discussion are several cute and fanciful "bulletins" describing hypothetical encounter groups for couples, business, education, the president of the U.S. and the premier of the U.S.S.R. and an interview with "the encounter politician" in 1983. These are entertaining and sometimes provoking.

He touches on many of the current issues in encounter with a delightful absence of footnotes: the training of group leaders, the group leader as a person, responsibility, and screening of participants. He also addresses some critics, e.g., the charge of brainwashing and encouraging acting out sexually.

I met Bill Schutz a couple of times in Bethel, Maine, in the early 1960's and I remember him well. At that time he was playing superbly the role of provocateur and enjoying the reputation of bad boy, primarily in terms of how sex and aggression were handled in his groups. While he has better arguments today and more of them, he is still fighting the same issues with the same delightful flare — ". . . honesty opens doors into a new life much like losing virginity allows for new levels of personal intimacy" . . . "It was like my penis was the answer in the back of the book" . . . "Bullshit [definition: words unconnected with feelings] is frequently a good fertilizer and makes the other material grow more fully."

I like H.C.E. for Schutz's honesty and for the book's readability. If the human potential movement is to survive, it has to continue to confront society. To a movement crying out for theory to guide it, H.C.E. offers some concepts. While no clear thinker has yet arrived to write the book, Bill Schutz has now done so three times. Each of his books has made a contribution. *Here Comes Everybody* says "the body is important, touching is possible, and fantasy is encouraged."

SMALL
BUT
SIGNIFICANT

Review of Rogers, C. R. *Carl Rogers on Encounter Groups.*
New York: Harper & Row, 1970. pp. vii + 172. $1.95

Reviewed by Willis D. Poland

As might be expected from the title, *Carl Rogers on Encounter Groups* is a highly personal account of his involvement in the encounter group movement. It is consistent with his more recent books in that it is not meant to be a scholarly work. The book is lucid, persuasive, and achieves balance and breadth from his perspective by not only focusing on the process but also on what happens to those who experience it.

Before presenting his own views, Rogers first describes the origin and scope of the trend toward groups. After pointing out that the planned, intensive small group experience is a rather recent but rapidly spreading social invention, he tries to account for its current popularity. It is his belief that the increasing dehumanization of our culture and the fact that we are sufficiently affluent to pay attention to our psychological needs account for the burgeoning interest in groups in this country. Since such group experiences lead to change, Rogers makes it clear that those opposed to change are currently and will continue to be vigorous in their opposition to the encounter movement.

For the small group practitioner the heart of this book is found in the two chapters which focus on the process and on being a facilitator in a group. In the chapter on process Rogers describes in great detail what he perceives happening in the groups which he facilitates. That this process parallels his views of what happens in therapy should come as no great surprise.

At the beginning of his groups there is little structure and considerable resistance to the expression of personal feelings and reactions. It is usually easier for the participants to talk about their past feelings at first. If the individual finds that the group is relatively safe and trustworthy, he will gradually express and explore more personally meaningful material, including his current interpersonal feelings in the group. The willingness of group members to share their impressions and their feelings results in the development of what Rogers calls a "healing capacity in the group." An important part of this process is giving and receiving feedback which may be in the form of a direct confrontation between two or more members. In his opinion such interaction leads from the cracking of facades, through considerable interpersonal involvement both during and outside the group sessions accompanied by developing closeness between members, to marked behavior change.

In order to balance the picture, Rogers stresses that there are risks involved in such an experience. These risks include the possibility that the behavior change will only be temporary or that the individual may open up areas of himself and then be left with problems not worked through. There is also some risk to ongoing relationships, particularly marital relationships, when only one partner is involved. This threat stems from either the isolated personal change which occurs outside of the marital context or the closeness which may develop between group members. To cope with this problem there is an increasing experimentation with couples groups.

One of the more difficult issues facing the encounter movement is the question of who is qualified to lead encounter groups. At the present time almost anyone who decides to lead an encounter group can usually find a ready supply of people who are willing to participate in whatever experience he devises for them. The major training facilities, such as NTL and Esalen, have skirted this issue by not giving formal credentials to those who receive training through their programs. Although Rogers does not face this issue squarely, he does provide some helpful guidelines in answering the question, "Can I be facilitative in a group?"

Consistent with his stance in individual therapy, Rogers states that he has no goal for a particular group. He believes that each group will develop its own potential and direction. His personal goal is to gradually become as much a participant in the group as a facilitator. In order to accomplish this he listens and responds to the meanings and feelings being communicated by the participants. He tries to operate in terms of his own feelings, which he trusts. At times this leads him to be confrontive of behaviors or attitudes that generate strong feelings in him.

The general impression created by Rogers is that his groups are unstructured and that participants are free to participate to whatever extent they wish. He does not find planned or structured exercises useful unless they fit spontaneously into whatever is happening at a given moment. He also engages in physical movement and contact only when it seems "real and spontaneous and appropriate."

The list of behaviors which he believes are nonfacilitative make quite clear his opposition to manipulation and the control of the group by the facilitator toward some end which he deems worthwhile. Ideally, the facilitator will be sufficiently free of his own problems so that he can become emotionally involved in the group and in this way facilitate the growth of others as well as himself.

Over one-third of the book is devoted to the question, "Does the encounter experience change behavior?" Citing both anecdotal and empirical data, Rogers answers this question in the affirmative. As a matter of fact, he is convinced that encounter experiences not only produce change in individuals but also promote institutional and organizational change. He points out that a number of studies have been done which support this conclusion. It is worth noting that most of the data he reports from his own groups are of a more personal, phenomenological nature. In his opinion, this type of study is far more valuable than the traditional "hard-headed," empirical approach since it provides "the deepest insights into what the experience has meant." It seems critical to this reviewer that both approaches be utilized if we are going to advance our knowledge about the encounter process and its effects on behavior.

Rogers concludes his book with a look to the future. He expresses the view that "the encounter group movement will be a growing counter-force to the dehumanization of our culture." He sees wide-ranging areas of application for the intensive group experience, including industry, churches, government, race relations, international tensions, families, and educational institutions. To help meet the need for trained leadership Rogers has been involved in the training of facilitators at the Center for Studies of the Person at La Jolla, California. The emphasis in this training program is on "the humanness of the person who is perceived as the facilitator, and the fact that he is the more effective as he is more real in his interactions with others."

Rogers has written a small but significant book. That he has written about encounter groups almost exclusively from his perspective is both a strength and a weakness of the book. His views are exceedingly important since he has been an influential person in the development and direction of the movement, but he does not have a corner on the market. Other works, such as Howard's *Please Touch* and Egan's *Encounter*, if read in conjunction with Rogers book, would provide a more adequate picture of the encounter movement as it currently exists. Nevertheless, it is exciting to experience Rogers through his book and to learn that he is growing and changing without losing his great respect for persons and their potential to grow.

THE CONTRACT
AND THE JOY

Review of Egan, G. *Encounter: Group Processes for Interpersonal Growth.* Belmont, Calif.: Brooks/Cole, 1970. pp. 424. $5.25.

Reviewed by Richard Heslin

This book can be looked at from three viewpoints. First, it is a summary of the relevant ideas of writers in the areas of personality, psychotherapy, sensitivity training, group dynamics, and interpersonal relations. Egan quotes these thinkers when they are seeing their subject most clearly and writing about it most eloquently. Second, the book presents a trenchant analysis of the whole encounter group experience: the happenings that are likely, those that are helpful, and those that are hurtful to interpersonal growth. Finally, the book presents Egan's version of the contract group. The titles of chapters three through ten in the book are also the major headings in the concept of contract; therefore, by looking at these chapters, we can get an overview of both the book and the contract experience.

In Chapter 1, "Introduction, the Contract Group in the Context of Laboratory Learning and Sensitivity Training," Egan discusses the growth in popularity of groups, tries to indicate the characteristics that define what laboratory training is, discusses who groups are intended for and what it is hoped they will gain from them, and introduces the concept of the contract group.

In "The Contract," he moves into detailed discussion of its use, its advantages (reduced expectation gap, reduced manipulation of members, reduced dependency, etc.), and its potential disadvantages if misused or misunderstood. A sample contract for an interpersonal growth group is described and discussed.

"Group Goals," as Egan sees them, are less a point to be reached by group members than they are a *level of functioning* the members move toward during the group experience. Some of these goals are 1) maintaining a strong "here and now" focus, 2) following the Rules of Immediacy (Use "I" rather than "people" or "one," avoid abstractions or generalities, speak to a particular person, and avoid "Why?" questions), 3) engaging in self-disclosure, 4) expressing feelings, 5) giving support, 6) engaging in responsible confrontation, 7) engaging in self-exploration as a response to confrontation, and 8) taking a stance against (individual or group) flight from encounter.

"The Laboratory Method," places emphasis on the laboratory aspects of laboratory training. It is because of its laboratory nature that the encounter group has some disadvantages, some special advantages, and also some things that are just different from everyday life. Some characteristics of the laboratory method are: learning from experience, the "cultural island" effect of a live-in residential laboratory, the provision of "psychological safety" to the participants, the use of others as sources of constructive feedback, a setting that is at the same time distinctly artificial and distinctly real, and an emphasis on experimentation with one's interpersonal style.

The role of the trainer is examined in "Leadership." The functions of the leader-member in a contract group are indicated as initial structuring, placing his knowledge and experience at the

258

service of the group, and discussing early the nature of the problems groups have with the leader, with tacit understandings, and with deviant members. He is a participant, a guardian of the contract (with the other members), and a role modeler. Leadership is expected to diffuse, and members are encouraged to assume leadership functions.

In "Total Human Expression: The Elements of Human Dialogue: Pathos, Logos, Poiesis," the task of communicating oneself to another is examined. In pathos, the ability of a person to experience emotions fully is discussed; in logos, the use of language to candidly communicate oneself to another; and in poiesis, the expression of meaningful emotion in language.

"Self Disclosure," deals with the pathogenic aspects of secrecy on one hand and on the other hand the forces in society and in the person that militate against disclosing oneself to another person. Shame and guilt are discussed as basic emotions associated with such secret material.

In "Supportive Behavior," Egan deals first with listening (hard listening, involved listening) as the first and basic ingredient for giving support to another person. Good listening is active and interactive. The good listener tries to feel the speaker's feeling and understand completely what he is being told. The good listener is then able to give support to other members for risking themselves, for disclosing themselves, for fulfilling the contract.

"Confrontation in Laboratory Training," concerns the problem of keeping the participant honest and responsible and of encouraging him to examine his motivations and beliefs in the light of his behavior. The confrontive situation is complex. If a confrontation is to result in self-examination by the confrontee with the idea that he may change his behavior following such self-examination, it must be in proportion to the psychological condition of the confrontee, the topic of confrontation, the closeness to the confrontee's definition of himself, the relationship between the confronter and the confrontee, and so on. Confrontation must be an act of concern about the other person and an indication of a desire to get involved with him if it is to be helpful.

In "A Stance Against Flight," Egan describes the behavior of both the individual in flight and the group in flight. The individual in flight may be cynical, silent, overly concerned with insight, overly ready to use humor, or he may deal in generalities, hide behind questions, or think of many reasons why it is impossible for him to benefit from the group. The group in flight may spend undue amounts of time "improving" the contract, analyzing past interactions, and engaging in serious non-contractual discussions. It may use procedures such as turn-taking, or dealing with one member at a time. Finally, it may adopt a problem/solution mode of interaction, ("Here is my problem, now what is the solution?") or limit group interaction by a number of tacit understandings about procedures, topics, or group goals. In general, flight can be recognized by its deadening effect on the group.

"Epilog," deals with some residual issues that do not fit neatly into the first ten chapters. First, Egan emphasizes the underlying goal of groups to move people toward a self-responsible, active, high-initiative approach to life. Second, he deals with research findings about the effectiveness of sensitivity training groups in general and about the member and leader characteristics most conducive to positive change in participants. He feels that methodological difficulties are formidable but not insurmountable and that the results obtained to date, although sometimes confusing, appear to indicate that the laboratory experience is a "powerful force for behavioral change."

Even if a reader does not agree with the concept of a group contract, the book is extremely useful for its discussion of encounter groups and the ideas of other theorists about such phenomena. Yet it is the idea of the contract that gives focus to the book. It is through looking at the contract as an alternative to the unstructured, high-ambiguity model of a growth group that the implied assumptions regarding what is growthful and what is important are addressed and clarified.

Encounter is a joy to read and a pleasure to review. It is perhaps the best presentation and analysis of the encounter group experience available today. I kept waiting for the point, somewhere around the middle of the book, where the discussion would become redundant enough for me to read faster. That point was never reached. Even when Egan amplifies an idea, the material is fresh and well presented.

Gerard Egan's *Encounter* should be required reading for anyone interested in facilitating awareness, honesty, and growth in themselves and others through group methods.

TOWARD AN ADEQUATE APPLIED BEHAVIORAL SCIENCE

Review of Golembiewski, R. T., and A. Blumberg.
Sensitivity Training and the Laboratory Approach.
Itasca, Ill.: Peakock, 1970. pp. xiii + 515. $9.50.

Reviewed by Robert B. LeLieuvre

With the plethora of writings on sensitivity training, one, at last, can find a book directed toward both novices and the more sophisticated. Golembiewski and Blumberg have edited such a book. Aiming at the widest possible audience, the editors offer a broad compilation of articles touching on most facets of the complex phenomenon. In addition to the thirty-seven selected articles, the editors proffer extensive editorial commentary to provide a rich, stereophonic view of the laboratory approach.

A blend of theory, research, impressionistic reporting, and skill-related input materials serves well to capture both the fundamentals and the evanescent qualities of laboratory training. The selections range from the concise but lofty "Goals and Meta-Goals of Laboratory Training," in which Bennis sets forth four major precepts of the human relations model, to the witty yet terrifying "Chief, Watch Out for Those T-Group Promoters!" written for the police chief's magazine, in which sensitivity training is compared to communist brainwashing techniques.

The Bennis and Shepard paper, "A Theory of Group Development," remains the single best summary of the phasic exigencies of the T-Group. The authors focus on the two major areas of internal uncertainty: 1.) dependence and authority relations, and 2.) interdependence and personal relations. Guiding the reader through the complex maze of actions and reactions, Bennis and Shepard emphasize the learnings, the conflicts, and the resolutions available to group members. By combining psychodynamic principles with a Lewinian model of group dynamics, the authors explore the nuances of dependence and interdependence, power and love, authority and intimacy. Stating that the major training goal is the establishment of valid communication, Bennis and Shepard point out that T-Group processes revolve around the examination of autistic responses to authority and intimacy and the formulation of provisional alternatives for members.

The major strengths of *Sensitivity Training and the Laboratory Approach* are its balance and diversity. The book is unquestionably valuable. Of import both to academicians and to practitioners are the last three sections: "IV. What Concerns Are There About T-Groups? Goals, Methods, and Results"; "V. Where Can T-Group Dynamics Be Used?: Applications in the Home, School, Office, and Community"; and "VI. How Can T-Group Dynamics Be Studied? Conceiving and Executing Research." Indeed these three sections are the strongest points in an already strong book.

In Section IV the focus is on the professional skirmish line vis-a-vis the emphasis on individual versus group dynamics. This controversy has recurred many times under various names: training versus therapy, clinical versus educational strategies of learning, small group theory versus the personal growth model. The crux of the controversy relates to two distinct sets of assumptions underlying training methods. A there-and-then focus is fundamental to the individual-therapeutic approach. The group-training model, however, stresses conscious, here-and-now events.

Argyris, in an article entitled "Conditions for Competence Acquisition and Therapy," cautions against the arbitrary interchange of these two models. Essentially, he argues that the goal orientations of the two differ. Therapy is based on a survival orientation, whereas, competence acquisition or training is growth oriented. Moreover the requisite expertise differs. On the one hand, training intervention rests on the modeling of minimally distorted, minimally evaluative, and directly validatable communication. Therapeutic intervention, on the other hand, is designed to probe the genesis of contemporary behavior and to interpret such behavior. In line with Argyris's position, Horwitz ("Transference in Training Groups and Therapy Groups") distinguishes between the two models on the basis of their differential encouragement and use of transference as an intervention technique. Training uses it minimally, while therapy relies on it heavily.

In another article ("On the Future of Laboratory Education") Argyris pushes his argument a step further. Focusing exclusively on the training movement, he calls to task the atheoretical existential-humanist tradition. That tradition demands an unconditional push toward complete openness. Argyris's main thrust is directed toward three fundamental humanist assumptions: 1.) that it is good to free a person to experience his world more fully in all situations; 2.) that events experienced cognitively are only partially experienced; and 3.) that the unconscious should be explored and exploited. The assumptions and the methods of humanistic training contain a strong, almost pathological, anti-intellectual bias. Argyris views the effects of such a bias within such an approach, the claimed positive results notwithstanding, as being less than beneficial. From his vantage point, these are: a rigid belief system anchored in a perception of a Messianic mission; a narcissistic tendency to experience feelings as ends in themselves; an arrogant stance disclaiming anyone but oneself as judge of effective learning; and a built-in lack of transfer of learnings and skills to the "real" world.

The most scathing indictment of training is offered by Odiorne in an article appropriately titled "The Trouble with Sensitivity Training." Citing a great deal of anecdotal evidence, that author criticizes the "cultish" practices of the groupies.

> The most damaging criticism of sensitivity training is that it has built into its system an automatic rejection of orderly, rational, conscious criticism. This itself is dangerous rigidity which should be corrected first. For a field of study to set itself above and immune to the attacks to which every scholar and writer must willingly submit his ideas is prime evidence of weakness. Nor must all such criticism be couched in the rules of the 'leaders' in the field. Valid science withstands every attack, including the specious and unfair. (p. 274, italics provided.)

Odiorne points out that research evidence on the effects of T-Groups is equivocal at best, a position corroborated by House ("T-Group Education and Leadership Effectiveness: A Review of the Empiric Literature and a Critical Evaluation"). Moreover, Odiorne charges that many laboratory experiences are duplicitous in their recruitment procedures. Various advertisements present training opportunities under the guise of "leadership training," management conferences," or "training seminars." That such duplicity borders on the unethical is evident. Odiorne simply asks that judgment be reserved until empirical evidence substantiates the claims.

Section V provides the reader with theoretical papers and case examples demonstrating the applicability of the laboratory method to divergent social systems. Touched are married couples, school systems, arbitration sessions, industry, and classrooms, to name a few. It is here that the crucial dilemma involved in training becomes crystal clear. That dilemma is maintaining the *status quo*, which is working, albeit not optimally, or instituting novel social experiments which appear questionable at best. That the whole world can be a T-Group is absurd. The burning

262

question is twofold: first, are the values and processes inherent in laboratory education functional; and second, if so, how might they be incorporated into the larger social context? As yet, there are no conclusive answers.

The strength of Section VI lies in the dispassionate tone in the presentation of critical research issues. The reader is swept into the vortex of the controversy over "pure science," emphasizing process inquiry as opposed to "applied science" stressing outcome inquiry. Both are essential to scientific advancement, yet their proponents, not unlike clinical researchers, blindly overstate the virtues of their particular case. That the editors favor the striking of a balance is no moot point.

House presents convincing evidence that "hard data" do not support unequivocally the proclaimed efficacy of training, as measured by transfer of learning to back-home situations. Harrison ("Problems in the Design and Interpretation of Research on Human Relations Training") provides extensive coverage of the methodological problems inherent in measurement. He concludes in a complex but not pessimistic note. Elegance of design is not likely. This difficulty, however, need not stand in the way of good research. Small incremental accumulations of knowledge are a necessary beginning, a stance reflected in the actual research articles offered by the editors.

With broad yet critical courage of the field, Golembiewski and Blumberg do readers a great service. They have put together the most comprehensive book to date on training, certainly no mean feat. Theirs is an accomplishment that has long been awaited, and they have constructed a base from which further evaluation, elaboration, and conceptualization can be conducted.

APPLYING BEHAVIORAL SCIENCE TO THE CLASSROOM

Review of Runkel, P., R. Harrison, and M. Runkel (eds.).
The Changing College Classroom. San Francisco, Jossey-Bass, 1969.
pp. xxi +359. $9.50.

Reviewed by Thomas Holman

For some five odd years I have been involved in teaching, counseling, and administration in a higher education setting. During those years I have become increasingly aware of and concerned about the personalization and/or humanization of what goes on in the name of "getting a college education." (Apparently I never gave it a second thought when I was so involved in the process "as student" for eleven years.) That area which I have become increasingly concerned about and aware of, with regard to this humanization, has been the realm of classroom teaching.

As a neophyte I was perfectly content to lecture five times a week and felt secure with my notes between me and the students. As I have gone on, however, my interest in students as persons and my belief that they have a lot to contribute, in terms of their own ability to teach themselves, have prompted me to become increasingly disenchanted with my role as "transmitter of facts" and constantly "on the lookout" for new and innovative approaches to teaching and learning in higher education.

It is apparent that a lot of persons called "professors" are doing many innovative things with regard to teaching and learning in higher education. It has also been apparent that there is a dearth of published material about innovative teaching and learning to get exciting ideas from, either with regard to theory or practice. Therefore, it was with great pleasure and excitement that I approached the book entitled *The Changing College Classroom*, and that pleasure and excitement continued "right on" through the last page.

The Changing College Classroom is divided into three parts entitled "Conflict," "New Practices," and "Designing Change."

Part I consists of articles by two student radicals (in the best sense of the word), which set the tone for conflict between the "traditional approach" to learning in the classroom vs. the "socially relevant approach." Their view is that "institutions of higher education are aging institutions in need of renewal and/or reform" (p. 3). Both are extremely critical of the theoretical basis on which traditional higher education rests and, by the way, do a very competent job of convincing the reader.

Part II is a compendium of case studies in innovative approaches to teaching and learning in various programs at various levels of higher education. It consists of a variety of concrete examples that can be put into practice by the individual teacher. These case studies demonstrate what is possible, "using only what any educator has in hand: himself, his subject, his students and *his understanding of teaching and learning.*" (p. 35, italics mine.)

Part III, entitled "Designing Change," turns to educational theory and "offers guides to the educator with which he can select techniques applicable to his own situation" (p. 291). With this broad introduction in mind, let me further share with you some of the scope and content of *The Changing College Classroom*, paying particular heed to Parts II and III. (I in no way mean to downplay Part I, but I am assuming that much of what is said by the authors is now "old hat" and needs not to be dwelt upon at any greater length.)

The new practices dealt with in Part II are, indeed, fascinating in terms of the variety of innovative teaching methods, both with regard to breadth and level of teaching methods (from the lowliest special class in freshman English to graduate level courses in public and adult education) and with regard to the variety of philosophical assumptions underlying them. A summary of Part II can best be stated by quoting, in part, the summary given by Leonard Lansky in the first paper in Part III. First of all, it is apparent, says Lansky, that each teacher has "taken a look at his own role and realized that to teach does not mean to lecture"; secondly, that each has "discovered that students could be resources for one another"; third, that "involvement lay inside the students in their needs, goals, skills, wishes, ideas, hopes, and fears"; fourth, they all learned that "the processes in the classroom were relevant to the subject matter"; and, fifth, that each teacher "got 'hung up' to some degree in the evaluation system" (the matter of grades). (pp. 292-294) The one inescapable conclusion seems to be that the teacher's *self-awareness* is the major requirement for changing the college classroom.

There are many implications as to the underlying attitudes and philosophies of learning dealt with in the several articles in section II, mostly focusing on openness and trust on the part of the teacher. These are best represented by two brief quotes: "The attitude that helped me most was the simple belief that, given a chance, most students would want to become excited, take a few risks, and become acquainted (with each other)" (Andrews, p. 131); and, paraphrasing Culbert (p. 219), "I told the students what needed to be done, but not how to do it."

Part III contains two excellent articles by Leonard Lansky and Roger Harrison. Both contain some sound assumptions and/or psychological theory which should be able to assist any concerned professor in planning the development of teaching/learning innovations.

Lansky lists some fourteen assumptions which are both educationally insightful and pragmatically useful. Quite frankly, they tie in very closely with many of the basic concerns or ideas of basic human relations laboratories. It is a pleasure, as an old T-grouper, to see that these concepts can be adapted to the classroom as well.

Harrison's article is entitled "Classroom Innovation: A Design Primer," and that is just what it is: thirty-seven pages of ideas, concepts and insights just waiting to be used by the well-intentioned classroom change agent. The basic value orientation underlying the chapter is that people (in the future) are going to be required to become increasingly responsive and adaptive to change, and that, as professors, we need to be equally concerned about the process of learning ("learning how to learn") as well as content. He continues on in excellent form to talk about three types of learning (conceptual, instrumental, and rote), an intriguing motivational model, and, lastly, gives some thoughts on how to deal with anxiety and failure when one is being innovative in the classroom. This article, in particular, is highly recommended reading.

I have tried, in a brief way, to share some of the interesting and exciting content of the book, *The Changing College Classroom*. My only hope is that I have intrigued teachers to glean from it those ideas that offer promise of re-humanizing the educational experience of college students.

A STEP
TOWARD DEFINITION

Review of *The Addison-Wesley Series on Organization Development.*
Reading, Mass.: Addison-Wesley, 1969. $3.50 each, or $17.50 for boxed set.
W. G. BENNIS. *Organization Development: Its Nature, Origins, and Prospects.* pp. viii+87.
R. BECKHARD. *Organization Development: Strategies and Methods.* pp. viii+119.
P. R. LAWRENCE and J. W. LORSCH. *Developing Organizations: Diagnosis and Action.* pp. x+101.
R. R. BLAKE and JANE S. MOUTON. *Building a Dynamic Corporation through Grid Organization Development.* pp. viii + 120.
R. E. WALTON. *Interpersonal Peacemaking: Confrontation and Third Party Consultation.* pp. viii+151.
E. H. SCHEIN. *Process Consultation: Its Role in Organization Development.* pp. ix+147.

Reviewed by Thomas Lyons

In a recent letter to the *Journal of Applied Behavioral Science* Vaill (1971) commented on the distinction between "organizational development," meaning development that occurs in organizations, and "organization development," meaning the development of an organization as a total unit. This series is devoted largely to organization development, although the two books by Walton and by Schein come to grips very concretely with the problems of organizational development in the service of OD.

Organization Development (OD) is defined by Bennis in his excellent overview of the field as "a response to change, a complex educational strategy intended to change the beliefs, attitudes, values, and structure of organizations so that they can better adapt to new technologies, markets, and challenges, and the dizzying rate of change itself " (p. 9).

OD relies on experience-based educational programs and interventions, using data generated from the client system itself, usually concentrating on the "people variables" in the client organizations. Its practitioners are often external change agents who develop collaborative relationships with organizational members involving mutual trust, joint determination of goals and means, and high mutual influence, and who share a social philosophy and normative goals common to much of the human potential movement.

Beckhard, in the other overview book of this series, defines OD as "an effort (1) planned, (2) organization-wide, (3) managed from the top, to (4) increase organization effectiveness and health through (5) planned interventions in the organization's 'processes,' using behavioral-science knowledge" (p. 9). Beckhard also describes OD as usually long-term (at least 2-3 years), *action-oriented* rather than merely training, focused on changing attitudes and/or behavior through experience-based learning activities primarily in group settings.

Despite the apparent similarity of these definitions to those of laboratory or sensitivity training, the authors in this series make it very clear that OD is *not* simply sensitivity training in organizations. The authors acknowledge the importance of the skills and learnings of laboratory training to the practice of OD but emphasize the much wider scope of activities, the more diverse background knowledge, and the greater analytic complexity demanded of the successful OD practitioner. Even Schein, who makes the analogy between a lab trainer and a process consultant, emphasizes that the major difference is in the greater complexity and difficulty of the OD task.

Both Bennis and Beckhard give overviews of this emerging field with surprisingly little overlap. The book by Bennis perhaps should be read first in the series. Besides defining what OD is and is not and giving examples of its broad range of activities, Bennis defines the background conditions for OD. In two particularly interesting chapters he presents answers to questions commonly asked about OD by professionals and practitioners. In another section he analyzes three failures in the use of lab training in OD and then offers propositions about the successful adoption of lab training in OD designs.

Beckhard contrasts OD to management development, training, and operations research. He discusses strategies and tactics such as team development, intergroup relations, goal-setting and planning, and personal education, and then analyzes consultant roles and activities in five detailed cases with differing change goals. Beckhard writes in an outline style, enumerating almost everything. Two of his lists may be of particular interest to the practitioner: (1) conditions for failure and for success in OD efforts, and (2) advantages and disadvantages of various methods of managing and staffing OD efforts with outside and internal resources. The last could be quite valuable to the prospective OD practitioner or contractor in listing possible OD roles, functions, styles, and services.

Of the six books, Lawrence and Lorsch present the heaviest reading and the most complex concepts in the most academic style, using a systems orientation. Fortunately they use interesting and pertinent case material to illustrate their concepts, which may be new to persons not well versed in sociologically-oriented organizational theory. They place heavy emphasis on the necessity of careful, complex, and thorough diagnosis of three major interfaces — the organizational-environment, the group-to-group, and the individual-organization — before tailoring each OD effort to fit an organization.

Lawrence and Lorsch state: "It is not that we like complex concepts, but that the real organizational world *is* complex and is so at each interface" (p. 92). The authors do not avoid the complexities of organizations. A good example is their discussion in the last chapter of alternative ways of handling a very practical dilemma facing OD planners — the need for high-quality, sophisticated solutions versus the need for large scale and intensive involvement and commitment by organizational members.

The organization, as opposed to organizational, development orientation is made very explicit by Blake and Mouton in their preface: "It should be read as a study of *organization* dynamics. It should not be read as a study of *individual* behavior." (Their italics). For three and a half bucks this is a good introduction to GOD (Grid OD) and its six phases: (1) learning about the Managerial Grid and team skills, (2) developing problem-solving teamwork, (3) developing company inter-unit coordination and cooperation, (4) developing an ideal corporate model guided by preselected readings, (5) implementing the ideal model, and, finally, (6) engaging in systematic critique of the changes and the present status of the organization. A dry but valuable contribution, especially for readers with little or no formal industrial administration background, is the Corporate Excellence Rubric explained and demonstrated in chapters 3-5. This catalogues a matrix for assessing corporate excellence of six functions (human resources, financial management, operations, marketing, R & D, and corporate activities) by three perspectives (current effectiveness, flexibility, and development) and by four orientations (internal or external, defensiveness or aggressiveness). The book is an exhortatory and brief description of a single, very successful, long-term, comprehensive, total-organization method of OD.

While the other books emphasize the organization level of OD, Walton and Schein make their contribution in dealing more with the nitty-gritty of the specific day-to-day activities of a consultant.

Walton presents and analyzes three detailed case histories of conflict in which he intervened as a third-party consultant. The concepts and the terminology he develops are understood easily because of clear formal definitions and because of references to the case material. He proposes a diagnostic model for conflict and methods of conflict control, suggests potential gains and risks of direct confrontation, and hypothesizes factors that contribute to successful confrontations. He defines strategic functions of consultants, develops alternative tactics for intervening, and considers optimal attributes of third-party consultants.

The strategic functions of a third-party consultant are: (1) assessing the motivation to reduce conflict, (2) trying to equalize situational power, (3) synchronizing initiative to confront with readiness for dialogue, (4) ensuring that differences are sufficiently explored and understood before moving toward integration, (5) assessing factors contributing to openness, (6) improving the reliability of communications, and (7) raising or lowering tension levels.

Walton discusses intervention tactics which illustrate the concrete activities of his practices. These are categorized as: being present and available in the confrontation, preliminary interviewing, structuring the context for the confrontation, intervening in the ongoing process, and assisting and setting up follow-up activities. This book could be read enjoyably and profitably by anyone interested in interpersonal interactions, whether they occur in organizations, families, or couples.

Schein defines OD as "an organization-wide kind of program, but its component parts are usually activities which the consultant carries out with individuals or small groups." One form of these activities comprise Process Consultation, "a set of activities on the part of the consultant which help the client to perceive, understand, and act upon . . . the various human interactions which occur in the normal flow of work, in the conduct of meetings, and in formal and informal encounters between members of the organization" (p. 9). He devotes the bulk of his book to what a process consultant looks for, how he starts, how he develops a relationship with a client, what kinds of interventions he makes, how the process is evaluated, and how it is terminated.

In six very short and clearly written chapters, Schein presents basic primers on the six kinds of processes he finds most crucial for organization performance: communication, member roles and functions in groups, group problem solving and decision making, group norms and growth, leadership and authority, and intergroup cooperation and competition. The reader who is already familiar with these basics is encouraged to go directly to the later chapters, in which he discusses consultant interventions.

In the second part of the book, Schein deals with specific activities of a process consultant: initially contacting a client; defining formal and psychological contracts; agreeing upon what to observe, when, and how; gathering data; using various methods of interventions, such as agenda setting, feedback sessions, coach-counseling, and structural suggestions; evaluating consultation results; and reducing involvement.

Individually, there is much to recommend about each of these volumes. Taken together, they represent a major step toward a clearer definition of the fuzzy field of O.D. Anyone seriously interested in O.D. should read all six. Anyone who merely wants to borrow or browse might look at Bennis' book for an overview or at Walton's and Schein's books for specifics and for the feeling of what consulting is like.

CONTRIBUTORS

B. Howard Arbes, Ph.D.
Intern in Counseling Psychology
University Counseling Center
Colorado State University
Fort Collins, Colorado 80521
    (303) 491-1101

Anthony G. Banet, Jr., Ph.D.
Director of Psychological Services
Marion County Mental Health Center
Indianapolis, Indiana 46202
    (317) 630-7791

Kenneth D. Benne, Ph.D.
Professor, Center for Applied Social Sciences
Boston University
Boston, Massachusetts 02215
    (617) 353-2000

Gerard Egan, S.J., Ph.D.
Assistant Professor of Psychology
Department of Psychology
Loyola University of Chicago
Chicago, Illinois 60626
    (312) 274-3000

Henry I. Feir, M.A.
820 Iowa Avenue
Iowa City, Iowa 52240
    (319) 354-1533

Norman A. Felsenthal, Ph.D.
Assistant Professor
Department of Communication
Purdue University
Lafayette, Indiana 47907
    (317) 494-8473

Robert N. Ford, Ph.D.
Personnel Director
Manpower Utilization
American Telephone and Telegraph Co.
195 Broadway
New York, New York 10007
    (212) 393-9800

Jack R. Gibb, Ph.D.
Consultant
8475 La Jolla Scenic Drive
La Jolla, California 92037
    (714) 453-0133

Gale Goldberg, M.S.W.
Assistant Professor
School of Social Administration

Temple University
Philadelphia, Pennsylvania 19122
    (215) 787-8621

Philip G. Hanson, Ph.D.
Director, Human Relations Training Laboratory
Veterans Administration Hospital
2002 Holcombe Boulevard
Houston, Texas 77031
    (713) 747-3000

Stanley M. Herman, Ph.D.
TRW Systems Group
One Space Park — E2/7042
Redondo Beach, California 90278
    (213) 536-4728

Richard Heslin, Ph.D.
Associate Professor
Department of Psychology
Purdue University
Lafayette, Indiana 47907
    (317) 749-3551

John L. Hipple, Ph.D.
Counselor, Student Counseling Center
University of Idaho
Moscow, Idaho 83843
    (208) 885-6111

Thomas R. Holman, Ph.D.
Associate Professor
Department of Psychology
Earlham College
Richmond, Indiana 47374
    (317) 962-6561 x 372

Francis V. Jessey, M.A.
Training Specialist
Southern New England Bell Telephone Co.
227 Church Street
New Haven, Connecticut 06510
    (203) 771-4212

Frank R. Johnson, M. Div.
Group Counselor, University Counseling Cente
Shoemaker Building
University of Maryland
College Park, Maryland 20742
    (301) 454-2931

John E. Jones, Ph.D.
Associate Professor
College of Education
University of Iowa

Iowa City, Iowa 52240
(319) 353-3187

Otto Kroeger, B.D.
Pastor, First Lutheran Church
43 Washington Street
Chambersburg, Pennsylvania 17201
(717) 264-2015

Robert B. Lelieuvre, Ph.D.
Assistant Professor
Department of Psychology
Indiana/Purdue University at Indianapolis
Indianapolis, Indiana 46204
(317) 264-7140

Richard H. Levin, Ph.D.
Professor, Department of Psychology
Apalachian State University
Boone, North Carolina 28607
(704) 264-8871

Thomas F. Lyons, Ph.D.
Research Associate
University of Michigan
Ann Arbor, Michigan 48104
(313) 763-1202

Ruth R. Middleman, Ed.D.
Professor, School of Social Administration
Temple University
Philadelphia, Pennsylvania 19122
(215) 787-8621

Kurt E. Olmosk, Ph.D.
Visiting Professor
University of Leeds
Leeds, Yorkshire, England
78-2274

J. William Pfeiffer, Ph.D.
Human Relations Consultant
P.O. Box 24402
Indianapolis, Indiana 46224
(317) 925-8217

Sandra L. Pfeiffer, Ed.S.
Counselor
Indiana/Purdue University at Indianapolis
Indianapolis, Indiana 46204
(317) 264-3986

Willis D. Poland, Ph.D.
Associate Professor of Psychology
and Senior Counselor
325 Pharmacy Building

University of Cincinnati
Cincinnati, Ohio 45221
(513) 475-2942

W. Brendan Reddy, Ph.D.
Program Director
Community Psychology Institute
109 W. Corry Street
Cincinnati, Ohio 45219
(513) 475-4680

Albert J. Robinson, M.S.
Senior Personnel Development Representative
Personnel Planning Division
Eli Lilly and Company
Indianapolis, Indiana 46225
(317) 261-3223

Brent Ruben, Ph.D.
Director, Institute for Communication Studies
Rutgers University
New Brunswick, New Jersey 08903
(201) 247-1766 x 6354

Steven J. Ruma, Ph.D.
President, International Association
of Applied Social Scientists, Inc.
Suite 300
1755 Massachusetts Avenue, N.W.
Washington, D.C. 20036
(202) 387-8985

John J. Sherwood, Ph.D.
Professor, Krannert Graduate School
of Industrial Administration
Purdue University
Lafayette, Indiana 47907
(317) 493-1882

Maury Smith, O.F.M., D.Min.
Program Director, Alverna
8140 Spring Mill Road
Indianapolis, Indiana 46260
(317) 255-1340

Thomas M. Thomson
Human Resources Management Program
U.S. Naval Base
Newport, Rhode Island 02840
(401) 841-4743

Paul Thoresen, Ph.D.
Staff Psychologist
Marion County Mental Health Center
Indianapolis, Indiana 46202
(317) 630-7791

Daniel B. Wile, Ph.D.
Associate Professor of Psychology
Counseling Services
California State College (Hayward)
25800 Hillary Street
Hayward, California 94542
(415) 884-3761

E. D. Yoes, Jr., M.A.
Assistant Director of Operations
Indiana Higher Education Telecommunications
System
1100 West Michigan Street
Indianapolis, Indiana 46202
(317) 264-7945